CONTEMPORARY ARISTOTELIAN ETHICS

CONTEMPORARY ARISTOTELIAN ETHICS

Alasdair MacIntyre, Martha Nussbaum, Robert Spaemann

ARTHUR MADIGAN, S.J.

University of Notre Dame Press

Notre Dame, Indiana

Published in the United States of America

Library of Congress Control Number: 2023946554

ISBN: 978-0-268-20759-5 (Hardback)
ISBN: 978-0-268-20758-8 (WebPDF)
ISBN: 978-0-268-20761-8 (Epub3)

CONTENTS

INTRODUCTION

In the fall of 1969, I enrolled in an introductory ethics course at the University of Toronto taught by David P. Gauthier, who went on to chair Toronto's graduate Department of Philosophy and later to teach at the University of Pittsburgh. This course was a wonderfully lucid and well-organized introduction to mainstream Anglo-American moral philosophy. We used William K. Frankena's *Ethics*, a summary of the main questions addressed in that moral philosophy and of the main answers to those questions. Included therein were various classical and contemporary readings.

Two aspects of the course left a deep impression on me. One was the opposition between deontological ethics and teleological ethics. I will have a good deal to say about deontological and teleological ethics in the pages that follow. For the moment, let me say, very roughly, that deontological ethics is a kind of ethics that focuses on duties and obligations, on what is right and what is wrong. A well-known example of deontological ethics is the ethics of Immanuel Kant, and perhaps the most famous, or infamous, example of Kant's ethics in practice is the claim that one may never tell a lie, not even to save a human life. Again very roughly, teleological ethics is an ethics that focuses on fulfillments and satisfactions, on what things are good and bad for human beings. A well-known example of teleological ethics is the utilitarianism of John Stuart Mill, who counseled that we should act in whatever way promotes the greatest possible good or satisfaction for the greatest number of human beings. The standard objection, of course, is that the utilitarian principle could be used to justify all sorts of injustices, such as the punishment of innocent people.

The other aspect of Gauthier's course that left a deep impression was G. E. M. Anscombe, "Modern Moral Philosophy," *Philosophy: The Journal of the Royal Institute of Philosophy* 33, no. 124 (1958): 1–19, with its criticism of both Kantian and utilitarian ethics. If Anscombe was right, the deontological ethics of Kant was incoherent and the teleological ethics of utilitarianism was really the abandonment of any ethics worthy of the name. In 1969, I was only beginning to understand the significance of Anscombe's argument.

In the fall of 1979, I began to teach philosophy at Boston College. When, on occasion, I had the opportunity to teach ethics, I went back to Gauthier's course, to Kant's *Groundwork for the Metaphysics of Morals* and to Mill's *Utilitarianism*, and to the problem of teleology and deontology. I tried to lead my students to appreciate the radical difference between the two and to make a reasoned choice in favor of one or the other. Most of them declined to choose. They insisted on affirming both deontology and teleology, refusing to accept the troubling implications of either. Disconcerting as it was for me, they wanted both. They knew better than I did.

In fall of 1981, I began to read Alasdair MacIntyre's *After Virtue*. It was the first sustained critique of modern ethics and modernity that I had ever read. He acknowledged a debt to Anscombe's "Modern Moral Philosophy," but MacIntyre offered a different and much more detailed analysis of what had gone wrong in modern ethics. He also outlined an alternative to that ethics: an updated version of Aristotle's ethics of the virtues. *After Virtue* opened up a new philosophical world.

In spring of 1986, at the Center for Hellenic Studies in Washington, DC, I read a manuscript version of Martha Nussbaum's *The Fragility of Goodness*. Here was a riveting example of how to read Greek philosophy in the light of Greek tragedy and Greek tragedy in the light of Greek philosophy. At the same time, *Fragility of Goodness* set me a problem. Impressed by MacIntyre's reading of Aristotle, and now attracted by Nussbaum's reading, I did not see how the two readings could be combined. MacIntyre read Aristotle with a view to diagnosing what had gone wrong with modern moral philosophy and to prescribing what should be done about it. Nussbaum did nothing of the kind. Her Aristotle was opposing Plato, or opposing a kind of Platonism that sought to deny or eliminate the dimensions of fragility and vulnerability that are inherent in human life. From this point on, as I began to teach electives on the *Nicomachean Ethics*, I went back and forth between readings influenced by MacIntyre and readings influenced by Nussbaum. This was a stimulating and fruitful experience for me, but it must have baffled my students.

Early in the 1990s, my friend and colleague Paul McNellis, S.J., introduced me to the work of Robert Spaemann, who was then teaching at the Ludwig-Maximilians-Universität in Munich, and whose work was only beginning to be noticed in the Anglo-American world. He persuaded me to read Spaemann's *Philosophische Essays*. The more I read, the more impressed I was. Here was someone analyzing modernity in a way that owed much to Aristotle and Aquinas, but also speaking a philosophical dialect that owed much to Kant and Hegel. Here was someone sensitive to the achievements of modernity, especially its awareness of human dignity, but also critical of modernity on many different counts. Here was another distinctive Aristotelian voice.

It took years for me to see it, but MacIntyre, Nussbaum, and Spaemann were weaning me away from my focus on the opposition between deontological and teleological ethics. Later than I should have, I woke up to the fact that the differences among their readings of Aristotle, or, better, their forms of Aristotelianism, were more significant than the differences between Kant and Mill that had held my attention for so long. This book is an attempt to pull together what I have learned from these three remarkable thinkers.

If MacIntyre, Nussbaum, and Spaemann are three of the more important figures in the revival of Aristotelian ethics, they are by no means its only representatives. It would have been worthwhile to study such Aristotelians as Henry Veatch and Mortimer Adler, to study the New Natural Law theory of Germain Grisez, John Finnis, and Joseph Boyle, and to study the influence of Philippa Foot, Rosalind Hursthouse, Timothy (now Sophie-Grace) Chappell, and others on Aristotelian ethics. The full history of the twentieth-century Aristotelian revival remains to be written, and it may be some time before anyone is in a position to write it. What has led me to focus on MacIntyre, Nussbaum, and Spaemann is that they have written not just for specialists but for educated and reflective general readers.

Time, as always, has marched on. MacIntyre's and Spaemann's more recent writings remain within the Aristotelian tradition, broadly understood. Nussbaum's more recent work has moved in different directions. In this book I have focused on her earlier Aristotelian writings.

I have written *Contemporary Aristotelian Ethics* for readers who have not yet read MacIntyre or Nussbaum or Spaemann, but who want to understand their thought and are ready to engage with it in some depth and detail. I have attempted to take such readers fairly deep into the details of their thinking about ethics, but this book cannot substitute for the study of their works themselves. I have also written for readers who have some familiarity with MacIntyre, Nussbaum, and/or Spaemann, and who want to explore alternative forms of Aristotelian ethics. I have written for philosophers who, perhaps not committed Aristotelians, take Aristotelian ethics seriously as a live philosophical option. But most of all, I have written the book for educated and reflective readers, the people whom MacIntyre calls "plain persons," that is, the readers that MacIntyre, Nussbaum, and Spaemann themselves are addressing.

My debts are many and various. Alasdair MacIntyre and Martha Nussbaum have helped me at various stages in the genesis of this book. Margaret Holland has ably and generously commented on chapter 1, about Anglo-American moral philosophy in the period 1950 to 1990. Christopher Stephen Lutz has ably and generously commented on chapter 2, on MacIntyre. Margaret Holland and Paulette Kidder have ably and generously commented on chapter 3, on Nussbaum. Jeremiah Alberg, Oliver O'Donovan, and Robert Sokolowski have ably and generously commented on chapter 4, on Spaemann. I have learned much from these scholars and should no doubt have learned more. They have saved me from many mistakes. The errors and infelicities that remain are, of course, my responsibility.

I am grateful to Boston College and to the Fitzgibbons family for entrusting me with the Albert J. Fitzgibbons Professorship. It has been an honor. I would also like to thank Boston College for its support of a sabbatical leave in academic year 2017–18, in which this book came close to completion, and to the staff of the Boston College Libraries, who have helped it to completion in more ways than they can know. I am deeply indebted to the students I have taught at Fordham University, Boston College, John Carroll University, Marquette University, and Le Moyne College. My greatest debt is to the Philosophy Department at Boston College. Most of the work for this book was done during the ups and downs of my six years as department chair, 2010–16. I am deeply grateful to my colleagues. In ways that I cannot yet articulate, those ups and downs have made this a better book than it might have been. Whatever our differences, we have respected one another's intellectual projects, and we have wanted the best for our students. As, I trust, did Aristotle.

My manuscript was received by University of Notre Dame Press in the summer of 2020 and was favorably reviewed. I thank the two reviewers for their helpful remarks and generous praise of my work. I would also like to thank two editors at UNDP: Stephen Little, who oversaw this project in its early stages, and Emily R. King, who has been overseeing the project since August 2022.

In the fall of 2020, I suffered two strokes, the first mild and the second not. I have been working very hard on my recovery and am making progress. I have received wonderful support from my Jesuit community, family, friends, and from the many physicians, nurses, and helpers who have seen to my immediate and long-term needs. They have been a blessing. I also thank Deborah De Chiara-Quenzer, a colleague and friend, who during this time helped me in completing the final stages of the project, including the communications with UNDP on my behalf.

Campion Center, Weston, Massachusetts
April 2023

ANGLO-AMERICAN MORAL PHILOSOPHY, 1950–1990

The last two decades of the twentieth century witnessed a remarkable revival of Aristotelian ethics in the Anglo-American philosophical world. This revival did not take place in a vacuum. It was in large part a response to a kind of ethics that was dominant in Anglo-American philosophical circles for most of the twentieth century and that has by no means disappeared. The revival cannot be properly understood without an understanding of that ethics. This first chapter will attempt to characterize Anglo-American moral philosophy not as it is today but as it was in the period roughly from 1950 to 1990.[1]

The choice of 1950 as a point of departure is an attempt to begin at a point where the influence of British analytic philosophy in North America was sufficiently advanced that one could speak of Anglo-American moral philosophy.[2] The choice of 1990 as a closing date is in recognition of two changes that had taken place in Anglo-American moral philosophy by that time: increased attention to the history of ethics and the recognition of virtue ethics as a field in its own right.[3]

I have based this chapter on a survey of introductory ethics textbooks from the period in question. None of these introductions is authoritative in itself, but taken together they convey a reliable idea of the issues that Anglo-American moral philosophers were discussing and the philosophical categories in which they were discussing them. They thus reflect the ethics to which the Aristotelian revival is in large part a response.[4]

I have consulted the following introductions: Ewing, *Ethics*; M. Warnock, *Ethics since 1900*; Frankena, *Ethics*; G. J. Warnock, *Contemporary Moral Philosophy*; Harman, *The Nature of Morality*; Rachels, *The Elements of Moral Philosophy*; and Raphael, *Moral Philosophy*. I have also consulted Kai Nielsen's article on the problems of ethics in Edwards, *Encyclopedia of Philosophy*.[5]

Someone who examines these introductory texts may at first be struck more by their dissimilarities than by their similarities. This should come as no surprise. Authors tend to draw on their distinctive experience as teachers. Publishers tend to claim that their introductions are different from, or better than, competing texts. Closer examination, however, discloses that these texts share a common core of authors, texts, and issues from the preceding two generations that they discuss, whatever else they may discuss. The following authors and titles capture this common core: G. E. Moore, *Principia Ethica* (1903); H. A. Prichard, "Does Moral Philosophy Rest on a Mistake?" (1912); W. D. Ross, *The Right and the Good* (1930); A. J. Ayer, *Language, Truth, and Logic* (1936); C. L. Stevenson, *Ethics and Language* (1944); and R. M. Hare, *The Language of Morals* (1952). The issues raised by these texts—the merits of naturalism and intuitionism, the relative priority of right and good, the positivist challenge to the meaningfulness of ethical language, and the responses to that challenge—are at the heart of Anglo-American moral philosophy in our period.[6]

Some of the introductions limit themselves to the common core of authors and issues, for example, Mary Warnock's *Ethics since 1900*, and Geoffrey Warnock's *Contemporary Moral Philosophy*. When the introductions go beyond this common core, they do so in three main ways.

The first way is historical. Some of the introductions go back beyond Moore to the utilitarianisms of Henry Sidgwick, John Stuart Mill, and Jeremy Bentham, of which Moore was critical. Some go back to Kant and Hume or even further back. The introductions by Ewing, Frankena, Harman, Rachels, and Raphael all include this kind of historical material.

A second way is by offering typologies of different ethical theories. In this they are recovering the approach of Henry Sidgwick, *The Methods of Ethics* (1874; 7th ed., 1906) and of C. D. Broad, *Five Types of Ethical Theory* (1930), but not necessarily following either of their classifications.

Frankena's typology of teleological ethics and deontological ethics, each with subtypes, seems to me the most explicit and detailed, but the introductions regularly contrast different normative theories with one another.

A third way distinguishes explicitly between first-order (or normative) ethics and second-order ethics (or metaethics) offering typologies of metaethics. When an introductory text does not mention metaethics or distinguish between normative ethics and metaethics, I take it that is because of the author's pedagogical judgment about what beginning students need to know, not ignorance of the distinction itself. Again, I find Frankena's delineation of naturalism, intuitionism, and noncognitivism to be the most explicit and detailed, but other introductions that talk about metaethics draw essentially the same distinctions. The technical terms in this paragraph will be explained shortly.

ANGLO-AMERICAN MORAL PHILOSOPHY, 1950–1990

Anglo-American ethics in our period was characterized by a widely shared conception of what ethics is: the attempt to clarify ethical concepts and to critically examine ethical theories and the arguments for and against them.[7] As a reflective activity, ethics does not simply accept the ethical views of parents, authoritative teachers, communities, and traditions. It subjects them to examination and criticism. Ethics is thus a matter of rational argument, of stating claims, explaining them, and giving reasons for them. Ethics includes both constructive arguments for various ethical theories and particular ethical claims and negative arguments against ethical theories and particular ethical claims.

Normative Ethics and Metaethics

Anglo-American ethics in this period takes for granted a distinction between first-order ethical questions and second-order ethical questions, or, as is more commonly said, between normative ethics and metaethics. The distinction is a tool of analysis and clarification. Most of the authors commonly studied in Anglo-American ethics—Hume, Kant, the utilitarians,

Moore, and Ross—did not themselves distinguish explicitly between normative ethics and metaethics.[8]

Broadly speaking, normative ethics considers questions about value (what things are good or bad, what makes them good or bad) and obligation (what things we are obliged to do, what things we are obliged not to do, and why). Normative ethics includes normative ethical theories (about which more below) and particular ethical judgments. Metaethics, by contrast, steps back from ethical principles and particular ethical judgments to consider what they mean and how they are or might be justified. Anglo-American ethics typically envisioned metaethics as neutral with respect to issues in normative ethics and particular ethical claims. At the same time, it treated metaethics as clarifying and establishing the bases on which normative ethics could proceed, or, as the case may be, exposing and demolishing the bases on which normative ethics might have tried to proceed.

Normative Ethical Theories: Teleological and Deontological

Three main families of normative ethical theories were in play: teleological ethics, deontological ethics, and divine command ethics. Let us begin with the first two. Here we need to distinguish between the broad senses of "teleological" and "deontological" and the stricter senses of these two terms.

In the broad sense, a teleological ethics is an ethics of fulfillment, that is, an ethical theory that focuses on what fulfills human beings (and in some versions, other sentient beings). In the broad sense, a deontological ethics is an ethics of obligation, that is, an ethics that focuses on duties or obligations that we have to one another and/or to ourselves (and in some versions, to other sentient beings). If we understand "teleological" and "deontological" in these broad senses, one and the same ethical theory can have both a teleological aspect and a deontological aspect. In such a case the question would then arise about whether one of these two aspects was prior to, more basic than the other. This question has been formulated as the question about the relative priority of the right and the good.[9] Is the right, what human beings ought to do and ought not to do, more basic than the good, what is good for human beings, what fulfills them? Or is the good more basic than the right? A teleological ethics would be an ethics in which good is prior to right. A deontological ethics, by contrast, would be an ethics in which right is prior to good. But so long as the terms are taken in their broad senses, it is possible to envision both a deontological ethics with important teleological features and a teleological ethics with important deontological features.

Alongside the broad sense, however, this ethics also knew of stricter definitions of teleological ethics and deontological ethics, such that the two were mutually exclusive. Thus Frankena:

> A teleological theory says that the basic or ultimate criterion or standard of what is morally right, wrong, obligatory, etc., is the nonmoral value that is brought into being. The final appeal, directly or indirectly, must be to the comparative amount of good produced, or rather to the comparative balance of good over evil produced. . . . Deontological theories deny what teleological theories affirm. They deny that the right, the obligatory, and the morally good are wholly, whether directly or indirectly, a function of what is nonmorally good or of what promotes the greatest balance of good over evil for self, one's society, or the world as a whole. They assert that there are other considerations that may make an action or rule right or obligatory besides the goodness or badness of its consequences—certain features of the act itself other than the value it brings into existence, for example, the fact that it keeps a promise, is just, or is commanded by God or by the state. Teleologists believe that there is one and only one basic or ultimate right-making characteristic, namely, the comparative value (nonmoral) of what is, probably will be, or is intended to be brought into being. Deontologists either deny that this characteristic is right-making at all or they insist that there are other basic or ultimate right-making characteristics as well.[10]

If we take teleological ethics and deontological ethics in these strict senses, there is no question of a theory's being both teleological and deontological. A theory can be one or the other but not both.

The early utilitarians were also hedonists, and introductions to ethics in our period typically included discussions of hedonism. "Hedonism" is a highly ambiguous term. Frankena helpfully distinguishes four different things that people mean by it. One is that happiness and pleasure are the same thing. A second is that all pleasures are intrinsically good. A third is that only pleasures are intrinsically good. A fourth is that pleasantness is the criterion of intrinsic goodness.[11]

Introductions to ethics typically distinguished between a purely quantitative hedonism, attributed to Jeremy Bentham, that recognizes differing *quantities* of pleasure and pain but not different *kinds* of pleasure and pain, and a qualitative hedonism, attributed to John Stuart Mill, that recognizes not merely different quantities of pleasure and pain but different types or species of pleasure and pain. These introductions pointed out that the original utilitarian project of arriving at decisions by comparing the amounts of pleasure and pain that would result from different courses of action presupposed quantitative hedonism. Recognition of the qualitative diversity of pleasures and pains made this kind of calculation much more complicated if not impossible.

Moral philosophers in this period knew very well that utilitarianism is not the only form of teleological ethics and that Kantianism is not the only form of deontological ethics. Nonetheless, their introductory texts tended to focus on the utilitarianisms of Bentham and John Stuart Mill as the principal (most important, influential, interesting) versions of teleological ethics and on the ethics of Kant as the principal version of deontological ethics. They typically highlighted Kant's insistence that genuine moral principles or maxims have to be universalizable, that is, they have to apply to every rational agent. Without going further into the complexities of Kant's categorical imperative, they might raise the question whether universalizability was a sufficient condition for something to count as a moral principle or maxim. They typically highlighted the utilitarian principle of the greatest happiness for the greatest number. They might go on to note that some utilitarians thought that agents should evaluate each and every moral decision by direct reference to that principle (act utilitarianism), but others thought the principle should be used to develop and evaluate moral rules, which agents then ought to follow even if on occasion following them resulted in a less satisfactory result (rule utilitarianism).

It is possible to draw a distinction between individual acts and general rules within deontological ethics, but deontological ethicians have generally presented our obligations in the form of rules. This raises a variety of questions. What are these rules? Where do they come from, or what are they based on? What should we do if rules happen to conflict? In an attempt to answer this last question, W. D. Ross proposed the idea of a prima facie duty, that is, a real duty that might on occasion have to yield to a higher or more important duty.[12] The notion of prima facie duties invites the further question of how we know which duties take precedence over other duties. That question would take us into metaethics, which we will consider shortly.

There was something attractive or appealing about utilitarianism: both its egalitarianism and its acute sensitivity to the effect of action on the welfare of people at large. Still, the principle of the greatest happiness for the greatest number might seem to justify actions that many people would not think were justifiable, such as the sacrifice of innocent persons to benefit larger groups or to protect those groups from harm. There was something attractive or appealing about Kantianism: its insistence on respect for persons. Still, Kant's ethics also appears to forbid any and all lying, even to people bent on committing murder.[13] The combination of attractive points and difficulties in Kantianism and utilitarianism invites a number of questions. Is it possible to devise a form of teleological ethics that is not subject to the difficulties of utilitarianism? Is it possible to devise a form of deontological ethics that is not subject to the difficulties of Kantianism? Is it possible, despite the incompatibility of teleological ethics and deontological ethics, strictly understood, to combine what is attractive in teleological ethics with what is attractive in deontological ethics?

Normative Ethical Theory: Divine Command

Anglo-American ethics recognized a third kind of normative ethical theory: divine command theory, also known as theological voluntarism. What divine command theories have in common is the idea that what it is right for people to do is what God commands them to do. Most if not all of these theories were developed in a Jewish or Christian context, with the biblical Ten Commandments as the prime examples of divine commands.

Not all introductions to ethics discussed divine command ethics, but some, such as Frankena's, recognized two different types of divine command theory. In the first kind, the divine commands are simply that, commands, commands whose content could be, or could have been, different from what it is. The content of the divine commands is fundamentally arbitrary. For example, it is wrong to steal, because God forbids it, but God could have commanded people to steal, and then it would be right, indeed obligatory, for people to steal. The second kind of divine command theory rejects the view that the content of the divine commands is arbitrary. It posits that God commands people to do what is good for them and to refrain from doing what is bad for them.[14]

Egoism and Altruism

Given that the best-known version of deontological ethics, Kantianism, the best-known version of teleological ethics, utilitarianism, and at least some forms of divine command ethics can place heavy demands on individuals, it was only natural that Anglo-American ethics should face the problem of self-interest and the competing claims of egoism and altruism.

Moral philosophers recognized two different kinds of egoism: psychological egoism and ethical egoism. Psychological egoism is the view, really a thesis in psychology, that as a matter of fact human beings always act with a view to their own self-interest as they perceive it. To take an example: If someone cites instances of apparently selfless or self-sacrificing behavior, the psychological egoist replies, "They are doing it because they think it is in their interest to do it. Otherwise they would not be doing it." Ethical egoism, by contrast, is not a factual claim but a normative claim: "People ought to act in their own self-interest." Commending ethical egoism presupposes that it is possible, if undesirable, for people not to act with a view to their own self-interest. If psychological egoism were true, there would be no point to commending ethical egoism. We would all be acting for our own self-interest, real or perceived, already. Nonetheless, people sometimes blur the line between ethical egoism and psychological egoism, or even appeal to psychological egoism in support of ethical egoism. Some of the moral philosophers of our period criticized that appeal as fallacious. Some argued that psychological egoism is either false or trivially true.[15]

To judge by the introductions to ethics, moral philosophers in our period were not of one mind about how to reply to ethical egoism or even how to formulate the issue.[16] One approach was to address the question, "Why should we be moral?" or "Why should we do what is right?" In response to this, Kurt Baier argued that a consistent egoist could not adopt specifically *moral* rules. Any rules that he or she might adopt would be merely rules of thumb, subject to self-interest, not genuinely moral rules, which would be superior to self-interest. He then developed what he called "the moral point of view," which he thought could serve as a criterion by which to distinguish true moral rules from false moral rules. Taking the moral point of view means doing things on principle, not out of self-interest. The principles in question are taken to apply to everyone, not just to some people. They must be for the good of everyone, not just the good of some people.[17] Baier argues that we have good self-interested reasons to adopt the moral point of view. I take it he means by that reasons genuinely to make that viewpoint our own, to adopt it as superior to considerations of self-interest, not just provisionally or as a rule of thumb: "The answer to our question 'Why should we be moral?' is therefore as follows. We should be moral because being moral is following rules designed to overrule self-interest whenever it is in the interest of everyone alike that such rules should be generally followed."[18] Very roughly, the argument is that pursuit of one's long-term self-interest makes it reasonable to accept limits on one's pursuit of short-term self-interest. The rational egoist ought to accept limitations on his or her egoism.

Frankena's reply to ethical egoism accepts Baier's distinction between the viewpoint of self-interest and the viewpoint of morality. "Prudentialism or living wholly by the principle of enlightened self-love just is not a kind of *morality*." "The moral point of view is *disinterested*, not 'interested.'"[19] He summarizes, more succinctly than Baier did, what the moral point of view actually is: "One is taking the moral point of view if one is not being egoistic, one is doing things on principle, one is willing to universalize one's principles, and in doing so one considers the good of everyone alike."[20] But, Frankena suggests, it is at least arguable that living morally is a form of excellent activity and a part of living the good life. It could make good sense for people who are trying to make a rational decision about how to lead their lives to adopt the moral point of view. Somewhat along the same line, Rachels presents three arguments in favor of ethical egoism and criticizes all three. He presents three arguments against it, criticizes the first and second, but finds that the third, from the arbitrariness of treating oneself differently from others, shows that ethical egoism fails as a moral theory.[21]

Statements of the moral point of view were open to the charge of stating a particular moral point of view, that of liberal modernity, not the viewpoint of morality as such. Thus Kai Nielsen wrote,

> However universalistic his intentions, what in fact [Kurt] Baier is doing is to characterize what is the moral point of view for a restricted cluster of moralities and most paradigmatically for liberal morality. It is a point of view which, by the very way it is characterized, is inescapably committed to regarding the "moralities" of slave societies, of caste societies, Nietzsche's conception of master morality and his conception of slave morality and (Nietzsche aside) the conception of morality held by Plato and Aristotle as not being opposing moralities all taking the moral point of view, but as not really being genuine moralities at all.

But theorists of the moral point of view could admit the charge, deny that the moralities of Plato, Aristotle, Nietzsche, or of slave and caste societies were in fact moralities, and say that morality and liberal morality are one and the same.[22]

Metaethical Theories: Naturalism, Intuitionism, Noncognitivism

Given the opposition between teleological ethics and deontological ethics, and the contrast between both of them and divine command ethics, the question naturally arises whether there are good reasons to accept or reject these theories, good reasons to prefer one approach to the others. This leads naturally to issues of metaethics, that is, issues about the meaning and justification of ethical claims and ethical theories. Our Anglo-American ethics recognized three main types of metaethical theories: naturalism (sometimes called definism), intuitionism (sometimes called nonnaturalism), and noncognitivism.[23]

The core idea of naturalism is that moral judgments, and in particular judgments of moral goodness and moral obligation, can be derived from facts that are not in and of themselves moral. One common version of naturalist metaethics is the view that ethical conclusions can be based on facts about what is good (beneficial) or bad (harmful) for human beings. The distinction between moral claims and nonmoral facts invites questions about the meaning and reference of the terms "moral" and "morality," questions that are taken more and more seriously in the latter part of our period.

The core idea of intuitionism is that moral goodness is not identical with any natural property. For any natural property, such as being pleasant, it is an open question whether it is good or not. Goodness is not something that we reason to but something that we intuit or recognize directly. Any attempt to reason from a natural property of a thing to the thing's being good begs the question whether that property is in fact good and commits (in the words of G. E. Moore) the naturalistic fallacy.[24] The intuitionist thus posits not just a distinction between facts and goods, facts and obligations, but an unbridgeable gap between them. The naturalist, by contrast, either denies the distinction or accepts it but argues that the gap between the two can be bridged.

The core idea of noncognitivism is that ethical theories and particular ethical judgments are not matters of knowledge. They are not known or knowable either in the way that the intuitionist thinks they are (by some direct intuition) or in the way that the naturalist thinks they are (by derivation from nonmoral facts). Noncognitivism thus denies the claims of naturalism and intuitionism. Noncognitivists typically also propose alternative accounts of ethical theories, particular judgments, and utterances, that is, of what they, the various theories, really are if they are not expressions of knowledge. One such account is the emotivism of A. J. Ayer and C. L. Stevenson, roughly the view that moral utterances are not truth claims but rather expressions of feeling or attitude.[25] Another is R. M. Hare's prescriptivism, roughly the view that the point of moral utterances is to influence people's behavior.[26]

Facts and Values, Is and Ought

Consideration of normative ethics and metaethics brings us to the matter of facts and values and to what is often called the "is–ought problem." Introductions to ethics commonly raised this problem apropos of a passage from book 3, part 1 of David Hume's *Treatise of Human Nature*, in which he argues, or has been taken to argue, that books of ethics generally commit the logical fallacy of passing from factual claims to claims about duties or obligations. The passage has been the focus of so much study and commentary that I will quote it here: "In every system of morality, which I have hitherto met with, I have always remark'd, that the author proceeds for some time in the ordinary way of reasoning, and establishes the being of a God, or makes observations concerning human affairs; when of a sudden I am surpriz'd to find, that instead of the usual copulations of propositions, *is*, and *is not*, I meet with no proposition that is not connected with an *ought*, or an *ought not*."

This sort of inference is often called the "modal fallacy," or a violation of "Hume's law." Whether or not this is the correct interpretation of the passage from Hume's *Treatise*, it surfaces the question about the relationship between factual claims and ethical claims, or, as some would put it, the relationship between nonmoral claims and moral claims.[27]

The issue about the relationships of fact and value, fact and obligation, gave rise to a considerable literature, with some contributors holding that there is no passing from factual claims to ethical claims and others holding that there is some way to do precisely that.[28] The details of these arguments need not concern us here. What united the two camps, however, was the assumption that there is enough of a difference between matters of fact and matters of value/obligation that the relationship between the two was a problem that needed to be faced. Some thinkers in our period questioned this assumption, perhaps most notably the Harvard philosopher Hilary Putnam.[29]

Relativism and Skepticism

Anglo-American moral philosophers in our period were well aware of issues about the objectivity and justification of ethical claims. These issues were central to the whole project of metaethics. Challenges to these claims went by the names of relativism, skepticism, and subjectivism. So far as I can tell, there was no general agreement about how these challenges should be met.

Frankena's distinction of three kinds of relativism is perspicuous.[30] The first of these is descriptive relativism, of which the best-known form is cultural relativism. This is the claim, in effect a thesis in sociology or anthropology, that different groups of people, different cultures, have substantively different ethics, that is, they recognize different things as good or bad, different things as obligatory or forbidden. At a certain level this is clearly true. What is disputed is how fundamental these differences are and what they do or do not entail for normative ethics.

The second type of relativism is normative relativism. Normative relativism asserts that different cultures *should* act on their different ethical beliefs or principles. Where descriptive relativism says that people in culture X and people in culture Y have and act on different ethical principles, normative relativism says that it is right for people in culture X to act on their ethical principles and right for people in culture Y to act on their different ethical principles. The Romans are right to do as the Romans do. If, for example, a certain culture regards the claims of honesty as taking precedence over the claims of family loyalty, then people in that culture ought to give precedence to the claims of honesty. But if a certain other culture regards family loyalty as taking precedence over honesty, then people in that culture ought to give precedence to the claims of family loyalty.

The third type of relativism is metaethical relativism. This is the view that there is no objective rational way of justifying ethical claims, and thus that different, even contradictory, ethical claims are equally justified, or rather equally unjustified. This would seem to be close to, if not identical with, ethical skepticism, which we will take up in a moment.

Some people have blurred the lines between descriptive or cultural relativism, on the one hand, and normative and metaethical relativism, on the other, or even appealed to cultural relativism in support of normative or metaethical relativism. Moral philosophers in our period tend to criticize those appeals as fallacious.[31] The differences between cultures, even if they go very deep, are not sufficient to establish that either normative or metaethical relativism is true.

Introductions to ethics in our period did not agree about how to describe the challenges of relativism and skepticism, much less about how to meet them. Ewing discusses skepticism on pages 26–27, 98, and 110–11 of his *Ethics* and then gives pages 111–15 to cultural relativism. He also discusses what he calls the subjective view of ethics on pages 26–27 and 156–57. Harman, whose index includes only proper names, has no discussion of skepticism or relativism, but his chapter 3 is entitled "Emotivism as Moderate Nihilism." Raphael has no index entries for "skepticism" or for "relativism" but does have a couple of entries for "subjectivism." Rachels has no entries for "skepticism" or for "relativism," but his second chapter is concerned with cultural relativism and his third chapter with subjectivism. Frankena does not discuss skepticism as such, presumably because he thinks his discussion of metaethical relativism says what needs to be said about it. Readers who look up "Ethical Skepticism" in Paul Edwards's *Encyclopedia of Philosophy* will be referred to "Emotive Theory of Ethics," "Ethical Relativism," and "Ethical Subjectivism."

Philosophers in our period apparently recognized that issues about the objectivity and justification of ethical claims were too complex and difficult to be treated, on anything beyond the simplest level, in introductions to ethics. On a higher or more technical level there was no general agreement about how these issues should best be treated.[32] In this situation, I would suggest that we draw a rough-and-ready distinction between two different contexts in which problems of objectivity, justification, relativism, skepticism, and subjectivism come up for discussion. The first context is theoretical: the continuing effort to come to terms with the legacies of Moore, Prichard, Ross, Ayer, Stevenson, Hare, and the heirs to their arguments. The second context is more obviously practical, not to say existential: addressing requests to justify particular claims about duties and obligations, or trying to answer the general question, "Why should I be moral?"

UNFINISHED BUSINESS

This section will highlight five sets of problems or difficulties that remained unsolved at the end of our period.

A first set of difficulties, at the level of normative ethics, may be called, for short, the problem of deontological and teleological ethics. It would seem that an adequate or viable ethics should include both a teleological aspect pertaining to happiness or satisfaction and a deontological aspect pertaining to obligation. But it would seem impossible, on a strict construal of the terms, for one and the same ethics to be both teleological and deontological. This set of difficulties includes the problem about the relative priority of the right and the good and the debate about the claims of Kantian and utilitarian ethics.

A second set of difficulties, also on the level of normative ethics, has to do with self-interest, egoism, and altruism. Given the demands that the best-known version of deontological ethics, Kantianism, the best-known version of teleological ethics, utilitarianism, and at least some forms of divine command ethics can place on individuals, it was only natural that Anglo-American ethics should face the issue of self-interest and the competing claims of egoism and altruism.

A third set of difficulties appeared at the level of metaethics. Naturalism, intuitionism, and noncognitivism seemed to be the only available forms of metaethics, but each was beset by serious difficulties. Naturalism seemed to reason invalidly from factual claims to claims about value or obligation. Intuitionism seemed unable to give a satisfactory account of its intuitions. To some, at least, the various forms of noncognitivism seemed not to be explaining the meaning and justification of ethical claims so much as explaining them away.

A fourth set of difficulties concerned the relation of facts to values and especially to obligations. Could either deontological ethics or teleological ethics be grounded or justified on the basis of facts about the world or about human beings? If so, how? Could the claims of naturalism or intuitionism be justified, and the claims of noncognitivism be refuted, on the basis of facts? If so, how?

A fifth set of difficulties concerned the appropriate responses to the challenges of skepticism and relativism. Even if the various forms of noncognitivist metaethics were less than fully satisfactory, the unresolved conflict between naturalism and intuitionism suggested that a skeptical stance toward ethical claims was in order. The variety of moral views in the Anglo-American world, not to mention the world generally, still seemed to count against the view that morality was something objective and knowable. The question, "Why should I be moral?" or, in a more sophisticated form, "Why should I adopt the moral point of view?" was still very much alive, both in its practical form, as a refusal to accept moral obligation until moral claims were demonstrated, and in its theoretical form, as a request that the objectivity of ethics be clarified and defended in response to ethical skepticism and relativism.

These five sets of problems were widely recognized, variously formulated, and endlessly debated in the Anglo-American academic ethics of our period.

It is sometimes suggested that the Anglo-American ethics of our period paid little or no attention to the history of ethics. The charge is not entirely fair. It paid close attention to a number of ethical theories and theorists: Hume, Kant, the utilitarians Jeremy Bentham and John Stuart Mill, the intuitionists (principally Moore, Prichard, and Ross), the emotivists (Ayer, Stevenson), and the prescriptivists (Hare). There is, however, some justice in the charge of inattention to history. In the preface to the first edition of *A Short History of Ethics* (1966), Alasdair MacIntyre wrote, "I wanted to give some account of Greek thought for those undergraduate students restricted to the treadmill of Hume, Kant, Mill, and Moore."[33] As late as 1986, James Rachels, in his "Suggestions for Further Reading," gives Aristotle ("whose name would not appear in the index of this book if it did not appear on this page") no more than a passing mention.[34] Anglo-American moral philosophy in our period took little account of the ethics of Plato, Aristotle, Thomas Aquinas and other scholastics, Kierkegaard, Nietzsche, and Sartre, Marx and Freud, Dewey and James.[35]

Apart from these historical lacunae, the moral philosophy of this period had little to say about the political, social, and economic contexts within which people live their ethical lives, or about the political, social, and economic implications of the ethical theories that they discuss. In the preface to the third edition of her *Ethics since 1900*, Mary Warnock admitted as much: "Perhaps the major change [between 1960 and 1978], and one to which I could not do anything like justice without substantial additions, is that it is no longer possible to distinguish moral from political philosophy as I briskly did in 1960. . . . The decision I came to in 1960 to omit political philosophy now seems naïve (as indeed it would always have seemed to some), and in any case impossible."[36] And the moral philosophy of our period did not have much to say about the notion of virtue or about individual virtues.[37]

CHALLENGES TO ANGLO-AMERICAN ETHICS

Some in our period admitted that all was not well within their tradition. Thus Geoffrey Warnock wrote in the Introduction to *Contemporary Moral Philosophy* (1967):

The case is, I believe, that the successive orthodoxies of moral philosophy in English in the present century have been, notwithstanding the often admirable acumen of their authors, remarkably barren. Certain questions about the nature and basis of moral judgment which have been regarded, at least in the past, as centrally important have not only not been examined in recent theories; those theories have seemed deliberately to hold that, on those questions, there is nothing whatever that can usefully be said. There seems to have occurred an extraordinary narrowing of the field; moral philosophy has been made to look, if not simple, then bald and jejune and, in its fruits, unrewarding.[38]

Five years later, Bernard Williams said:

Contemporary moral philosophy has found an original way of being boring, which is by not discussing moral issues at all. Or, rather, it is not so much that a style of moral philosophy has been evolved which cuts the connection with moral issues altogether—that, if it were possible, would have had the interest of being remarkable; but the desire to reduce revealed moral commitment to a minimum and to use moral arguments in the role of being uncontentiously illustrative leaves an impression that all the important issues are off the page, somewhere, and that great caution and little imagination have been used in letting tiny corners of them appear.[39]

By 1985, Williams had broadened his criticism to include what he called "morality" or "the morality system," the morality of which Kantianism and utilitarianism are species.[40]

Some were working to make progress on the issues noted at the end of the preceding section. Thus Frankena's *Ethics* not only surveyed the different normative and metaethical theories, but also proposed a theory of obligation designed to reconcile the claims of deontological and teleological ethics. And John Rawls's *A Theory of Justice* (1971) could be understood as crafting an ethics that would be both deontological and teleological, combining a concern for fairness that had roots in Kant with a concern for outcomes that had roots in the utilitarian tradition, all in a form that would be applicable to an advanced industrial democracy. Mary Warnock's postscript to *Ethics since 1900* had a good deal to say about Rawls and about other developments in Anglo-American moral philosophy, including attention to the history of ethics, to the question what morality itself is, and to the field of moral psychology, citing the work of Anthony Kenny, Donald Davidson, and Charles Taylor. As she saw it, "Ethics since 1960 has become a practical subject, and therefore more urgent and more interesting."[41]

The most direct attack on the dominant Anglo-American ethics came from a pupil of Ludwig Wittgenstein. In "Modern Moral Philosophy" (1958), Elizabeth Anscombe advanced three theses. The first was that it was not profitable for philosophers to do moral philosophy at that time, because they were lacking an adequate philosophical psychology. That is, they lacked adequate understandings of such crucial items as action, intention, pleasure, wanting, human nature, virtue, and human flourishing.[42]

Anscombe's second thesis was that philosophers should stop using the concepts of moral obligation, moral duty, moral right and wrong, and the specifically moral sense of "ought," because these are survivals from an earlier type of ethics, the Hebrew and Christian ethics of divine law, that no longer survives. Modern moral philosophy rejects the Hebrew-Christian ethics of divine law, but inconsistently keeps on using concepts that have their origin in that ethics.[43]

Anscombe's third thesis was that the differences between well-known English moral philosophers from the utilitarian Henry Sidgwick (1838–1900) to the 1950s were of little importance. As she tells the story, Sidgwick departed decisively from Hebrew-Christian ethics when he asserted that the morally right action is the action that produces the best possible consequences; whereas Hebrew-Christian ethics taught that certain types of actions are wrong in and of themselves, regardless of their consequences. And later English moral philosophers—Moore, Ross, Nowell-Smith, Hare—have followed Sidgwick in rejecting the Hebrew-Christian tradition. English moral philosophy since Sidgwick has been consequentialist, as is shown by its willingness to entertain the possibility that it might on occasion be morally right to do an unjust action, such as the judicial condemnation of an innocent person for the benefit of a group. "And that is my complaint."[44]

For all their painstaking work, then, Anglo-American moral philosophers in the years 1950 to 1990 did not succeed in resolving the problems that they themselves had recognized: the competing claims of deontological and teleological ethics, of Kantian and utilitarian ethics, of egoism and altruism, of naturalist, intuitionist, and noncognitivist metaethics, the relationship between fact and value, is and ought, and the challenges of relativism and skepticism. They had done much to clarify these issues, but they were nowhere near resolving them. They had yet to take full account of the history of ethics and to work out the relations between ethics and politics. Perhaps most importantly, some of them were calling into question the basic category of morality.

Contemporary Aristotelians have addressed the problems of Anglo-American moral philosophy in very different ways. One measure, by no means the only measure, by which to evaluate the various forms of contemporary Aristotelianism is the degree to which they have solved or made progress toward solving these problems.

FURTHER REMARKS

The preceding account of the issues faced was arrived at first of all by surveying a number of introductory ethics textbooks. The account is confirmed by an examination of anthologies of readings in ethical theory. Thus *Readings in Ethical Theory*, edited by Wilfrid Sellars and John Hospers (1952), has the following chapter headings:[45]

Introductory
A Sample Ethical Theory (Utilitarianism)
Moore and the Naturalistic Fallacy
The Development of Ethical Intuitionism
The Naturalistic Rejoinder
The Emotive Theory
The Psychology of Conduct and the Concept of Obligation
Moral Freedom, Guilt, and Responsibility
The Problem of Justification

Despite their very general title, Sellars and Hospers say in their preface that their aim "has been to provide a balanced and firsthand account of the theoretical controversies that have developed in ethics since the publication in 1903 of Moore's *Principia Ethica*." They say it again in the preface to their second edition (1970), which covers essentially the same ground and retains many of the readings from the first edition, but with different chapter headings:[46]

Introductory
The Analysis of Ethical Concepts

Theories of Normative Ethics
Rights, Justice, Punishment, and Responsibility
Ethics and Psychology[47]

A sampling of books that were more than introductory points in the same direction. These more advanced books recognize the same basic agenda as the introductory textbooks, discuss them in greater detail, and introduce additional topics that go beyond them. A few examples will make this point. We meet the core issues raised by Moore, Ross, Ayer, Stevenson, and Hare once again in W. D. Hudson's *Modern Moral Philosophy* (1970).[48] The table of contents is too long to quote in full, but here are the chapter titles:

Moral Discourse and Moral Philosophy
Moral Discourse and Theories of Meaning
The Intuitionist Theory
The Emotivist Theory
Prescriptivism
Descriptivism
Action and Responsibility

We have already seen that Bernard Williams's *Morality: An Introduction to Ethics* (1972) challenges the then-current Anglo-American ethics. Still, it includes the following chapters:

The Amoralist
Subjectivism: First Thoughts
Interlude: Relativism
Subjectivism: Further Thoughts
"Good"
Goodness and Roles
Moral Standards and the Distinguishing Mark of Man
God, Morality, and Prudence
What Is Morality About?
Utilitarianism

J. L. Mackie's *Ethics: Inventing Right and Wrong* (1977) has the following chapter titles:[49]

The Subjectivity of Values
The Meaning of "Good"
Obligations and Reasons
Universalization
The Object of Morality
Utilitarianism
Consequentialism and Deontology
Elements of a Practical Morality
Determinism, Responsibility, and Choice
Religion, Law, and Politics

These more advanced works, therefore, tend to confirm our account of Anglo-American moral philosophy in the period 1950 to 1990.[50]

CHAPTER TWO

ALASDAIR MACINTYRE'S REVOLUTIONARY ARISTOTELIANISM

Alasdair MacIntyre was born January 12, 1929, in Glasgow, Scotland. In an interview for *Cogito*, he divided his philosophical career into three parts. The first ran from 1949, when he began graduate school, to 1971, when he arrived in the United States. This he characterized as a period of "heterogeneous, badly organized, sometimes fragmented and often frustrating and messy enquiries." Raised as a Christian, for part of this period he aspired to be both a Christian and a Marxist, but eventually concluded that he could not be either a Christian or a Marxist. His second period, 1971–77, was "an interim period of sometimes painfully self-critical reflection," in which he began to take seriously "the possibility that the history both of modern morality and of modern moral philosophy could only be written adequately from an Aristotelian point of view."[1] MacIntyre's Aristotelian reflections led him to embrace theism and Catholic Christianity.[2]

MacIntyre's third period, from 1977 to the present, is the period of his best-known books: *After Virtue* (1981), *Whose Justice? Which Rationality?* (1988), *Three Rival Versions of Moral Enquiry* (1990), *Dependent Rational Animals* (1999), *Ethics in the Conflicts of Modernity* (2016), and others. Since 1971 he has taught at Boston University, the University of Notre Dame, Vanderbilt University, Duke University, and once again at Notre Dame, where he is now professor emeritus.

Even within his third period, MacIntyre's philosophical output has been vast. A brief account of his position is bound to be highly selective. I focus on *After Virtue, Dependent Rational Animals*, and *Ethics in the Conflicts of Modernity*. *After Virtue* is foundational to MacIntyre's project, and he reaffirmed its main theses in his 2007 prologue to the third edition. *Dependent Rational Animals* supplies the biological and metaphysical grounding that MacIntyre found he needed for the claims of *After Virtue*. *Ethics in the Conflicts of Modernity* is the latest extended statement of his position. I also draw on several of his published essays, which sometimes provide more recent and more concise expressions of his views.

MacIntyre has authored a number of statements clarifying his positions. Particularly helpful are those in the collections *After MacIntyre*,[3] *Revolutionary Aristotelianism*,[4] *Virtue and Politics*,[5] and *What Happened in and to Moral Philosophy in the Twentieth Century?*,[6] along with his interviews with Thomas D. Pearson and Alex Voorhoeve.[7] Likewise helpful are the 1995 preface to the second edition of *A Short History of Ethics*[8] and the prefaces to his *Selected Essays*.[9] These shorter pieces offer helpful guidance for the interpretation of his books.

AFTER VIRTUE

To understand his position in the third period (1977–), one might well begin with "Notes from the Moral Wilderness."[10] At a time when the atrocities of Stalin had recently come to light and were being widely condemned, MacIntyre asked on what basis they were being condemned, and he concluded that the autonomous morality of liberalism, a morality grounded not in fact but in personal choice, provided no sufficient basis for the condemnation. This criticism of the morality of liberalism is a key to understanding MacIntyre's position in *After Virtue* and *Ethics in the Conflicts of Modernity*.[11]

Another piece that announces several of the themes of MacIntyre's later work is his 1975 review of C. B. Macpherson's *Democratic Theory: Essays in Retrieval*.[12] Macpherson (1911–87) was a Canadian political theorist. His fundamental work was *The Political Theory of Possessive Individualism: Hobbes to Locke*.[13] Possessive individualism, as Macpherson understands it, includes the following assumptions: "(i) What makes a man human is freedom from dependence on the wills of others. (ii) Freedom from dependence on others means freedom from any relations with others except those relations which the individual enters voluntarily with a view to his own interest. (iii) The individual is essentially the proprietor of his own person and capacities, for which he owes nothing to society."[14] Macpherson started out as a liberal in the tradition of John Stuart Mill, but he came to think that this brand of liberalism had been infected by the possessive individualism of the seventeenth century. In response, he tried to develop a different kind of liberalism, which MacIntyre in his review termed a "cooperative and creative individualism," as opposed to possessive individualism. He thought that Macpherson was right to criticize liberalism and possessive individualism, but that he should have taken his criticism a good deal further.[15] The review also anticipates two other aspects of MacIntyre's later work: his criticism of social contract theory and his rejection of some forms of contemporary rights talk.[16]

MacIntyre's criticism of liberal individualism rests not only on theoretical grounds but also on moral and political grounds:

> So in history, as in theory, I conclude that Macpherson concedes too much to the contemporary inheritors, enlightened as they may seem to be, of that possessive individualism which Macpherson has so unerringly diagnosed in the seventeenth century. The heirs of the writings of Hobbes and Locke are the contemporary versions of contract, of private rights and of utility. They are the philosophies of the contemporary men of property—both private property and state property—just as their intellectual ancestors were the philosophical spokesmen for those who in the name of contracts, rights and utility, stole away our common land. Individualism is and always was the doctrine of successful thieves from the community.[17]

Criticisms of liberalism, individualism, social contract theory, and rights talk will be constants in MacIntyre's later work.

The Emotivist Situation

After Virtue begins with the "disquieting suggestion" that the language that advanced Western societies use to talk about morality is in grave disorder: "What we possess, if this view is true, are the fragments of a conceptual scheme, parts which now lack those contexts from which their significance derived."[18] MacIntyre says that we are living in what he calls an "emotivist situation." Emotivism is the metaethical view, espoused by C. L. Stevenson and others, that moral utterances are expressions of feeling that have no cognitive content and that are, in that sense, meaningless. And so MacIntyre rejects emotivism as an account of the meaning of moral language, but he accepts it as an acute diagnosis of the way that G. E. Moore and his friends were in fact using moral language.[19] As MacIntyre sees it, Moore and his friends were behaving "as if their disagreements over what is good were being settled by an appeal to an objective and impersonal criterion; but in fact the stronger and psychologically more adroit will was prevailing."[20] He suggests that the emotivists saw clearly enough how Moore and his friends were using moral language, but that they then (mistakenly) took this as the basis for a general account of the meaning of moral language. He suggests "that they did in fact confuse moral utterance at Cambridge (and in other places with a similar inheritance) after 1903 with moral utterance as such, and that they therefore presented what was in essentials a correct account of the former as though it were an account of the latter."[21]

Ours is an emotivist situation, then, not in the sense that the emotivist theory of meaning is true, but in the sense that many elements of our contemporary moral language no longer have a clear and definite meaning. They are survivals of an earlier moral language, now separated from the original context in which they once made sense.[22]

The emotivist situation is characterized by unsettleable disagreements over moral matters, unsettleable in large part because the contending parties never make intellectual contact with one another.[23] It is also marked by manipulative social relations and pervasive fictions.[24] Thus we have the prominence of rights talk, despite the fact that natural rights are (in MacIntyre's much-controverted view) fictions.[25] We have the prominence of protest, understood not as a rational argument addressed to opponents, but as utterance addressed to people who already agree. We have the prominence of unmasking: interpreting other people's moral talk as the expression of unacknowledged motives and interests.[26]

The Enlightenment Project

The emotivist situation results from the failure of what MacIntyre calls the "Enlightenment project of justifying morality." Why did Enlightenment thinkers think that they needed to justify morality? The answer lies in the late medieval and early modern periods. The Christian Middle Ages had recognized three interrelated terms: human beings as they are; human beings as they could be if they actualized their nature, attaining their *telos*; and a set of virtues and precepts as the bridge that could take human beings from what they are to what they could be. When the later Middle Ages rejected the notions of essential nature and teleology, they rejected the idea of human beings as they could be if they actualized their nature. This rejection removed the virtues and precepts from their original teleological context, and so left unclear the relationship between humans as they are and the former bridge of virtues and precepts.[27]

MacIntyre documents the failure of the Enlightenment project through three case studies: the failed attempts of Diderot and Hume to base traditional morality on desires and passions; the failed attempt of Kant to base it on pure practical reason; and the failed attempt of Kierkegaard to base it on sheer choice or decision. In each case, MacIntyre finds a deep-seated discrepancy between the ethical content that was being defended and the manner in which it was being defended.[28] The general pattern of ethical argument in the Enlightenment was inference from facts about human nature as it is (de facto) to conclusions about the content and authority of moral rules (de jure). The task was to find a connection between the plain facts of human nature and a set of moral rules drawn mainly from the predecessor culture. This kind of argument did not work and cannot work. The Aristotelian tradition, by contrast, had regarded "human being" as a functional or teleological concept, a concept that carries standards of evaluation within it. The late Middle Ages lost the idea that human being is a functional concept. Lacking that functional concept, the Enlightenment lost the connection between is and ought. Thus the Enlightenment project was doomed to fail.[29]

Nietzsche or Aristotle?

The first half of *After Virtue* is mostly critical narrative. The second half is largely narrative but also presents a constructive argument. The transition from one to the other takes place in chapter 9, titled "Nietzsche or Aristotle?" Here MacIntyre argues that the emotivist situation is really a situation of self-assertion in the Nietzschean sense of that term. Nietzsche found expressions of objectivity to be merely expressions of subjective will. It was he who most acutely diagnosed the failure of the Enlightenment project and of the whole long development that started with the rejection of Aristotle in the fourteenth through the seventeenth centuries. The Marxist and Weberian analyses of society reduce to Nietzsche's analysis. In fact, the whole long attempt to do without Aristotle boils down to Nietzsche. Hence someone who hesitates to accept Nietzsche's interpretation of morality ought to reconsider the modern rejection of Aristotle.[30]

Practices, Goods, and Virtues

MacIntyre outlines a contemporary Aristotelian position in three stages. In the first stage, he argues that certain activities, which he calls "practices," are essential to a good human life.[31] In chapter 14 of *After Virtue*, he defines a practice as "any coherent and complex form of socially established cooperative human activity through which goods internal to that form of activity are realized in the course of trying to achieve those standards of excellence which are appropriate to, and partially definitive of, that form of activity."[32] Examples of practices include football and farming, the arts and the sciences, and (in certain contexts, but unfortunately not in ours) politics.

Practices are an essential part of a good human life, because they have what MacIntyre calls "internal goods," that is, goods that can only be achieved by engaging in the relevant practice. The only way to enjoy the goods internal to playing chess is to play chess, and the only way to enjoy the goods internal to playing football is to play football. Practices may also bring with them external goods, such as financial payments. Someone may be paid for playing chess. Someone else may be paid the same amount for playing football. But the internal goods and the achievement of excellence in these practices are inseparable from the practices themselves.[33]

MacIntyre gives a preliminary and tentative definition of virtue as "an acquired human quality the possession and exercise of which tends to enable us to achieve those goods which are internal to practices and the lack of which effectively prevents us from achieving any such goods."[34] Pursuit of external goods does not necessarily require the virtues. The pursuit of internal goods does. If someone is being paid simply to win at football or soccer, he or she might win by cheating and still get paid. But, MacIntyre argues, attaining excellence in practices and achieving the internal goods of practices require at least the virtues of honesty, justice, and courage. To attain the goods internal to a practice, to meet and to raise the standards of excellence in a practice, one cannot cheat. One must face and admit the facts about oneself, one's abilities, and one's achievements. One must be prepared to resist the pressures and desires that would stand in the way of the practice. Those who do not exercise these virtues exclude themselves from practices and from their corresponding internal goods.[35]

The terminology of practices and internal goods is not Aristotle's, but MacIntyre sees his account as Aristotelian, on three counts: "First it requires for its completion a cogent elaboration of just those distinctions and concepts which Aristotle's account requires: voluntariness, the distinction between the intellectual virtues and the virtues of character, the relationship of both to natural abilities and to the passions and the structure of practical reasoning."[36] Second, it can accommodate the Aristotelian account of pleasure as specified by and supervening on activity, but not the utilitarian account of pleasure as something that can be pursued as a goal and something that is summable.[37] Third, MacIntyre's account of the virtues "links evaluation and explanation in a characteristically Aristotelian way. From an Aristotelian standpoint to identify certain actions as manifesting or failing to manifest a virtue or virtues is never only to evaluate; it is also to take the first step towards explaining why those actions rather than some others were performed."[38] On this account, as opposed to any view that restricts explanations to bare facts, virtues and vices can function as explanations: "Why did you give back that money?" "Because it was the just thing to do."

MacIntyre does not mean, however, that we ought to return to the position of the historical Aristotle. He objects to certain of the historical Aristotle's views, in particular to what he calls Aristotle's "metaphysical biology." He proposes to place an Aristotelian understanding of the virtues on what he terms a "socially teleological" basis rather than a biologically teleological basis.[39] He recognizes, however, that this first stage of his definition of the virtues, basing the virtues on practices, yields only a partial and preliminary account of them.[40]

Narrative Unity, Community, and Tradition

In chapter 15 of *After Virtue*, MacIntyre introduces the second and third stages of his Aristotelian analysis: the narrative unity of a human life and the concept of a tradition. Practices do not exist in isolation. They exist in the context of human lives. The notion of a bare action, that is, of physical behavior apart from intention and further contexts, is unintelligible. Human action is intelligible only in the context of intentions, which in turn have their contexts. Humans are storytelling animals, and narrative structure is a property not only of our stories but also of our lives. We are accountable to explain to others how our actions fit into our lives, and we can ask the same of them.[41]

Part of life's being a narrative is that, if it is at all meaningful, it is heading to a *telos*:[42] "There is no present which is not informed by some image of some future and an image of the future which always presents itself in the form of a *telos*—or of a variety of ends or goals—towards which we are either moving or failing to move in the present."[43] And we cannot exercise the virtues or seek the good qua isolated individuals. The virtues, once again truthfulness, justice, and courage, are

> those dispositions which will not only sustain practices and enable us to achieve the goods internal to practices, but which will also sustain us in the relevant kind of quest for the good, by enabling us to overcome the harms, temptations, dangers, and distractions which we encounter, and which will furnish us with increasing self-knowledge

and increasing knowledge of the good. The catalogue of the virtues will therefore include the virtues required to sustain the kind of households and the kind of political communities in which men and women can seek for the good together and the virtues necessary for philosophical enquiry about the character of the good.[44]

Practices, the quest for the good, and community all require traditions in order to maintain and reinforce the standards involved in the practices. The word "tradition" may suggest something unchanging, a sense associated with the conservatism of Edmund Burke, but MacIntyre stresses instead the dynamic character of tradition:[45] "A living tradition . . . is an historically extended, socially embodied argument, and an argument precisely in part about the goods which constitute that tradition."[46] A tradition that does not change is dying or dead.

Individuals owe a large part of their identities to the histories and traditions in which they stand, and those histories and traditions are the contexts within which they carry on their quests for the good. The very shape of the good, at least at the outset of our quest, comes from the social context in which we start, the communities to which we belong, the history or tradition of which we are bearers. And once again, no tradition can be maintained without a commitment to truthfulness, justice, and courage: "The virtues find their point and purpose not only in sustaining those relationships necessary if the variety of goods internal to practices are to be achieved and not only in sustaining the form of an individual life in which that individual may seek out his or her good as the good of his or her whole life, but also in sustaining those traditions which provide both practices and individual lives with their necessary historical context."[47]

Practices, traditions, and communities typically require the support of institutions. Still, their relationship to institutions is ambiguous. Institutions tend to make themselves their own ends, neglecting or even stifling the practices, goods, and virtues that they were founded to serve and promote. The remedy, of course, is not to try to do without institutions. That would be impossible. The remedy is to cultivate the virtues of truthfulness, justice, and courage, precisely in order to keep institutions on the right track.[48]

Here is MacIntyre's overall conclusion: "It is that on the one hand we still, in spite of the efforts of three centuries of moral philosophy and one of sociology, lack any coherent rationally defensible statement of a liberal individualist point of view; and that, on the other hand, the Aristotelian tradition can be restated in a way that restores intelligibility and rationality to our moral and social attitudes and commitments."[49]

The Enlightenment project has failed, as it had to fail. We are living in an emotivist situation. We face a choice between the position of Nietzsche and some form of Aristotelianism. The Aristotelian tradition can be expressed and defended in terms of internal goods, practices, the narrative unity of human life, the need for communities, traditions, and institutions, and the need for the virtues of justice, truthfulness, and courage to sustain them. In the practical order, "what matters at this stage is the construction of local forms of community within which civility and the intellectual and moral life can be sustained through the new dark ages that are already upon us. . . . We are waiting not for a Godot, but for another— doubtless very different—St. Benedict."[50]

Some readers have taken this remark as counseling withdrawal from the contemporary world. In the 2007 prologue to *After Virtue*, MacIntyre comments as follows: "Benedict's greatness lay in making possible a quite new kind of institution, that of the monastery of prayer, learning, and labor, in which and around which communities could not only survive, but flourish in a period of social and cultural darkness. . . . it was my intention to suggest, when I wrote that last sentence in 1980, that ours too is a time of waiting for new and unpredictable possibilities of renewal. It is also a time for resisting as prudently and courageously and justly and temperately as possible the dominant social, economic, and political order of advanced modernity."[51] That is hardly a counsel of withdrawal.

BEYOND *AFTER VIRTUE*

The last chapter of *After Virtue* points the way to a further development of MacIntyre's project, one that provides a systematic account of the notion of rationality that was presupposed in the arguments of that book.[52] This turned out to be *Whose Justice? Which Rationality?*[53] The book is largely concerned with differences between Aristotle and Hume and their respective traditions. Its systematic account of rationality is stated in chapter 18, "The Rationality of Traditions." For the purposes of this chapter, however, I am going to draw instead on his "Moral Relativism, Truth and Justification" (1994). Besides giving us MacIntyre's view on how we might possibly make progress in philosophy, this essay will also give us his take on the problem of relativism, which has been a major concern in Anglo-American moral philosophy.

Rationality and Tradition

"Often, if not always, moral relativism is a response to the discovery of systematic and apparently ineliminable disagreement between the proponents of rival moral points of view, each of whom claims rational justification for their own standpoint and none of whom seems able, except by their own standards, to rebut the claims of their rivals," MacIntyre states.[54] We have met this kind of disagreement in the emotivist situation. From this some conclude (correctly, in MacIntyre's view) that all rational justification is internal to and relative to the standards of a particular standpoint. Correctly, in his view, for he recognizes no universal or impartial standpoint from which one could pass judgment on particular points of view. And some conclude (incorrectly, in his view) that this is an area of judgment in which no claim to truth can be sustained.[55]

Against this MacIntyre argues that, given a substantive conception of truth (truth as the adequacy of the intellect to its object, as opposed to truth as rational justification and truth as pragmatic commitment), it is possible, under certain conditions, for a moral standpoint to show itself superior to one or more of its rivals.[56] For a tradition to show itself superior to a rival tradition, its adherents have to accept the burden of justification that comes with a realist theory of truth. They have to offer explanations of why the adherents of the rival tradition see things as they do, and these explanations have to be specific, detailed, and so open to testing and possible refutation. They have to face the distinctive problems, difficulties, and weaknesses of their own standpoint. And they have to be able to understand their own moral standpoint from another point of view than their own.

When people understand their own moral standpoint from one different from their own, that opens up the possibility that this other standpoint will explain why they have not been able to deal with problems that have arisen within their own. And so progress in rational inquiry about the moral life is possible, not in the sense that someone speaking from a supposedly universal or impartial standpoint passes judgment on particular standpoints, but in the sense that adherents of a particular tradition can on occasion recognize that their standpoint has problems that it cannot solve and that to solve those problems they need the assistance of another tradition.[57] But even if one tradition has the resources to solve a problem that has arisen in another tradition, there is no guarantee that adherents of the latter tradition will recognize that fact: "So on fundamental matters, moral or philosophical, the existence of continuing disagreement, even between highly intelligent people, should not lead us to suppose that there are not adequate resources available for the rational resolution of such disagreement."[58]

MacIntyre's response to the problem of relativism in ethical theory is thus that it is at least possible, under certain conditions, to show that one ethical standpoint is superior to some other standpoint. But the conditions are stringent, and MacIntyre does not hold out much hope that any one standpoint, even his own, will decisively defeat its rivals. In the postscript to the second edition of *After Virtue*, responding to a criticism from William K. Frankena, he quotes with approval a passage from David Lewis: "Philosophical theories are never refuted conclusively. (Or hardly ever, Gödel and Gettier may have done it.) The theory survives its refutation—at a price. . . . Our 'intuitions' are simply opinions; our philosophical theories are the same . . . a reasonable task for the philosopher is to bring them into equilibrium. Our common task is to find out what equilibria there are that can withstand examination, but it remains for each of us to come to rest in one or other of them. . . . Once the menu of well-worked out theories is before us, philosophy is a matter of opinion."[59] This approving reference to Lewis brings out an aspect of MacIntyre's view of rationality that might otherwise be missed. He is not a relativist, he believes that philosophical issues, even central philosophical issues, are settleable, and he believes that in certain circumstances one philosophical tradition can show itself superior to a rival tradition, but he also believes that definitive proof is rarely, if ever, possible.

A New Perspective on Marxism

MacIntyre's first book was *Marxism: An Interpretation* (1953).[60] In 1968, he published a revised version under the title *Marxism and Christianity*.[61] In 1995, he published a further revision of *Marxism and Christianity*.[62] In the introduction to this revision he narrates how his stance toward Marxism had changed between 1953 and 1995.[63] In 2006, he wrote of this introduction: "It reasserts the truth of that in Marxism which has survived every critique and it attempts, although too briefly, to suggest how Marxist, Aristotelian, and Christian insights need to be integrated in any ethics and politics that is able to reckon with contemporary realities."[64] This chapter is not the place to discuss the evolution of MacIntyre's thinking about Marxism, but a brief account of what he retains from Marxism will fill out the position of *After Virtue* and prepare the way for *Ethics in the Conflicts of Modernity*.

First and foremost, MacIntyre accepts Marx's critique of capitalism and in particular the theory of surplus value: "The needs of capital formation impose upon capitalists and upon those who manage their enterprises a need to extract from the work of their employees a surplus which is at the future disposal of capital and not of labor."[65] The necessarily conflicting interests of capital and labor make it impossible, at the economic level, for a capitalist society to have a common good. Even if capitalism has provided a rising standard of living, this does not alter the fact of exploitation. Further, capitalism systematically miseducates people. It teaches them "to believe that what they should aim at and hope for is not what they deserve, but whatever they may happen to want. The attempt is to get them to regard themselves primarily as consumers whose practical and productive activities are no more than a means to consumption."[66] Capitalism teaches people to regard what the Greeks called *pleonexia*, "acquisitiveness," as a virtue, when in fact it is a vice, the vice opposed to justice. It "provides systematic incentives to develop a type of character that has a propensity to injustice."[67] Thus capitalism is bad even for those who succeed by its standards.

Social democracy, the attempt to use the state to cure the evils of capitalism, is a mistake: "Those who make the conquest of state power their aim are always in the end conquered by it and, in becoming the instruments of the state, themselves become in time the instruments of one of the several versions of modern capitalism."[68] Liberalism—here MacIntyre calls it "secular liberalism"—is not the answer to the evils of capitalism. It is "the moral and political counterpart and expression of developing capitalism."[69]

MacIntyre rejects liberal social democracy for three reasons. First, when trade unions try to work through the system, they become domesticated and eventually lose their power. Second, "liberalism is the politics of a set of elites, whose members through their control of party machines and of the media, predetermine for the most part the range of political choices open to the vast mass of ordinary voters. . . . Liberalism thus ensures the exclusion of most people from any possibility of active and rational participation in determining the form of community in which they live."[70] Third, and most importantly:

> The moral individualism of liberalism is itself a solvent of participatory community. For liberalism in its practice as well as in much of its theory promotes a vision of the social world as an arena in which each individual, in pursuit of the achievement of whatever she or he takes to be her or his good, needs to be protected from other such individuals by the enforcement of individual rights. Moral argument within liberalism cannot therefore begin from some conception of a genuinely common good that is more and other than the sum of the preferences of individuals. But argument to, from, and about such a conception of the common good is integral to the practice of participatory community.[71]

If capitalism is evil and liberal social democracy is not the answer, what are we to do? MacIntyre calls for "a politics of self-defense for all those local societies that aspire to achieve some relatively self-sufficient and independent form of participatory practice-based community and that therefore need to protect themselves from the corrosive effects of capitalism and the depredations of state power. And in the end the relevance of theorizing to practice is to be tested by what theorizing can contribute, indirectly or directly, to such a politics."[72]

MacIntyre does not accept Marx or Marxism uncritically. On the contrary, he holds that Marxism so far has largely failed, mainly because Marxist theorizing has become detached from revolutionary practice. At the end of the "Three Perspectives on Marxism," he criticizes Marx for not pressing further certain questions that he had posed in his own *Theses on Feuerbach*.[73]

A Politics of Common Goods

What does MacIntyre propose by way of an alternative to capitalism and liberalism? Two texts outline the answer. One is "Politics, Philosophy and the Common Good" (1997).[74] The other is chapter 11 of *Whose Justice? Which Rationality?*

By "politics," MacIntyre understands a community's discussion and deliberation about its goods and how they are to be ordered. By this standard, the politics of the contemporary nation state fails to be politics. It has no room for debate about first principles or for discussion that appeals to first principles or for a politics of the common good.[75] For basically the same reasons that we have seen, MacIntyre remains critical of liberalism and of the individualism that he thinks is part and parcel of it. Liberalism is, despite appearances and professions, a politics of elites: "Modern Western societies are oligarchies disguised as liberal democracies."[76] MacIntyre dismisses present-day conservatism as a viable alternative to liberalism. What passes for conservatism is really just a species of liberalism and shares its problematic assumptions.[77]

On the positive side, MacIntyre stresses the importance of communities in which members act cooperatively in pursuit of acknowledged common goods. Such communities are almost necessarily small and local. These local communities have goods that are common in the strong sense of that term: not merely aggregates of the goods of individuals but goods that are genuinely shared:[78] "Such are those goods not only achieved by means of cooperative activity and shared understanding of their significance, but in key part constituted by cooperative activity and shared understanding of their significance, goods such as the excellence in cooperative activity achieved by fishing crews and by string quartets, by farming households and by teams of research scientists."[79]

He recognizes that local communities can and often do have their defects, but MacIntyre believes that they are the only places where common goods can be pursued and where political discussion about the ordering of those goods can be carried on. Only small communities can meet the three characteristics that genuine politics requires: their members have a large degree of shared understanding of goods, virtues, and rules; their relationships are not deformed by compartmentalization (the modern tendency for people to think and act differently in different contexts and social roles); and they are protected from the incursions of the state and the "free" market economy.[80] The "free" market necessarily presupposes an individualist conception of common good, as opposed to the conception of common good that a community needs if it is to be a genuine political community, that is, a community that inquires into its goods and how to order them. He also believes that markets above a small local level are not really free: "Market relationships in contemporary capitalism are for the most part relations imposed both on labor and on small producers, rather than in any sense freely chosen."[81]

MacIntyre's emphasis on the importance of communities and common goods has led some observers to classify him as a communitarian. He rejects this label on the grounds that communitarianism's theoretical critique of liberalism is practically ineffectual, that its account of common goods is vague and elusive, and that it mistakenly assumes that the values that can be achieved in relatively small communities can also be realized in the modern nation-state.[82]

Toward the end of "Politics, Philosophy and the Common Good," MacIntyre faces the objection that his approach to politics is a recipe for utopian ineffectiveness. In response, he admits that any worthwhile politics of local community will have to be aware of the power of the nation-state and the influence of national and international markets. But small-scale political communities can and must be wary and antagonistic in their dealings with the state and the market economy. Whenever possible, these local communities should challenge the state and the market to justify their claims to authority: "For the state and the market economy are so structured as to subvert and undermine the politics of local community. Between the one politics and the other there can only be continuing conflict."[83]

Chapter 11 of *Whose Justice? Which Rationality?* is entitled "Aquinas on Practical Rationality and Justice."[84] This was first published in 1988, but MacIntyre reaffirmed it in "Natural Law as Subversive: The Case of Aquinas" (2006). There he said he would argue "that at the level of theoretical enquiry Aquinas defined, both for his contemporaries and for us, a set of legal, political, and moral possibilities for structuring communal life, practically as well as theoretically alternative to those which were in fact realized, and I have argued elsewhere that this alternative was and is rationally and morally superior to that which was in fact realized in and by the emerging nation-state and its later bureaucratic heirs."[85]

Fundamental to Aquinas's alternative possibilities is distributive justice: "The requirements of distributive justice are satisfied when each person receives in proportion to his or her contribution, that is, receives what is due in respect of their status, office, and function and how well they fill it and so contribute to the good of all."[86] Aquinas's understanding of justice has implications for the legal system: "Justice in the administration of justice requires respect of jurisdiction, no irrelevant discrimination between persons, no unfounded accusations, truth-telling by everyone in court, that if a poor person has no one to defend him or her here and now but this particular lawyer, this particular lawyer defend that poor person, and that no lawyer knowingly defend an unjust cause. Exorbitant legal fees, like all other exorbitant prices . . . are a form of theft (*ST* IIa-IIae, 67–71)."[87]

Aquinas's conception of justice recognizes the legitimacy of private property, but "ownership is limited by the necessities of human need."[88] Beyond that, his ideas about justice in the economic sphere are strongly opposed to key elements of the capitalist economy:

In what would now be called the economic sphere Aquinas distinguishes between the value of a thing and what it is worth to a particular person, a distinction which lacks application in the modern economics of free markets. The justice of a price is not only a matter of the value of a thing but in most types of cases it is such. Trade is a legitimate activity when it is undertaken by someone "for the sake of public utility so that necessary things should not be lacking from the life of one's *patria*, and he seeks money, not as if an end, but as if a wage for labor" (*S. T.* II-IIae, 77,4). Deception and exorbitant pricing are prohibited unconditionally, and so is usury.[89]

In today's English, "usury" means charging an excessive rate of interest. Aquinas understands usury in the broader biblical sense of taking any interest at all. MacIntyre says that Aquinas could have distinguished between lending money at interest to someone simply to make more money and lending money at interest as a form of partnership: "That he did not [so distinguish] is not unimportant, for it is quite clear that any such return upon investment, which was not either a *stipendium laboris* [payment for labor] or compensation for a need unmet because of that investment, would have been regarded by him as usury. The standard commercial and financial practices of capitalism are as incompatible with Aquinas' conception of justice as are the standard practices of the kind of adversarial system of legal justice in which lawyers often defend those whom they know to be guilty."[90]

Aquinas takes a stringent view of what counts as a just law, holding that unjust laws do not require obedience and in fact do not merit the name of law:

> And so also insofar as unjust regimes approach the character of tyrannies, they lose all claim to our obedience (*S. T.* IIa-IIae, 42, 2; cf. *De Regno*, cap. 3). What is bad about tyranny is that it subverts the virtues of its subjects; the best regime is that whose order best conduces to education into the virtues in the interest of the good of all. Hence the modern liberal conception of government as securing a minimum order, within which individuals may pursue their own freely chosen ends, protected by and large from the moral interference of government, is also incompatible with Aquinas' account of a just order.[91]

MacIntyre went on to develop similar political views in *Dependent Rational Animals* and *Ethics in the Conflicts of Modernity*. They will strike many, perhaps most, readers as unrealistic. But lest the reader think that

MacIntyre the political thinker is simply lost in the thirteenth century, let me quote from a statement that he published during the United States presidential campaign of 2004: "What then are the right political questions? One of them is: What do we owe our children? And the answer is that we owe them the best chance that we can give them of protection and fostering from the moment of conception onwards. And we can only achieve that if we give them the best chance that we can both of a flourishing family life, in which the work of their parents is fairly and adequately rewarded, and of an education which will enable them to flourish. These two sentences, if fully spelled out, amount to a politics."[92] Such a politics, he added, would be unacceptable to both major U.S. political parties.

Dependent Rational Animals

In the mid-1980s, MacIntyre began to identify himself not just as an Aristotelian but as a Thomistic Aristotelian. Why this shift? As he put it in the 2007 prologue to *After Virtue*, he had become convinced that Aquinas "was in some respects a better Aristotelian than Aristotle, that not only was he an excellent interpreter of Aristotle's texts, but that he had been able to extend and deepen both Aristotle's metaphysical and his moral enquiries."[93] MacIntyre had also come to think that the position of *After Virtue* required a metaphysical grounding. In the prologue, he wrote, "I had now learned from Aquinas that my attempt to provide an account of the human good purely in social terms, in terms of practices, traditions, and the narrative unity of human lives, was bound to be inadequate until I had provided it with a metaphysical grounding. It is only because human beings have an end towards which they are directed by reason of their specific nature, that practices, traditions, and the like are able to function as they do."[94] This notion of a natural end (*telos*) becomes increasingly prominent in MacIntyre's later work.

Dependent Rational Animals picks up some of the central themes of *After Virtue* and anticipates several of the themes of *Ethics in the Conflicts of Modernity*. Its distinctive contribution, however, is to place the ethics of *After Virtue* in the context of biology and the human life cycle. It considers the implications of the facts that human beings are born helpless, once again become helpless as they grow old, and even in adult life are always liable to become helpless and dependent on others. This biological grounding points to a further case for the virtues and a fuller list of the virtues than that found in *After Virtue*. This richer understanding of the virtues involves an appreciation of the importance of common activities and common goods, a rejection of the sharp distinction between one person's goods and other people's goods, and a further criticism of the modern nation-state.

In a significant shift from *After Virtue*, MacIntyre admits that he was wrong to judge that an ethics independent of biology was possible:

> Although there is indeed good reason to repudiate important elements in Aristotle's biology, I now judge that I was in error in supposing an ethics independent of biology to be possible . . . and this for two distinct, but related reasons. The first is that no account of the goods, rules and virtues that are definitive of our moral life can be adequate that does not explain—or at least point us towards an explanation—how that form of life is possible for beings who are biologically constituted as we are. . . . Secondly, a failure to understand that condition and the light thrown upon it by a comparison between humans and members of other intelligent species will obscure crucial features of that development. One such [feature], of immense importance on its own account, is the nature and extent of human vulnerability and disability.[95] And by not reckoning adequately with this central feature of human life I had necessarily failed to notice some other important aspects of the part that the virtues play in human life.[96]

Dependent Rational Animals focuses attention on two sets of facts. The first set is about what we share with other intelligent animal species, with dolphins in particular.[97] The second set is about the vulnerability and disability that pervade our lives, especially in early childhood, old age, and times when we are sick or injured:

> From those starting points I attempted to answer the question of what it would be for thus vulnerable and dependent rational animals

to flourish and what qualities of character we would need, if we were to be able to receive from others what we need to receive from them. The answer that I have sketched is that in order to flourish, we need both those virtues that enable us to function as independent and accountable practical reasoners and those virtues that enable us to acknowledge the nature and extent of our dependence on others. Both the acquisition and the exercise of those virtues are possible only insofar as we participate in social relationships of giving and receiving, social relationships governed by and partially defined by the norms of the natural law.[98]

Dependent Rational Animals thus complements the case for the virtues made in *After Virtue*. Given our initial animal condition, the development of human beings into independent practical reasoners requires the education of desires and the acquisition of the relevant virtues: "What are the qualities that a child must develop, first to redirect and transform her or his desires, and subsequently to direct them consistently towards the goods of the different stages of her or his life? They are the intellectual and moral virtues. It is because failure to acquire those virtues makes it impossible for us to achieve this transition that the virtues have the place and function that they do in human life."[99]

Given that many of our human goods cannot be achieved apart from the common goods of various groups, we need the virtues required to sustain those groups, or what MacIntyre calls the "virtues of giving and receiving":

We become independent practical reasoners through participation in a set of relationships to certain particular others who are able to give us what we need. When we have become independent practical reasoners, we will often, although not perhaps always, also have acquired what we need, if we are to be able to give to those others who are now in need of what formerly we needed. We find ourselves placed at some particular point within a network of relationships of giving and receiving in which, generally and characteristically, what and how far we are able to give depends in part on what and how far we received.[100]

Being dependent in all sorts of ways, we need what MacIntyre calls the "virtues of acknowledged dependence," "such virtues as those of knowing how to exhibit gratitude, without allowing that gratitude to be a burden, courtesy towards the graceless giver, and forbearance towards the inadequate giver. The exercise of these latter virtues always involves a truthful acknowledgement of dependence."[101]

In chapters 10, 11, and 12 of *Dependent Rational Animals*, MacIntyre develops his views on community and politics. Once again he insists on the importance of genuinely common goods, that is, goods that can only be achieved by people acting in common, and of the virtues of acknowledged dependence that action in common requires. Alluding to Adam Smith's remark in *The Wealth of Nations* that we do not expect butchers, brewers, or bakers to act out of benevolence but out of self-interest, he writes:

> Adam Smith's contrast between self-interested market behavior on the one hand and altruistic, benevolent behavior on the other, obscures from view just those types of activity in which the goods to be achieved are neither mine-rather-than-others' nor others'-rather-than-mine, but instead are goods that can only be mine insofar as they are also those of others, that are genuinely common goods, as the goods of networks of giving and receiving are. But if we need to act for the sake of such common goods, in order to achieve our flourishing as rational animals, then we also need to have transformed our initial desires in a way that enables us to recognize the inadequacy of any simple classification of desires as either egoistic or altruistic.[102]

Besides the virtues of independent practical reasoning and the virtues of acknowledged dependence, MacIntyre draws on Aquinas to recognize the virtue of liberality (just generosity) and the virtue of *misericordia* (mercy), which he understands as including recognition and relief of the needs even of people outside our own groups.[103]

The modern nation-state cannot sustain the goods and virtues that we need for the good life: "The modern state cannot provide a political framework informed by the just generosity necessary to achieve the common goods of networks of giving and receiving."[104] Neither can the modern family: it is simply too small a unit to achieve what the virtues of acknowledged dependence require. What we need, he says, is local communities within which the goods of families, schools, and workplaces can be achieved: "Generally and characteristically then the goods of family life are achieved in and with the goods of various types of local community. And generally and characteristically the common good of a family can only be achieved in the course of achieving the common goods of the local community of which it is a part."[105]

The Natural Law

Natural law is not a category in Aristotle's ethics and politics, and it was not part of MacIntyre's constructive position in *After Virtue*. In *Dependent Rational Animals*, he presents it, following Aquinas, as a necessary condition for a community to deliberate about and pursue its common good: "The precepts of the natural law are those precepts promulgated by God through reason without conformity to which human beings cannot achieve their human good."[106] Also following Aquinas, he points out that these precepts include not only negative prohibitions but also positive prescriptions to carry out the requirements of the virtues: "The precepts of the natural law however include much more than rules. For among the precepts of the natural law are precepts that enjoin us to do whatever the virtues require of us ([*S. T.* I-II] 94, 3). We are enjoined to do whatever it is that courage or justice or temperateness demand on this or that occasion and always, in so acting, to act prudently."[107] MacIntyre has elaborated his view of natural law in a series of articles/book chapters. The account here will draw mainly on "Theories of Natural Law in the Culture of Advanced Modernity" (2000) and "Intractable Moral Disagreements" (2009):[108]

> What then are Aquinas's claims concerning the natural law? He argues that the first principles, the fundamental precepts, of that law give expression to the first principle of practical reason: that good is to be done and pursued and evil to be avoided. The goods that we as human beings have it in us to pursue are threefold: the goods of our physical nature, that is, the goods of preserving our lives and health from dangers that threaten our continued existence; the goods of our

animal nature, including the good of sexuality and the goods to be achieved by educating and caring for our children; and the goods that belong to our nature as *rational* animals, the goods of knowledge, both of nature and of God, and the goods of a social life informed by the precepts of reason (*ST* Ia-IIae 94, 2).

There are therefore several distinct precepts of the natural law, each a precept of reason directed to our common good that enjoins the achievement of one or more of these shared human goods or forbids what endangers that achievement. Notable examples are: never take an innocent life or inflict gratuitous harm; respect the property of others; shun ignorance and cultivate understanding; do not lie.[109]

The precepts of the natural law are directed to the common good in the sense that "the goods that they enjoin are goods for each of us, not *qua* individual, but *qua* member of this family or that household, *qua* participant in the life of this workplace or that political community. And they are therefore goods that we can achieve only in the company of others, including not only those others with whom we share the life of family, household, or workplace, or political community, but also strangers with whom we interact in less structured ways."[110]

Why does natural law, so understood, have authority or binding force?

Because on the one hand the happiness of rational agents can only be achieved through, and in part consists in, relationships with others that are informed by unconditional obedience to the precepts of the natural law. Whatever might be achieved through violating these precepts, even from benevolent motives, it would not and could not be the happiness of a rational agent. And, on the other hand, rational agents are and cannot but be directed towards the achievement of the kind of happiness that is specifically theirs and, were the precepts of the natural law not to guide them towards this end, it would be quite unclear what the point of conformity to them would be.[111]

For human beings to live and work together, achieve common goods, and carry on inquiries and deliberations, they have to respect the precepts of the natural law.

MacIntyre presents the precepts of the natural law as necessary conditions presupposed in the activities of shared inquiry and deliberation.

> The life that expresses our shared human nature is a life of practical inquiry and practical reasoning, and we cannot but presuppose the precepts of the natural law in asking and answering those fundamental questions through our everyday activities and practices. Generally and characteristically, the social relationships through which we are able to learn how to identify our individual and common goods correctly and adequately are those relationships governed and defined by the precepts of the natural law. I have to learn about my good and about the common good from family and friends, but also from others within my own community, from the members of other communities, and from strangers; from those much older than I and from those much younger. But how can I have relationships of adequate cooperative inquiry and learning except with those whom I can trust without qualification? And how can I trust without qualification, unless I recognize myself and others as mutually bound by such precepts as those that enjoin that we *never* do violence of any sort to innocent human life, that we *always* refrain from theft and fraud, that we *always* tell each other the truth, and that we *always* uphold justice in all our relationships.[112]

Aquinas teaches that the precepts of the natural law "are one and the same for everyone, that they are unchanging and unchangeable, that they are known to be what they are by all human beings insofar as they are rational, and that knowledge of them cannot be abolished from the human heart."[113] Why, then, is the natural law so commonly ignored or denied today? MacIntyre's answer is that modern individualism and modernity's preoccupation with the antithesis between self-regarding principles and other-regarding principles, or between egoism and altruism, have made it difficult or impossible for many people to recognize the force of the natural law:

> During our upbringing, morality is commonly presented to us in terms of two distinct sets of principles, self-regarding principles and

other-regarding principles. The individual is therefore commonly taught to ask not, "How should we in our familial and communal relationships act together?" but "How far should I regard only the promotion of my own happiness and the protection of my own rights, and how far should I also have regard for the happiness of others and the rights of others?" Underlying this latter question is a conception of society as primarily constituted, not as a web of familial and communal relationships, but as a set of individuals to each of whom everyone else is an "other."[114]

This preoccupation with the difference between the individual's interests and the interests of others obscures people's awareness of the extent to which they are social beings, beings whose individual goods in many cases cannot be achieved apart from the achievement of common goods. It leads people to think that it is up to them to choose the moral principles on which they will act.[115] People who distinguish sharply between their goods and other people's goods, and who think they are faced with a choice about moral principles, will be unable to appreciate why the natural law has the binding force that it does. Modernity has largely rejected the understanding of human nature that the natural law presupposes and so has miseducated large numbers of people in just this way. But this fact does not refute the theory of the natural law. On the contrary, the fact that the theory can explain why people reject it is a point in the theory's favor.[116]

Aquinas's doctrine of natural law is centuries old. To many ears the very words "natural law" may suggest something old-fashioned and restrictive. MacIntyre's take on natural law is strikingly different. He regards it as subversive: subversive in the past, as a challenge to the rulers and governments of the thirteenth century, and potentially subversive today insofar as it gives plain persons a ground from which to challenge the institutions and practices of modernity. Aquinas's is "the only account of natural law that not only is able to explain its own rejection, but also justifies plain persons in regarding themselves as already having within themselves the resources afforded by a knowledge of fundamental law, resources by means of which they can judge the claims to jurisdiction over them of any system of positive law."[117]

Natural law is not one of MacIntyre's main themes in *Ethics in the Conflicts of Modernity*, but he does address the role that the natural law plays in resistance to the dominant order:

> The positive laws of particular societies have the character of genuine law only insofar as they are in conformity with the natural law. So plain persons, by the exercise of reason in reflecting with others on how they are to achieve their common goods, are able to put in question the actions of those with authority and power. And, insofar as such plain persons understand what at the level of everyday practice the virtues require of them, they are also able to understand what the virtues require of their rulers, especially by way of justice. The consideration of what rationality requires of rulers and ruled becomes a prologue to radical social critique.[118]

Surviving Academic Moral Philosophy

In March 2009, a conference was held at University College Dublin to mark MacIntyre's eightieth birthday. The theme of the conference is expressed in the title of its proceedings, *What Happened in and to Moral Philosophy in the Twentieth Century?* MacIntyre's opening address, "On Having Survived the Academic Moral Philosophy of the Twentieth Century," recalls many of the themes of *After Virtue* and *Dependent Rational Animals* and anticipates many of the themes of *Ethics in the Conflicts of Modernity*. At the same time, it brings out three distinctive points.[119]

The first is a fuller statement of the conditions of human flourishing. MacIntyre is defending the Aristotelian thesis that human beings have a distinctive function against the contention of Stuart Hampshire, Isaiah Berlin, and others that there is no such function:

> To this it can be replied that there are indeed many different ways of leading a good human life, but that there are at least four sets of goods that are characteristically needed by every human individual if she or he is to flourish. First, without *adequate nutrition, clothing, shelter, physical exercise, education, and opportunity to work* no one is likely to

be able to develop his or her powers—physical, intellectual, moral, aesthetic—adequately. Second, everyone benefits from *affectionate support by, well-designed instruction from, and critical interaction with family, friends, and colleagues.* Third, without *an institutional frame- work that provides stability and security over time* a variety of forms of association, exchange, and long-term planning are impossible. And fourth, if an individual is to become and sustain her- or himself as an independent rational agent, she or he needs *powers of practical ratio- nality, of self-knowledge, of communication, and of inquiry and under- standing.* Lives that are significantly defective in any one of these respects are judged worse, that is, less choiceworthy, than lives that are not.[120]

Second, MacIntyre uses the distinction between theory and practice to characterize the difference between Kantianism and utilitarianism and his own Thomistic Aristotelianism. Kantianism and utilitarianism, he contends, are two forms of academic moral philosophy, while his Tho- mistic Aristotelianism is not one more form of academic moral phi- losophy, but rather a form of practice: "It Is Only at the Level of Practice That We Can Become Aristotelians" (section title).[121] The practice in question is our own moral development, and specifically the education of our desires:

> We learn what place in our individual and common lives to give to
> each of a variety of goods, that is, only through a discipline of learn-
> ing, during which we discover what we have hitherto cared for too
> much and what too little and, as we correct our inclinations, discover
> also that our judgments are informed by an at first inchoate but
> gradually more and more determinate conception of a final good, of
> an end, one in the light of which every other good finds its due place,
> an end indeed final but not remote, one to which here and now our
> actions turn out to be increasingly directed as we learn to give no
> more and no less than their due to other goods.[122]

MacIntyre will have much more to say about this final end in *Ethics in the Conflicts of Modernity*. For the moment, the point to notice is his claim that the practical discipline of educating our desires requires us to become Aristotelians:

> This discovery of a directedness in ourselves toward a final end is initially a discovery of what is presupposed by our practice, as it issues in a transformation of ourselves through the development of habits of feeling, thought, choice, and action that are the virtues, habits without which—even if in partial and imperfect forms—we are unable to move toward being fully rational agents. Only secondarily, as we articulate at the level of theory the concepts and arguments presupposed by and informing our practice, are we able to recognize that we have had to become some sort of Aristotelian. I am not suggesting that in order to become an Aristotelian one first has to become virtuous—even a slender acquaintance with Aristotelians would be enough to dispose of that claim. I am saying that it is only through recognition at the level of practice of our need for the virtues, and through practical experience of how the exercise of the virtues stands to the achievement of goods, that a number of Aristotle's philosophical arguments become compelling.
>
> To have become such an Aristotelian is to have found good reasons for rejecting both utilitarianism and Kantianism. What renders any form of consequentialism unacceptable is the discovery of the place that relationships structured by unconditional commitments must have in any life directed toward the achievement of common goods, commitments, it turns out, to the exceptionless, if sometimes complex, precepts of the natural law. What makes Kantian ethics unacceptable is not only that our regard for those precepts depends upon their enabling us to achieve our common goods but also that the Kantian conception of practical rationality is inadequate in just those respects in which it differs from Aristotelian *phronêsis* or Thomistic *prudentia*.[123]

I take it that the key difference between Kantian practical reason, on the one hand, and Aristotelian practical wisdom and Thomistic prudence, on the other, is that the latter are informed by substantive conceptions of what is good and what is bad for human beings.

MacIntyre has often been described as a theorist of virtue ethics. This he denies: "It is therefore of some importance that in arriving at a certain kind of Aristotelian standpoint I was not taking up one more theoretical position within the ongoing debates of contemporary moral philosophy. It is because I have been thought to have done just this that I have been unjustly accused of being one of the protagonists of so-called virtue ethics, something that the genuine protagonists of virtue ethics are happy to join me in denying."[124]

Third, "On Having Survived" sheds light on how MacIntyre sees his Thomism and his Marxism as complementary. What Thomism and Marxism both gave him is a standpoint external to and independent of the academic moral philosophy of the twentieth century. In the final section, he speaks of "the importance for the moral philosopher of living on the margins, intellectually as well as politically, a necessary condition for being able to see things as they are. The two standpoints without which I would have been unable to understand either modern morality or twentieth-century moral philosophy are those of Thomism and of Marxism, and I therefore owe a large and unpayable debt of gratitude to those who sustained and enriched those marginal movements of thought in the inhospitable intellectual climate of capitalist modernity."[125]

ETHICS IN THE CONFLICTS OF MODERNITY

Ethics in the Conflicts of Modernity is the latest extended statement of MacIntyre's Aristotelianism. Although it was written, as he says, for reflective readers who are not professional philosophers, it is a subtle and complex book. Rather than stating his position at the outset, he confronts a view that he calls "expressivism," another view that he calls "Morality" (with a capital M), and a political, social, and economic reality that he calls the "dominant order." He unfolds his Aristotelianism—at the outset he calls it NeoAristotelianism, in the latter part of the book Thomistic Aristotelianism—in and through confrontations with expressivism, Morality, and the dominant order.[126]

A Question and an Impasse

Ethics in the Conflicts of Modernity begins with an eminently practical question: How should we think about our desires? How we answer this question and what we desire have a great deal to do with whether our lives go well or poorly. MacIntyre thinks—and he recognizes that most academic philosophers will disagree with him—that two answers to the question most deserve consideration: expressivism and NeoAristotelianism.[127]

Expressivism is an updated version of emotivism with roots in Hume. It is the metaethical view that ethical convictions are nothing more than expressions of prerational commitments. To the question about how we should think about our desires, the expressivist answers: any way we choose. If we experience a conflict between desires, we have to choose between them. If we experience a conflict between a desire and a belief or conviction, we also have a choice to make. But for expressivism there are no reasons why we should choose one way rather than another. There is no fact of the matter, no truth waiting to be discovered, about what human beings should or should not desire, or about how they ought to live.[128] The other answer, which MacIntyre calls NeoAristotelian, is the direct opposite of expressivism: we should desire those things, and only those things, that we have good reason to desire.[129] Neither side convinces the other. The impasse between expressivism and NeoAristotelianism seems to be unresolvable.[130]

Expressivism, Morality, and the Dominant Order

Expressivism cannot be understood without an understanding of what MacIntyre means by "Morality." This he sets forth in chapter 3 of *Ethics in the Conflicts of Modernity*. By "Morality" he means the distinctive morality of modernity, the morality of which Kantianism, utilitarianism, and contractarianism are species. Morality is a secular doctrine that developed in response to the religious divisions of the early modern period. Its universal rules are held to bind all human agents, whatever the culture or social order to which they belong. It presupposes a sharp distinction

between fact and value, between factual judgments and evaluative judgments. It also presupposes a sharp distinction between each individual's
interests and the interests of other individuals, and so makes the competing claims of egoism and altruism central to moral philosophy. The rules
of Morality function as a set of constraints on individuals, setting limits
on how and how far they may pursue their interests and satisfy their
desires.[131]

Agents operating within the framework of Morality face conflicts between universal principles that they are supposed to obey without exception and a requirement to maximize, or at least to protect, human well-
being. Two familiar examples: whether or not to torture a terrorist to
extract information that may save lives; whether or not to prevent a crash
that will kill many people, if the only way to do so involves intentionally
causing the death of an innocent bystander. Readers will recognize these
as conflicts between Kantian ethics and utilitarian ethics. At the practical
level, people oscillate between these two positions, now following one,
now following the other.[132]

Morality with a capital M differs from Aristotelian morality in several
important respects. In Aristotelian morality, the point of conforming to
moral precepts is that not doing so will keep us from flourishing, from
achieving the goods that are proper to us as human beings. For Morality,
it is unclear whether there even are such human goods. Aristotelian morality supposes that individuals can achieve their own individual goods
only in and through achieving common goods, that is, goods that they
share with other people. Morality has no place for genuine goods, individual or common. Aristotelian morality, by contrast, treats ethics and
politics together as parts of a single inquiry. Morality draws sharp distinctions between different dimensions of life: ethical, political, legal, social,
aesthetic, and economic.[133]

Morality is by no means the same as expressivism. Adherents of Kantianism, utilitarianism, or any other species of Morality are necessarily
committed to denying expressivism. But when they try to say why we
should follow the rules of Morality, why we should be moral, they give different answers. They do not accept one another's answers. In particular,
Kantians cannot accept utilitarian answers, and vice versa. Expressivists
conclude that the adherents of Morality seem to have no reason or justi-

fication for their claims. Morality seems unable to meet the challenge of expressivism.[134]

MacIntyre sees other objections to Morality. Two concepts central to Morality are those of utility, understood as the satisfaction of preferences, and human rights. But people's preferences depend on their prior moral formation and so the satisfaction of preferences cannot provide an independent standard by which to make moral judgments.[135] And natural rights, MacIntyre argues once again, are philosophical fictions.[136]

MacIntyre's position on rights in *Ethics in the Conflicts of Modernity* is more nuanced than it was in *After Virtue*. There he wrote, "There are no such [natural or human] rights, and belief in them is one with belief in witches and in unicorns."[137] In *Ethics in the Conflicts of Modernity*, he criticizes "appeals to human rights, *understood as rights attaching to each and every human individual qua human individual.*"[138] This qualification leaves the door open for him to affirm human rights, understood in a sufficiently different way. And that is what we find in his 2007 response to a paper by Bill Bowring:

> It matters that eighteenth century claims, whether American or French, that there are rights that attach to individuals as such and that ascriptions of such rights can function as first and evident premises in our practical reasoning, are mistaken, that human rights thus conceived are fictions. We need to reach conclusions about what rights human beings have or should have, but these are to be derived from quite other types of premise, from premises about the common good and about what both justice and generosity, virtues that are directed towards the common good, require in this or that particular situation.[139]

MacIntyre cites another objection to Morality that comes from Oscar Wilde: May there not be situations where the claims of art and beauty take precedence over the claims of morality?[140] He cites yet another from D. H. Lawrence: Might morality miseducate us, leading us not to recognize, or to deny, our deepest desires?[141] And he cites two more objections that come from Bernard Williams. The universal impersonal rules of morality— what Williams means by morality comes close to what MacIntyre calls

Morality—cannot come to terms with the sheer complexity of our practical lives. Nor can these rules come to terms with the importance of
projects and commitments that matter to us precisely because they are *our*
projects and commitments.[142]

These objections to Morality are serious. Morality, however, is more
than a set of theoretical claims against which one can raise theoretical objections. It also plays an important role by supporting what MacIntyre
calls the "dominant order" and cannot be understood without reference to
that order. If the dominant order is problematic, as MacIntyre thinks it is,
then the Morality that supports it is problematic.

MacIntyre explains what he means by the "dominant order" in chapter 2 of *Ethics in the Conflicts of Modernity*. He means the capitalist order
with all that that implies, in particular the conflict of capital and labor,
the consumer society, and the liberal political systems and bureaucratic institutions that accompany advanced capitalist economies. The key to understanding capitalism as an economic system is Marx's theory of surplus
value: workers are paid wages that are less than the value that they produce, and this surplus is the source of profits and of further investments.[143]

But this is not all. For the capitalist system to work, it is important
that workers not recognize what is going on. They and their labor have
become commodities to be bought and sold, but that is not how they are
supposed to see it: "The relations of exchange through which those who
own the means of production appropriate the unpaid labor of productive
workers are disguised by their legal form as the contractual relations of
free individuals, each of them seeking what she or he takes to be best for
her or himself. And as capitalism becomes the dominant economic mode
of production and exchange, so this way of thinking about oneself and
one's relationships becomes the dominant mode of social and moral
thought, both among theorists and in everyday life."[144]

As MacIntyre sees it, following Marx, people in the European Middle
Ages, using an Aristotelian idiom, had been able to pose critical questions
about their social roles and relationships.[145] This changed with the advent
of modernity and Morality. Happiness was no longer understood as Aristotelian *eudaimonia* or Thomistic *beatitudo* but as a psychological state in
which an individual's desires have been satisfied.[146] There was no longer

any place for such Aristotelian and Thomistic notions as those of an end, a common good, or the natural law. Thus "the question for each individual became 'Why should I not pursue the satisfaction of my desires with unbridled egoism, resorting to force or to fraud whenever necessary?' and the case for morality became the case for altruism."[147]

The exploitation of labor by capital, with its consequent increasing inequalities of income, educational opportunity, and political power, is bad enough. But the English Distributists or Distributivists, who included Hilaire Belloc, G. K. Chesterton, Vincent McNabb, O.P., and other English Dominicans, identified an even worse evil: a deformation of desire, or a deformation of people's thinking about their desires:

> From a Distributist point of view, what is amiss with capitalism is not only what it does to the unemployed and the poor, but also what it does to the rich and to better paid workers and managers. Human beings can achieve their common and their individual goods only through concerted actions that require cooperative relationships informed by the norms of the natural law and, in order to achieve those goods, they must develop their powers as rational agents. However, the social order of capitalism not only recurrently imposes types of social relationship that violate these norms, it also miseducates and wrongly directs desires—something that Marxist critics of capitalism have also recognized—so that for many of every social class the satisfaction of their desires and the development of their powers become incompatible. What they want is too often what they have no good reason to want. Those of every class who succeed in getting what they want under capitalism are likely, therefore, just because they so often do not want what they need, to lead impoverished lives.[148]

Morality provides what MacIntyre calls an "ethics-of-the-state" and an "ethics-of-the-market." These support the dominant order by limiting individuals' pursuit of their desires.[149] Morality will "impose constraints both on their choice of goals and on the means that they may adopt in order to achieve those goals. It will do this by imposing constraints on the ways in which and the extent to which they may attempt to satisfy their desires and to further their interests. Morality is in this way indispensable for the functioning of the ethics-of-the-state and the ethics-of-the-market, since individuals can only function as modernity requires them to function, if their desires are expressed, contained, and ordered in certain ways."[150]

MacIntyre's criticism of the dominant order extends to academic economics. First, this economics supposes and promotes an oversimplified view of agents and practical rationality. It regards people as individual maximizers of preferences and encourages its students to understand themselves in this way. It understands practical rationality as the efficient maximization of preferences under conditions of uncertainty, or in other words, as rational risk-taking, and encourages its students to adopt this understanding of rationality.[151]

Second, academic economics inculcates an overly optimistic view of the capitalist market: "For that in capitalism which tends toward crisis and destruction was relegated to the margins of study as matters of hazard and accident."[152] Academic economists understand crises as caused by factors external to the market, not, as Marx understood them, as stemming from the logic of capitalism itself. Academic economics thus prevents Marx's critique of capitalism from being heard.

Third, academic proponents of capitalism see free market economies as the only engines of growth, as measured by gross domestic product, and therefore of prosperity. They accept "gross inequalities and the recurring unemployment and regeneration of poverty that result from even the best economic policies" as "effects that must be accepted for the sake of the benefits of long-term growth and with it world-wide reduction in the harshest poverty in underdeveloped countries."[153] But this mindset underestimates the uncertainties of markets, discounts the influence of wider social factors, and leads traders to underrate the likelihood of failure and to put at risk "not only their employers' and their investors' money, but the livelihoods of large numbers of people, unknown to them and unconsidered by them, something which the narrowness of their education in academic economics or in business studies helps them to put out of mind."[154]

MacIntyre's indictment of the dominant order and with it of Morality continues in chapter 4 of *Ethics in the Conflicts of Modernity*. The profit-driven capitalist economy undermines the kind of work that supports the life of communities and the development of excellence: "The common goods of those at work together are achieved in producing goods and services that contribute to the life of the community and in becoming excellent at producing them. But enterprises that are unprofitable are always in time eliminated and profitability may dictate the production of what is less than good, perhaps harmful or trivializing, while managerial control of the workplace may result in methods of work that are inimical to excellence."[155]

When families and households fail to prosper, they are generally aware of it: "Workplaces by contrast may be organized so that the work performed by individuals is never more than a cost-effective means to ends imposed by others for the sake of high productivity and profitability. In periods of prosperity for this or that industry, such individuals may be relatively highly paid for doing work that it is not otherwise worthwhile to do. But note that in order to say this, we have to speak and judge in a way that is incompatible with the standard vocabulary of academic economics."[156] To speak of work as worthwhile or not worthwhile is to appeal to a standard independent of markets and preferences.

MacIntyre sums up his case against the dominant order:

> The exploitative structures of both free market and state capitalism make it often difficult and sometimes impossible to achieve the goods of the workplace through excellent work. The political structures of modern states that exclude most citizens from participation in extended and informed deliberation on issues of crucial importance to their lives make it often difficult and sometimes impossible to achieve the goods of local community. The influence of Morality in normative and evaluative thinking makes it often difficult and sometimes impossible for the claims of the virtues to be understood, let alone acknowledged in our common lives. So too the culture that entertains and distracts makes it often difficult and sometimes impossible to develop those imaginative powers that are of the first importance for living the life of the virtues. We therefore have to live *against* the cultural grain, just as we have to learn to act as economic, political, and moral antagonists of the dominant order.[157]

The Thomistic Aristotelian Alternative

In chapter 4 of *Ethics in the Conflicts of Modernity*, MacIntyre deploys Thomistic Aristotelianism in response to expressivism, Morality, and the dominant order. In his preface, MacIntyre says that Thomistic Aristotelianism provides resources for describing the dominant order as it actually is: "My argument is designed to show that it is only from a Thomistic Aristotelian perspective that we are able to characterize adequately some key features of the social order of advanced modernity and that Thomistic Aristotelianism, when informed by Marx's insights, is able to provide us with the resources for constructing a contemporary politics and ethics, one that enables and requires us to act against modernity from within modernity."[158]

Thomistic Aristotelianism is first of all an answer to the question of how we should think about our desires. At the outset of chapter 5, MacIntyre says that chapters 1 through 4 have established a complex theoretical conclusion: "It is [1] that agents do well only if and when they act to satisfy only those desires whose objects they have good reason to desire, [2] that only agents who are sound and effective practical reasoners so act, [3] that such agents must be disposed to act as the virtues require, and [4] that such agents will be directed in their actions toward the achievement of their final end."[159] These four claims are the core of what MacIntyre means by Thomistic Aristotelianism.

Claim (1) answers the question about desires with which *Ethics in the Conflicts of Modernity* began. We should desire, and try to be or do or have those things, and only those things, that we have good reason to desire. The contrast with expressivism is clear: "To act for a good reason is to act for the sake of achieving some good or avoiding some evil. . . . we have a good reason to want some particular object of desire only if and when to act so as to achieve the object of that desire is to act so as to achieve some good."[160] This supposes that there are genuine goods, both things that are good for us qua engaged in this or that form of activity and things that are good for us qua human beings. Of course, a good reason to act in a certain way is not necessarily a sufficient reason to act. Asking whether we have sufficient reason to act in a certain way is asking "what good or goods are or might be at stake in my acting so as to satisfy it rather than some other desire."[161]

In chapter 1, MacIntyre offers an initial account of the practical reasonableness introduced by claim (2): "We have to become . . . agents who desire to act as reason directs, who desire to act for the sake of the good and the best, and who have a second order desire that this desire for the good and the best is a desire that we will satisfy. It is the central characteristic of human beings that they are born with the potentiality of becoming reasoning and desiring animals of this kind."[162]

What MacIntyre says about practical reasonableness is to be understood in the context of what he said about practices, virtues, and communities in *After Virtue* and *Dependent Rational Animals*. People become practically reasonable agents through a complex set of experiences in family, school, workplace, and politics, experiences that initiate them into a range of practices. Initiation into practices involves recognition of the goods internal to practices, both individual and common, training in the virtues and skills required by practices, and reflection on how the goods of practices are to be ordered. These experiences teach people the difference between simply wanting something and having good reason to want it, between mere objects of desire and genuine goods. They have to have learned to be accountable, to respond to other people's questions about their actions, and to pose such questions to themselves.[163]

People developing as practical reasoners need to become reflective about their reasons for action, about the ways that they have rank ordered goods in the past, and about whether or not they have been justified in making those rankings. They need to progress beyond their first identifications of goods, practices, and the virtues required by practices, to a stage of integrating those goods into a flourishing life. They become self-aware by learning from and correcting their mistakes.[164]

Agents who are practically reasonable "will . . . have learned to take seriously the judgments of perceptive others. . . . They will have learned to suspect themselves in types of situation in which in the past they have become victims of their own desires. They will have learned to give due weight to constraints such as those that the norms of justice impose."[165] They "must have found resources for identifying and dealing with two important sources of practical error. One arises from the danger that we all confront of being led astray by our feelings and affections. . . . The other arises from the sometimes distorting and misleading influences of our own social and cultural order on our beliefs, attitudes, and choices."[166] They will in particular have learned to question the presuppositions of their own culture and tradition, "to put in question that particular tradition's distortions and errors and so, often enough, engaging in a quarrel with some dominant forms of their own political and moral culture."[167] Much of *Ethics in the Conflicts of Modernity* is just such a quarrel.

Since the inquiry into what is good and what is better is necessarily a shared inquiry, the virtues mentioned in claim (3) must include the truthfulness, justice, and courage that are required for any community of inquiry to function. Presumably they also include the other virtues for which MacIntyre argued in *Dependent Rational Animals*: the virtues of the independent practical reasoner, the virtues of acknowledged dependence, and the virtues of just generosity and mercy.

Rationality, Narrative, and Justification

Claim (4), that practically reasonable agents will be directed toward the achievement of their final end, points toward MacIntyre's thesis that a certain kind of narrative, one informed by a NeoAristotelian or Thomistic Aristotelian conception of human activity, is necessary for understanding the place of desires and practical reasoning in our practical and moral life.[168] What kind of narrative is this?

It is, first of all, a teleological narrative, a narrative of progress toward an end. Of course, a person may not be consciously pursuing such an end. A person may at first have only the most general conception of what such an end might be. But reflective agents, in the course of making practical judgments and choices, become aware of failures and successes in their practical reasoning. They become aware that their lives are not yet perfect or complete. They become aware of what MacIntyre calls a directedness, "an uneven movement toward some end state about which they often can say very little."[169]

Such a narrative will be the story not of an individual in isolation but of a person interacting with other persons. It will be the story of the person's practical reasoning and of how the person learned from his or her failures as a practical reasoner. It will be the story of the person's successes and failures in achieving particular ends or goods and through them moving toward a final end or good. It will be a story of increasing direct-edness and integration:[170] "Of any life which has come to an ending or is about to come to an ending . . . we can ask 'What, if anything, makes this life, qua the life of a human being, significantly imperfect and incomplete? What is or was lacking in it which would have brought it to completion?' To answer these questions is to have found application for the concept of a final end for human beings and to have posed the problems about the relationship between our ends and our endings, about how we should tell the stories of lives that go well and lives that go badly."[171]

What leads people to formulate such narratives?

> We generally become aware of the narrative structure of our lives in-frequently and in either of two ways, when we reflect upon how to make ourselves intelligible to others by telling them the relevant parts of our story or when we have some particular reason to ask "How has my life gone so far?" and "How must I act if it is to go well in future?" It is in answering these sometimes harsh practical questions that the question "What is the good for me?" with its narrative presupposi-tions is also answered. What occasions the asking of these questions is a need to make critical choices at points in our lives in which alter-native futures open up.[172]

What kind of final end or good is MacIntyre talking about? Ulti-mately, and here he follows Aquinas, the end is God or the vision of God. This is the metaphysical *telos* that his ethics requires. He recognizes that the existence of God is both controverted and crucial to his position, but he says that arguing for the existence of God lies beyond the scope of the book.[173]

MacIntyre does not, of course, mean either that all or most human beings understand themselves to be progressing toward God or that they need to understand themselves in this way in order to be in fact progress-ing toward God. People's conceptions of their final end may be quite in-determinate. For that matter, he recognizes that not everyone experiences his or her life in narrative terms. In response to a criticism from Galen

Strawson, he writes, "It is not at all my view that human beings most of the time *experience* their lives as narratives, something that would involve a remarkable and unfortunate degree of self-dramatization."[174]

How can Thomistic Aristotelianism, or for that matter any comparable position, be justified? MacIntyre distinguishes two different kinds of justification, theoretical and practical. Narrative plays a central role in both. At the theoretical level, Thomistic Aristotelianism faces questions and objections from other theories. It is too much to ask of a theory that it refute its rivals in ways that their adherents accept, but it is not too much to expect that it respond to the strongest objections lodged against it. To be justified theoretically, Thomistic Aristotelianism has to respond to these challenges. Typically the response takes the form of what MacIntyre calls a "third-person narrative" of how the Aristotelian tradition has developed, how it has faced questions and objections, and how it does so now.[175] I take it this is essentially the same position as that developed in chapter 18 of *Whose Justice? Which Rationality?* and in "Moral Relativism, Truth and Justification."

At the practical level, however, justification takes a very different form. Here it is not a matter of theory confronting theory but of persons, not necessarily theorists, meeting other persons, not necessarily theorists. Typically, a response to a question of the form "Why do you do that?" takes the form of a first-person narrative, in which a person tells some part of his or her story, explaining how they have come to rank goods as they do, why they think that way of ranking goods is better than their earlier way of ranking them, and why they have confidence in their judgments. An Aristotelian narrative will be framed in terms of goods and practical reasonableness. The quality of the response will depend on the quality of the person's narrative and on their ability to articulate it, while the success of the justification will depend on the ability of the questioner or objector to appreciate the narrative.[176]

In this context, MacIntyre outlines three conditions that Thomistic Aristotelians need to meet if they are to consider their position justified. First, they need to have identified the strongest objections of their critics and to have good reason to reject these objections. Second, they need to explain "the mistakes made by those critics and why their objections are found compelling by those who advance them."[177] But third, they also need to have what MacIntyre calls "sociological self-knowledge": "To have sociological self-knowledge is to know who you and those around you are in terms of your and their roles and relationships to each other, to the common goods of family, workplace, and school, and to the structures through which power and money are distributed. It is to understand what in those roles and relationships is consonant with the exercise of rational agency and what through the contingencies of an imposed set of structures inhibits or distorts that exercise."[178] When it comes to justification, MacIntyre says, "It is therefore important for all of us that we should not be open to the charge that in some respects we reason as we do, in justifying either our theoretical commitments or our practical conclusions, because of some lack of sociological self-knowledge."[179]

Once Again the Impasse

Ethics in the Conflicts of Modernity began with the question of how we should think about our desires and with the impasse between the expressivist answer and the NeoAristotelian answer. We have reviewed MacIntyre's confrontations with Morality and the dominant order and his presentation of the Thomistic Aristotelian answer. Are we any closer to resolving the impasse between expressivism and NeoAristotelianism?

We are not to expect a decisive refutation of expressivism. MacIntyre returns to the passage from David Lewis that he cited in the postscript to the second edition of *After Virtue*:

> "The reader," he [Lewis] wrote, "in search of knock-down arguments in favor of my theories will be disappointed," and this because philosophical theories are only rarely, if ever, refutable by knock-down arguments. What we learn from the objections advanced against our theories is the price that we will have to pay, the philosophical commitments that we will have to take on board if they are to escape refutation. The question then is "which prices are worth paying" and "On this question we may still differ." What weight we give to each of our prephilosophical opinions is up to us. "Once the menu of

well-worked-out theories is before us, philosophy is a matter of opinion."[180]

However, *Ethics in the Conflicts of Modernity* marshals a number of considerations against expressivism. First, expressivism does not take into account the possibility that an agent might desire something precisely because that something is good, and so it gives an inadequate account of the range of possible motivations that may move an agent to desire and to act.[181]

Second, expressivism is vulnerable to a criticism lodged by Bernard Williams: "that what expressivists say about the relationship between our moral convictions and judgments and our emotions is at too high a level of generality and so fails to capture the significant relationships between particular emotions or aspects of emotions and our convictions and judgments."[182]

Third, expressivism is vulnerable to another criticism from Williams. Expressivism appears to treat moral principles as things about which we could decide, when (MacIntyre quotes Williams) "we see a man's genuine convictions as coming from somewhere deeper in him than that." MacIntyre comments: "Our deliberations, so it seems, must begin from convictions for some of which we can give no further reason, convictions that, although they are not to be understood as the emotivists understood them, are expressed in emotion, so that an observer would be unable to characterize either those convictions or the relevant emotions independently of one another."[183]

Fourth, expressivism performs an important service by criticizing the family of theories that make up Morality, but it shares with Morality the assumption of a sharp distinction between facts and values, between judgments of fact and evaluative judgments.[184] This renders expressivism less than helpful for answering the question about how to understand desires in a way that will promote human flourishing. This point can be spelled out in two complementary ways. First, if thinking about desires in a way that would promote human flourishing requires thinking about them in terms of the claim that agents do well only if and when they act to satisfy only those desires whose objects they have good reason to desire, the distinction between having and not having good reason to desire something is part of what expressivism denies. Second, if thinking about desires in a way that would promote human flourishing requires thinking about lives in terms of reasons, goods, practical reasonableness, and directedness toward a final end, expressivism has no place for these concepts.

Fifth, MacIntyre thinks that expressivists can have expressivist narratives of their lives, narratives that do without the categories of reasons, goods, practical reasonableness, and directedness, but he believes that this comes at a cost: "What NeoAristotelians claim . . . is that, in so understanding themselves, expressivists are unable to reckon with important aspects of themselves and that their activities over extended periods of time can only be characterized and understood adequately in Aristotelian terms. So their own histories of themselves will always be defective histories."[185] MacIntyre acknowledges that Thomistic Aristotelians cannot compel expressivists to agree to this point. If expressivists come to agree, it will be through reflection on their own lives.

REVISITING ANGLO-AMERICAN MORAL PHILOSOPHY

Anglo-American moral philosophy in the period 1950 to 1990 found itself grappling with five sets of problems: (1) the competing claims of deontological, especially Kantian, ethics and teleological, especially utilitarian, ethics; (2) the competing claims of egoism and altruism; (3) the competing claims of naturalism, intuitionism, and noncognitivism in metaethics; (4) the relations between fact and value, is and ought; and (5) the challenges of relativism and skepticism. Without suggesting that MacIntyre made it his project to solve these problems precisely as posed, I find that he addresses them in a number of different ways.

He holds that neither Kantian nor utilitarian ethics can give a convincing account of itself, and that neither can carry out the Enlightenment project of justifying morality. There is no real point either to trying to decide between them or to trying to reconcile them. What is needed is a whole different approach, which he finds in Aristotle, the Aristotelian tradition, and Thomistic Aristotelianism. Within this tradition, the good is prior to the right. Right practical reasoning is to be understood in the light of the goods that we pursue. The duties that good parents or wise and benevolent rulers prescribe are the means by which to achieve human goods, including the goods of shared inquiry and of various forms of community.[186]

The so-called problem of egoism and altruism rests on a pernicious mistake: the tendency in modernity to see human beings as individuals with largely competing private interests, in contrast to the Aristotelian tradition's stress on genuinely common goods achieved in and through cooperative activities.

In metaethics, MacIntyre is opposed to intuitionism and to noncognitivism. His position is a form of naturalism, but in no sense a crude inference from facts to values or obligations. On the contrary, his position is that human being is a functional or teleological concept that has standards embedded within it and that human flourishing and failure to flourish are matters of a kind of empirical judgments that ordinary people can and do make, when they are not under the spell of erroneous theories, and that they are right to make. This does not, of course, rule out the possibility of errors in those judgments. But the idea that there is a gap to be bridged between fact and value, is and ought, is one more mistake of modernity.[187]

MacIntyre's response to relativism is complex. He believes that relativism itself is largely a response to the seeming impossibility of resolving disputes between competing ethical theories and traditions. The core of his response to it is to outline a set of conditions under which such disputes might conceivably be resolved. In *Whose Justice? Which Rationality?*, "Moral Relativism, Truth and Justification," and other works, MacIntyre has argued that it is possible, under certain conditions, for a tradition to show itself to be superior to a competing tradition and for adherents of the latter tradition to recognize that fact. In *Ethics in the Conflicts of Modernity*, he distinguishes how justification works at the level of theory and at the level of practice. Justification at the level of theory calls for a third-person narrative about the progress of a tradition. Justification at the level of practice calls for an agent's first-person narrative of his or her history as a practical reasoner. MacIntyre rejects the attempt to settle disputes from some supposed impartial universal standpoint. There is no such standpoint. People who think they are speaking from it are really speaking from one or other particular standpoint. One of the mistakes of modernity has been to suppose that its distinctive form of morality, Morality, occupies such a universal standpoint.

I am not aware that MacIntyre has a treatment of ethical skepticism as such, distinct from his discussions of emotivism, expressivism, and relativism. But if the question that lies behind ethical skepticism is "Why should I be moral?" his response is clear: because people achieve human goods through the shared activities of communities (families, schools, workplaces, and so on) and these shared activities and the deliberations of the relevant communities require cultivating the virtues and obeying the prescriptions of the natural law.

MacIntyre has a comprehensive, if controversial, set of responses to the problems of our period of Anglo-American moral philosophy. The title "On Having Survived the Academic Moral Philosophy of the Twentieth Century" makes clear what he thinks of this kind of moral philosophy.[188] As he indicates early in *Ethics and the Conflicts of Modernity*, he is "committed to holding that academic moral philosophy at some point in its past history took a wrong turning, marched off in the wrong direction, set itself the task . . . of climbing the wrong mountain."[189]

Our period's moral philosophy has been charged with neglecting history or with focusing on an unduly narrow core of texts and authors. From his *A Short History of Ethics* (1966) through the later project that one of his colleagues called "An Interminably Long History of Ethics," MacIntyre has insisted on the centrality of history and narrative to making progress on the problems of ethics.[190] Anglo-American moral philosophy has also been charged with neglecting the social and political dimensions of ethics. MacIntyre, by contrast, has had these dimensions in view from the very beginning of his career. The ethics of his latest work is inseparable from his social, political, and economic analyses, analyses indebted to both the Aristotelian-Thomistic tradition and to the Marxist tradition. If the moral philosophy of 1950 to 1990 neglected the virtues, MacIntyre has played a major role in reversing that neglect. This is not, however, to say that MacIntyre considers himself a proponent of virtue ethics. He does not.[191]

MACINTYRE'S APPROPRIATION OF ARISTOTLE

How should we characterize MacIntyre's version of Aristotelianism? The place to start, I think, is with Aristotle's occasional remark that he is giving an outline (*tupos*) of what needs to be said in ethics.[192] MacIntyre's Aristotelianism is an attempt to fill in the details of what Aristotle outlined and to supply deeper grounds for, and therefore deeper understanding of, claims that Aristotle made. In *After Virtue*, for instance, he takes a basically Aristotelian account of the virtues and situates it in the contexts of practice, community, and tradition. In *Dependent Rational Animals*, he situates the account from *After Virtue* within the contexts of human animality and the human life cycle, thus lengthening the list of the virtues and providing the account with a biological grounding. In *Ethics in the Conflicts of Modernity*, he places this enlarged account in the context of the question how we ought to think about our desires, thus deepening the understanding of practical rationality and of how individuals become practically reasonable.

In all this, MacIntyre has held fast to important, and sometimes neglected, Aristotelian themes: the inseparability of ethics from social and political embodiment, the dependence of individuals on communities, and the crucial importance of common goods. At the same time, he has not hesitated to follow Aquinas in providing Aristotle's ethics with a metaphysical grounding and an elaboration in terms of natural law, and to draw on Marx for insights into the workings of a capitalist economy and its corresponding form of society. MacIntyre's Aristotelianism (NeoAristotelianism, Thomistic Aristotelianism) is thus not a relic of historical interest but a well-developed competitor with modern and contemporary understandings. I set aside the charge that MacIntyre is caught up in nostalgia for ancient, medieval, or other premodern ways of life. No doubt he thinks, and says, that Aristotle and other ancients and medievals got certain things right that many moderns got wrong, and continue to get wrong. But however controversial those claims may be, they are claims to be debated, not dismissed with a blanket charge of nostalgia.

SOME QUESTIONS

In this section I will try to identify some questions that should be raised about MacIntyre's Thomistic Aristotelianism.

First, what are the "conflicts of modernity" to which MacIntyre refers in the title of *Ethics in the Conflicts of Modernity* (2016)? Someone familiar with his earlier work might think first of the conflict of Aristotle and Nietzsche that structured *After Virtue*, or of the conflict between Aristotle and Hume that structured *Whose Justice? Which Rationality?*, or of the conflict among "Encyclopaedia," "Genealogy," and "Tradition" that structured *Three Rival Versions of Moral Enquiry*. Someone familiar with Anglo-American moral philosophy might think of the conflicts between deontological and teleological ethics, Kantian and utilitarian ethics, egoism and altruism, the conflict among naturalistic, intuitionist, and noncognitivist metaethics, the conflicts about facts and values, is and ought, or the conflicts about relativism and skepticism. These theoretical conflicts do indeed figure in the book, along with the practical conflicts of modern capitalism, especially the conflict of capital and labor. But the conflicts that structure *Ethics in the Conflicts of Modernity* are the conflict between Morality (with its support of the dominant order) and expressivism and the conflicts between both of these and Aristotelianism (NeoAristotelianism, Thomistic Aristotelianism). And these are not simply conflicts between theories. They are also conflicts between individuals and groups and within individuals and groups, individuals and groups who are divided between their loyalties to Morality and the dominant order and their loyalties, at least implicit, to Aristotelian ways of thinking, feeling, and acting.

A second question concerns MacIntyre's decision to supplement the sociological teleology of *After Virtue* with the biological teleology of *Dependent Rational Animals* and the metaphysical teleology of *Ethics in the Conflicts of Modernity*. "Decision" is not really the right word. As MacIntyre sees it, he came to recognize the need to ground his position in biology and metaphysics. But there is deep disagreement among philosophers about whether ethics needs to be grounded on any other form of knowledge besides itself. And many philosophers are suspicious of any form of grounding that could be described as metaphysical. This, then, is a question that must be raised but cannot be answered here.

A third question concerns MacIntyre's account of why we should follow the precepts of the natural law: because doing so is essential to shared inquiry, the functioning of groups, their achievement of common goods, and the achievement of many of the goods of individuals.[193] Supposing that this argument is sound as far as it goes, one might still question whether it gets to the heart of the matter. One might think that the case for the natural law rests not only on the requirements of cooperation and shared inquiry but on a more basic recognition of other persons as persons. If, for instance, the natural law places limits on how people may treat their opponents in war, those limits would seem to stem from what every human being owes every other human being qua human being, not just qua cooperator in shared inquiry or any other activity. (Here I leave aside MacIntyre's controversial rejection of natural rights.)

A fourth question concerns MacIntyre's Marxism, or the use to which he puts Marxism. Many academics, philosophers and free market economists, and most U.S. politicians, will doubt that much is to be learned from Marx or from Marxism, unless perhaps from what is widely taken to be their failure.[194] Favorable reference to Marx or to Marxism may also raise suspicions in Thomistic and allied Catholic circles. Here it is important to be clear that materialism and atheism form no part of MacIntyre's Marxism.[195] But the theory of surplus value and the labor theory of value are integral to it, and objections to these theories, if sustained, would count against important elements of MacIntyre's position.

A fifth question concerns the concrete political implications of MacIntyre's position. It was Kelvin Knight who coined the phrase "revolutionary Aristotelianism" to describe MacIntyre's position.[196] MacIntyre has accepted the description.[197] He is not, however, advocating an attempt to take over nation-states through their own political processes, much less advocating armed revolution. But he has often insisted on the need to cultivate forms of local community that distance themselves, to the extent they can, from the corrupting influences of the state and the market. He continues this theme in his latest work. In at least one place he seems to go further, but how much further is unclear: "Those with the most power and money . . . have identified themselves as having an interest that can only be served and a status that can only be preserved if the common goods of family, workplace, and school are not served. Disagreement with them . . . is therefore of a very different kind from most other theoretical and philosophical disagreements. It is and should be pursued as a prologue to prolonged social conflict."[198] It remains to be seen what this invitation to prolonged social conflict amounts to.

A sixth question, perhaps the most general of all, concerns MacIntyre's reservations about modernity and especially about liberal individualism. MacIntyre has acknowledged many positive contributions of modernity, but, if we accept the distinction between boosters and knockers of modernity that Charles Taylor draws in *The Ethics of Authenticity*, MacIntyre must surely be counted among the knockers. Many recent Aristotelians, however, have placed more emphasis on the positive contributions of modernity. They have tried to make an alliance, or even a synthesis, with liberalism.[199] In chapter 3, we will study just such a version of contemporary Aristotelianism: the liberal Aristotelianism of Martha Nussbaum.

FURTHER READING

This chapter has concentrated on a selection of books and essays from MacIntyre's third period. I have mentioned very few of his earlier writings. The chapter has had, alas, almost nothing to say about *Three Rival Versions of Moral Enquiry: Encyclopaedia, Genealogy, and Tradition* (Notre Dame, IN: University of Notre Dame Press, 1990), and nothing to say about *Edith Stein: A Philosophical Prologue 1913–1922* (Lanham, MD: Rowman and Littlefield, 2006).

The best general introduction to MacIntyre's work is Christopher Stephen Lutz, "Alasdair Chalmers MacIntyre (1929–)," *Internet Encyclopedia of Philosophy*.[200] This includes selective and partially annotated bibliographies of MacIntyre's work from 1953 to 2013, arranged chronologically, and of relevant secondary literature down to 2014. Jack Russell Weinstein, *On MacIntyre* (Belmont, CA: Wadsworth/Thomson Learning, 2003), is a brief but useful introduction to MacIntyre's work, leading up to a defense of his conceptions of tradition and rationality. Edward Clayton, "Political Philosophy of Alasdair MacIntyre," *Internet Encyclopedia of*

Philosophy,[201] is helpful, but the most recent items in the bibliography are from 2003.

A bibliography of MacIntyre's work from 1953 to 1974, arranged chronologically, appears in Paul Blackledge and Neil Davidson, eds., *Alasdair MacIntyre's Engagement with Marxism: Selected Writings 1953–1974* (Leiden: Brill, 2008), lvii–lxix. A bibliography of MacIntyre's work down to 1993, also arranged chronologically, is in John Horton and Susan Mendus, eds., *After MacIntyre: Critical Perspectives on the Work of Alasdair MacIntyre* (Notre Dame, IN: University of Notre Dame Press, 1994), 305–18. A very full bibliography, arranged chronologically and running down to 2006, is in Thomas D. D'Andrea, *Tradition, Rationality, and Virtue: The Thought of Alasdair MacIntyre* (Aldershot: Ashgate, 2006). Also useful, arranged chronologically and running down to 2010, is the bibliography in Paul Blackledge and Kelvin Knight, eds., *Virtue and Politics: Alasdair MacIntyre's Revolutionary Aristotelianism* (Notre Dame, IN: University of Notre Dame Press, 2011), 345–52.

Readers who want to understand MacIntyre, but without specializing in his work, should, I think, focus on *After Virtue, Whose Justice? Which Rationality?, Dependent Rational Animals*, and *Ethics in the Conflicts of Modernity*, along with the papers that MacIntyre included in the two volumes of his *Selected Essays* and those included in Kelvin Knight, ed., *The MacIntyre Reader* (Notre Dame, IN: University of Notre Dame Press, 1998). MacIntyre's briefer statements, such as those cited at the outset of this chapter, are helpful guides to the interpretation of his longer works. The interviews with Giovanna Borradori and with *Cogito* in *The MacIntyre Reader*, and with Alex Voorhoeve in *Conversations on Ethics* are particularly helpful and clarifying, as are the other interviews cited at the beginning of this chapter. Christopher Stephen Lutz, *Reading Alasdair MacIntyre's "After Virtue"* (London: Continuum, 2012), is especially helpful on *After Virtue* and on much else besides. On a much smaller scale, see Arthur Madigan, S.J., "Alasdair MacIntyre: Reflections on a Philosophical Identity, Suggestions for a Philosophical Project," in *What Happened in and to Moral Philosophy in the Twentieth Century? Philosophical Essays in Honor of Alasdair MacIntyre*, ed. Fran O'Rourke (Notre Dame, IN: University of Notre Dame Press, 2013), 122–44.

This chapter has had little to say about MacIntyre's views on education and their relation to his criticism of the dominant economic, social, and political order. On this, see MacIntyre, "The Idea of an Educated Public," in *Education and Values: The Richard Peters Lectures, Spring Term, 1985*, ed. Graham Haydon (London: University of London Institute of Education, 1987), 15–36; "Reconceiving the University as an Institution and the Lecture as a Genre," in *Three Rival Versions of Moral Enquiry*; "How Is Intellectual Excellence in Philosophy to be Understood by a Catholic Philosopher? What Has Philosophy to Contribute to Catholic Intellectual Excellence?," in *Current Issues in Catholic Higher Education* 12 (1991): 47–50; "Aquinas's Critique of Education: Against His Own Age, against Ours," in *Philosophers on Education: Historical Perspectives*, ed. Amélie Oksenberg Rorty (London: Routledge, 1998), 95–108; "Catholic Universities: Dangers, Hopes, Choices," in *Higher Learning & Catholic Traditions*, ed. Robert E. Sullivan (Notre Dame, IN: University of Notre Dame Press, 2001), 1–21; the interview "Alasdair MacIntyre on Education: In Dialogue with Joseph Dunne," *Journal of Philosophy of Education* 36 (2002): 1–19; "The End of Education: The Fragmentation of the American University," *Commonweal*, October 20, 2006, 10–14; MacIntyre's interview with Liam Kavanagh in *Expositions* 6 (2012): 1–8; and "Philosophical Education against Contemporary Culture," *Proceedings of the American Catholic Philosophical Association* 87 (2013): 43–56.[202]

There is a large secondary literature on MacIntyre, the greater part of it written before his most recent work appeared. I have referenced several collections of essays on MacIntyre's work at the outset of this chapter. Kelvin Knight's "Guide to Further Reading" in *The MacIntyre Reader*, 276–94, is a very helpful introduction to the secondary literature up to the time of its publication in 1998. I hope that a second edition of *The MacIntyre Reader* will include an updated version of this guide.

Peter McMylor, *Alasdair MacIntyre: Critic of Modernity* (London: Routledge, 1994), presents the significance of MacIntyre's work to a social-scientific audience. Michael Fuller, *Making Sense of MacIntyre* (Aldershot: Ashgate, 1998), brings MacIntyre into a critical dialogue with Richard Rorty and Donald Davidson. Christopher Stephen Lutz, *Tradition in the Ethics of Alasdair MacIntyre: Relativism, Thomism, and Philosophy*

(Lanham, MD: Lexington Books, 2004), focuses on MacIntyre's conceptions of tradition and rationality, arguing that for MacIntyre rationality both is constituted by tradition and constitutes tradition. The book also has much to say about MacIntyre's Thomism, defending him against the charge of importing theological presuppositions into his philosophy. Thomas D. D'Andrea, *Tradition, Rationality, and Virtue* (Aldershot: Ashgate, 2006), gives a very full account of MacIntyre's development prior to *After Virtue*, then presents *After Virtue, Whose Justice? Which Rationality?*, and *Three Rival Versions of Moral Enquiry*, and concludes with an examination of criticisms of MacIntyre's position. Jeffery L. Nicholas, *Reason, Tradition, and the Good: MacIntyre's Tradition-Constituted Reason and Frankfurt School Critical Theory* (Notre Dame, IN: University of Notre Dame Press, 2012), brings MacIntyre's Thomistic Aristotelianism into dialogue with the Marxist tradition of Frankfurt School critical theory. Christopher Stephen Lutz, "No One Is Minding the Store: MacIntyre's Critique of Modern Liberal Individualism," *Perspectives on Political Science* 44 (2015): 115–21, is a very helpful concise introduction to MacIntyre's challenge to liberalism. I have written on the political dimension of MacIntyre's thought in Arthur Madigan, S.J., "Alasdair MacIntyre on Political Thinking and the Tasks of Politics," in *Political Philosophy in the Twentieth Century: Authors and Arguments*, ed. Catherine H. Zuckert (Cambridge: Cambridge University Press, 2011), 252–63.

Two recent publications are Ron Beadle and Geoff Moore, eds., *Learning from MacIntyre* (Eugene, OR: Wipf and Stock/Pickwick, 2020), which presents essays by scholars on MacIntyre's contributions to a variety of topics and his influence in a number of fields; and Émile Perreau-Saussine, *Alasdair MacIntyre: An Intellectual Biography*, trans. Nathan Pinkoski (Notre Dame, IN: University of Notre Dame Press, 2022), which translates from French to English Perreau-Saussine's 2005 work on MacIntyre's intellectual journey.

A recent collection of articles on MacIntyre is the special issue of the *American Catholic Philosophical Quarterly* 88 (2014), edited by Christopher Stephen Lutz. An older but still valuable collection is Mark C. Murphy, ed., *Alasdair MacIntyre* (Cambridge: Cambridge University Press, 2003).

The Roman Catholic theologian Tracey Rowland makes extensive use of MacIntyre to develop a postmodern Augustinian Thomism in Rowland, *Culture and the Thomist Tradition after Vatican II* (London: Routledge, 2003). The political scientist Jason Blakely has used the work of MacIntyre and Charles Taylor in an attempt to integrate empirical social science and normative political theory in Blakely, *Alasdair MacIntyre, Charles Taylor, and the Demise of Naturalism: Reunifying Political Theory and Social Science* (Notre Dame, IN: University of Notre Dame Press, 2016).

The International Society for MacIntyrean Enquiry (ISME) has met annually or almost annually since 2007. Adjustments were made in 2020 and 2021 because of COVID-19. "ISME is dedicated to the theoretical and practical pursuit of the human good and seeks to bring together the different traditions that are informed by this Aristotelian principle."[203]

A number of papers from the ISME's 2010 conference in Vilnius, Lithuania, appear in Andrius Bielskis and Kelvin Knight, eds., *Virtue and Economy: Essays on Morality and Markets* (Farnham: Ashgate, 2015). The editors write, "So far Aristotelian philosophy has been strong on ethics and politics, but it has been much weaker on economics. This volume seeks to fill the lacuna."

CHAPTER THREE

THE LIBERAL ARISTOTELIANISM
OF MARTHA NUSSBAUM

Martha Craven Nussbaum (born 1947) is currently the Ernst Freund Distinguished Service Professor of Law and Ethics in the University of Chicago, with appointments in the law school and in philosophy and associate membership in divinity, political science, and the classics. She has authored a long line of books, edited or coedited another long line of books, and published scores of articles and reviews. In 1988, the year she was elected to the American Academy of Arts and Sciences, she was among those interviewed for what became *Bill Moyers: A World of Ideas*. She has been profiled in the *New York Times Sunday Magazine* and *The New Yorker*. She has received more than fifty honorary degrees and numerous awards, such as the Prince of Asturias Award, the Kyoto Prize in Arts and Philosophy, the Don M. Randel Award for Humanistic Studies of the American Academy of Arts and Sciences, the honor of delivering the 2017 Jefferson Lecture in the Humanities, and the 2018 Berggruen Prize for Philosophy and Culture. She has taken stands on issues of the day, perhaps most publicly in the Colorado lawsuit *Evans v. Romer* (1996). Her work with the World Institute for Development Economics Research of the United Nations University, her long-standing involvement with India, her collaboration with the Nobel Prize–winning economist Amartya Sen, and her activities with the Human Development and Capability Association (to mention but a few of her many engagements) have given her a breadth of experience and perspective that is exceptional for an academic philosopher. Her achievements have been recognized by the academic and humanitarian establishments of the United States and many other nations. She is arguably the most celebrated American philosopher of her generation.

Nussbaum's first book, a study of Aristotle's *De Motu Animalium*, appeared in 1978.[1] Since then, her thought has developed in many different directions. This chapter, in a book devoted to contemporary forms of Aristotelian ethics, will focus on Aristotelian elements that I find in her earlier work: in *The Fragility of Goodness* (1986); in a series of essays in which she develops the position of *Fragility of Goodness* and works out the political dimensions of her ethics; and to some extent in *Creating Capabilities* (2011), a book-length statement of her capabilities approach to human development. Nussbaum's intellectual interests have changed significantly since the publication of *Fragility of Goodness*, and her philosophical position has shifted away from Aristotelianism in the direction of a consequentialism that owes much to John Stuart Mill. This chapter will not attempt to cover her later work on the emotions and on political and legal philosophy. Thus, despite my use of the present tense in exposition of her earlier writings, the Aristotelianism that I find in them is not to be taken as her current position. By the same token, any criticisms that I may make of that Aristotelianism are not to be taken as touching her current position.[2]

Nussbaum's philosophical position in the work that I shall study is explicitly Aristotelian, but her version of Aristotelianism takes account of insights from many other sources: Hellenistic philosophy, in particular the Stoics, among the ancients; Kant, Mill, and Marx among the moderns; John Rawls, Hilary Putnam, and Bernard Williams among contemporaries. Her exposition of Aristotle in these early works is generally sympathetic and for the most part expresses her own views at the time of writing, but she has not hesitated to correct or dismiss certain of Aristotle's views. Her appropriation of Aristotle has always been critical and discerning.

THE FRAGILITY OF GOODNESS

The Method of Appearances

Fundamental to Nussbaum's Aristotelianism is her account of Aristotle's "method of appearances"; "appearances" is her rendering of Aristotle's word *phainomena* at *Nicomachean Ethics* 7.1, 1145b3. Here is her translation of the relevant passage: "Here, as in all other cases, we must set down the appearances (*phainomena*) and, first working through the puzzles (*diaporêsantas*), in this way go on to show, if possible, the truth of all the beliefs we hold (*ta endoxa*) about these experiences; and, if this is not possible, the truth of the greatest number and the most authoritative. For if the difficulties are resolved and the beliefs (*endoxa*) are left in place, we will have done enough showing (1145b1ff.)."[3]

On Nussbaum's reading, Aristotle is committed to a conception of philosophical method that may be called "saving the appearances." As she explains, appearances are not "observed facts" in a Baconian sense, prior to interpretation and theorizing. They are facts as they appear to us, as we experience and interpret them. The plural "we" is important. The first step in the method is to set forth the appearances, both ordinary beliefs and scientific or philosophical theories, about whatever subject is in question. Typically, the appearances are not entirely consistent with one another; they pose puzzles or dilemmas. The second step is to state these puzzles or dilemmas as clearly as possible and to try to resolve them. The third step is to state a consistent position, but consistency by itself is not all that the method requires. The eventual position has to preserve the appearances with which we started: perhaps not all of them, but most of them and the most basic or authoritative among them.[4]

Why would Aristotle work so hard simply to save "appearances"? "When Aristotle declares that his aim, in science and metaphysics as well as in ethics, is to save the appearances and their truth, he is not, then, saying something cozy and acceptable. Viewed against the background of Eleatic and Platonic philosophizing, these remarks have, instead, a defiant look. Aristotle is promising to rehabilitate the discredited measure or standard of tragic and Protagorean anthropocentrism. He promises to do his philosophical work in a place from which Plato and Parmenides had spent their careers contriving an exit."[5]

Nussbaum then goes on to argue that a range of passages in Aristotle illustrate his use of this method of appearances. For present purposes, her treatment of Aristotle's defense of the principle of noncontradiction in *Metaphysics* 4 is especially relevant, since someone might think of this principle as more than an appearance, as more basic than anything that we may think or say. Here Nussbaum underlines the fact that Aristotle's response to someone who denies the principle focuses on whether the denier will say something or not: "First, he says, you must find out whether this person will say anything to you or not. If he will not say anything, then you can stop worrying about him. 'It is comical to look for something to say to someone who won't say anything. A person like that, insofar as he is like that, is pretty well like a vegetable' (1006a13–15). But if he *does* say something, something definite, then you can go on to show him that in so doing he is in fact believing and making use of the very principle he attacks."[6]

Nussbaum's response to the question whether the principle of noncontradiction is an a priori principle gives a helpful clarification of the position that she, with evident approval, attributes to Aristotle:

> It is certainly *a priori* if an *a priori* principle is one that is basic or unrevisable, relative to a certain body of knowledge (what has sometimes been called the "contextual *a priori*"). It is even *a priori* in a somewhat stronger sense: it is so basic that it cannot significantly be defended, explained, or questioned at all from within the appearances, that is to say, the lives and practices of human beings, as long as human beings are anything like us. But it is not an *a priori* principle if that is a principle that can be shown to hold independently of all experience and all ways of life, all conceptual schemes. This is the question that we are in no position either to ask or to answer.[7]

Nussbaum then cites Aristotle's dismissal of the Platonic Forms in *Posterior Analytics* 1.22, 83a32–34: "So goodbye to the Platonic Forms. They are *teretismata* [meaningless sounds] and have nothing to do with our speech." But it is important not to misunderstand this dismissal of the Forms: "To say 'goodbye' to the forms is not to assert that they do not exist entirely outside of the world of our thought and language. That we could not say either. Even the contrast between the world as it is for us and the world as it is behind or apart from our thought may not be a contrast that the defender of a human internal truth should allow himself or herself to make using human language."[8]

Another text that bears on Nussbaum's understanding of Aristotle's method is his defense of the study of animals in *Parts of Animals* 1.5:

> He addresses some students who had evidently protested against the study of animals and their form and matter, asking for something more sublime. He tells them that this reluctance is actually a kind of self-contempt: for they are, after all, creatures of flesh and blood themselves (*PA* 654a27–31). That they need to be reminded of this fact is a sign of the depth of Platonism; or, rather, a sign that Platonism appeals to an already deep tendency in us towards shame at the messy, unclear stuff of which our humanity is made. We could generalize Aristotle's point by saying that the opponent of the return to appearances is likely to be a person not at peace with his humanity; and that this is an inner problem for that person, not a defect of the method.[9]

The method of appearances, then, "is a kind of realism, neither idealism of any sort nor skepticism. It has no tendency to confine us to internal representations, nor to ask us to suspend or qualify our deeply grounded judgments. It is fully hospitable to truth, to necessity (properly understood), and to a full-blooded notion of objectivity. It is not relativism, since it insists that truth is one for all thinking, language-using beings. It is a realism, however, that articulates very carefully the limits within which any realism must live."[10]

Can a method of "saving the appearances" ever be sure of making contact with a reality beyond or beneath or above those appearances? The question is misplaced. It suggests that we could have contact with a reality beyond appearances, when in fact our whole activity of referring and communicating takes place *within* the circle of appearances, within the circle of our thought and language. The whole idea of passing through the appearances to a reality beyond them was a futile Platonic dream. It is Aristotle's merit to have seen its futility.[11]

Nonscientific Deliberation

The Platonic project of getting beyond appearance to reality was an attempt to show that the good human life is in fact invulnerable to the chances and changes of the phenomenal world. That attempt risks turning our life into a different life from the one that we actually live. Aristotle's viewpoint, which Nussbaum shares, is by contrast resolutely anthropocentric. So long as we are dealing with *our* lives—and we have no other lives to deal with—we must remain within the ambit of the appearances. We have no access to a Platonic "god's-eye view" of the world.[12] What is left for us is to deal with life's contingencies, or better, with life's opportunities, opportunities that are inseparable from fragility and vulnerability. And the way to deal with life is practical nonscientific deliberation:[13] "Aristotle says two anti-Platonic things about practical deliberation. First, that it is not and cannot be scientific: 'That practical wisdom is not scientific understanding (*epistêmê*) is obvious' (*EN* 1142a23–4). Second, that the appropriate criterion of correct choice is a thoroughly human being, the person of practical wisdom. This person does not attempt to take up a stand outside of the conditions of human life, but bases his or her judgment on long and broad experience of these conditions."[14] It is perfectly reasonable, within the circle of appearances, to ask about the shape of the good life, as it is reasonable to consider what is distinctive about human beings, what differentiates us from minerals, vegetables, and even from other animals. Still, "our question about the good life must, like any question whatever, be asked and answered within the appearances."[15]

In *Nicomachean Ethics* 1.7, Aristotle articulates what has come to be called his "function argument." Scholars differ about the interpretation of this argument, but this much at least is clear, that Aristotle thinks that human beings have a distinctive function, unique to the human species, that this function is reason (*logos*), however that is understood, and that this distinctive human function is crucial for the understanding of what human happiness or fulfillment (*eudaimonia*) is. Nussbaum comments on the argument as follows: "We begin an ethical treatise by looking at the characteristic functioning of humans—both its shared and its distinctive elements—because we want a life which includes whatever it is that makes us us."[16] On her reading, Aristotle "argues that the values that are constitutive of a good human life are plural and incommensurable; and that a perception of particular cases takes precedence, in ethical judgment, over general rules and accounts."[17] General principles do not tell us very much. They are "perspicuous descriptive summaries of good judgments, valid only to the extent to which they correctly describe such judgments. They are normative only insofar as they transmit in economical form the normative force of the good concrete decisions of the wise person and because we wish for various reasons to be guided by that person's choices."[18]

Talk about the superiority of experience to the principles, which are merely formulations or distillations of experience, might suggest to some an uncontrolled relativism or situationalism. One might think that we were faced with a choice: either accept the Platonic view that any genuinely objective understanding of particulars depends on a grasp of universal criteria or principles, or fall into subjectivism. Nussbaum's Aristotle is not bound by this dilemma:

> We must insist that Aristotelian practical wisdom is not a type of rootless situational perception that rejects all guidance from ongoing commitments and values. The person of practical wisdom is a person of good character, that is to say, a person who has internalized through early training certain ethical values and a certain conception of the good human life as the more or less harmonious pursuit of these. He or she will be concerned about friendship, justice, courage, moderation, generosity; his desires will be formed in accordance with these concerns; and he will derive from this internalized conception of value many ongoing guidelines for action, pointers as to what to look for in a particular situation.[19]

Reliance on universal principles and a fall into subjectivism are not the only two possibilities: "It is now time to say that the particular case would be surd and unintelligible without the guiding and sorting power of the universal. . . . Nor does particular judgment have the kind of rootedness and focus required for goodness of character without a core of commitment to a general conception—albeit one that is continually evolving, ready for surprise, and not rigid. There is in effect a two-way illumination between particular and universal."[20]

Nussbaum's Aristotle recognizes certain types of desire, feeling, and passion as necessary conditions for certain kinds of ethical knowledge: "The experienced person confronting a new situation does not attempt to face it with the intellect 'itself by itself.' He or she faces it, instead, with desires informed by deliberation and deliberations informed by desire, and responds to it appropriately in both passion and act. Frequently the perception of the salient features will be achieved in a way that relies centrally upon the discriminating power of passion." Citing *De Anima* 3.7, 431b2 and following, Nussbaum goes on to explain that for Aristotle our desires mark out for us certain elements or features of situations, mark them out as pleasant or painful, to be pursued or to be avoided, "and we might say that it is really desire itself that does the marking, showing us the sort of situation that we are dealing with."[21]

Animality and Neediness

Fragility of Goodness has much to say about the fragility of the human condition. I will summarize this material under two main headings: (1) animality and neediness, and (2) vulnerability to conflict and tragedy.

It is of fundamental importance to Nussbaum's Aristotle that human beings are animals, not just souls inhabiting or informing bodies. This is not just a truism of biology. It is basic to the human ethical situation, because animality entails neediness and rules out self-sufficiency. Aristotle "will argue for a picture of the causes of action that permits us to see our neediness *vis-à-vis* the world as not inimical to, but at the very heart of, our ethical value."[22]

Animality is the basis of the *orexis* (appetite), the focused neediness that essentially characterizes human beings and is the principle of their activity. Once we understand what it means for us to be animals, dependent on and in constant interaction with an environment, we will see that by far the greatest part of what we cherish is bound up with our animality: "Without being-affected, as Aristotle explicitly reminds us, there will be cleverness and even contemplative wisdom, but not, for example, gentleness, or courage, or love—praiseworthy elements of the person without which a human life would not be a good one (*EE* 1220a11–13)."[23]

Animal action in the world is therefore neither mechanical nor mindless, but rather rich and complex. Human neediness, love, and desire pervade human rationality: "Appropriate eating, drinking, and sexual activity has intrinsic value, not in spite of, but because of the way in which it satisfies contingent needs; and to be needy is not a bad, but an appropriate thing for a human being to be."[24]

Conflict and Tragedy

The final chapters of *Fragility of Goodness* spell out in detail that fragility to which our world and our needy animality destine us and from which our reason cannot rescue us. Chapter 11 explores the fragility of human activities, including the most valuable among them, and in particular their vulnerability to interference and interruption. Circumstances can interfere with excellent activity in a variety of ways. They may deprive us of things that we need as instruments for activity, such as financial resources. They may take away the people who would benefit from our activities, such as families or friends. Sometimes these hindrances to activity may be quickly removable, but sometimes they may be long-lasting. It might thus seem desirable for us to step outside these limiting conditions. But that seeming deliverance would mean discarding the most central human values: "It is plain that these central human values [justice, courage, generosity, moderation]—which are, in the bulk of Aristotle's ethical writings, treated as ends in themselves, important constituents of human *eudaimonia*—cannot be found in a life without shortage, risk, need, and limitation. Their nature *and* their goodness are constituted by the fragile nature of human life."[25]

Chapter 12 discusses a further aspect of our human fragility. Some of our most valued goods are relational, that is, they involve or even consist in relations that we form with other humans. Such would be membership and participation in a political community. Political and social activities possess intrinsic value and not only instrumental value, but they are notoriously risky and unstable. Friendships, especially the best sort of friendships, have many conditions (for example, the good character of the parties, their liking each another, their having time to spend together, their trusting each other) and are vulnerable to happenings in the world (absence, the changes in temperament brought on by aging, and death). To retreat from these dimensions of fragility and vulnerability would drastically impoverish human life.[26]

Chapters 11 and 13 of *Fragility of Goodness* discuss the possibility of tragedy affecting human life. Nussbaum distinguishes various instances of tragedy. The case of Priam shows how a person who has developed a good character and acted well throughout life can in the end be deprived of family, friends, and almost everything that made it possible for him to act well.[27] The case of Oedipus shows how a person of good character may, as a result of excusable ignorance, or as a result of circumstances, commit a terrible act that impedes or even destroys his happiness.[28] The case of Agamemnon shows how a person may be caught in a terrible conflict between goods.[29] The case of Hecuba in Euripides's play of that name shows how a person's character may be so ravaged by suffering, sorrow, and betrayal that she leaves the framework of human trust, association, and community, and becomes in effect a subhuman animal, isolated from the rest of humanity, ultimately turned into stone.[30]

In an extended review of *Fragility of Goodness*, the Canadian philosopher Charles Taylor suggested that Plato's position was marked not only by an aversion to human vulnerability but also by a positive aspiration to transcendence. He raised the question whether Nussbaum's Aristotle, or Nussbaum herself, regarded this aspiration to transcendence as something negative, or whether they each regarded the aspiration to transcendence as part of the complete human good.[31] Nussbaum recognized the importance of Taylor's question in her "Transcending Humanity." Speaking in her own name rather than in Aristotle's, she wrote that in her view "there is a great deal of room for transcendence of our ordinary humanity—transcendence, we might say, of an *internal* and human sort." On the same page she wrote that her argument "urges us to reject as incoherent the aspiration to leave behind altogether the constitutive conditions of our humanity, and to seek for a life that is really the life of another sort of being—as if it were a higher and better life for *us*."[32]

BEYOND *FRAGILITY OF GOODNESS*

In 2001, Nussbaum published an updated edition of *Fragility of Goodness*. The preface to this new edition sums up the most important aspects of her philosophical development in the years 1986–2001. Four points stand out. First and foremost, she confirms her commitment to the major theses of *Fragility of Goodness*: "I still support most of the arguments of *Fragility*, both interpretive and substantive. For example, I still think that Aristotle's conception of the human being, and of practical deliberation, is of great importance for contemporary ethical and political thought; and I believe that the depiction of the plurality of goods and of conflicts among them that we find in both the poets and Aristotle offers insights that are absent from much of contemporary social reasoning."[33]

Second, in the years after publishing *Fragility of Goodness*, Nussbaum made the nature of the emotions a central theme of her work. She came to accept the Stoic view that emotions are not unintelligent forces but rather judgments of value. She has gone on to explore the emotions in a series of major books, but the aspect that she mentions in the 2001 preface is the possibility of educating people's emotions in a way that can transform society: "While the Stoic view thus poses some problems for anyone who would rely on the guidance of emotion, it also holds out hopes for societal enlightenment that are ignored by at least some Enlightenment theories, for example Kant's, which tends to treat emotions as relatively unintelligent elements of human nature. The Stoic view suggests that while change is not easy, it is possible for the personality as a whole to become an enlightened one, by combating the value judgments that constitute unwise anger and hatred."[34]

Third, Nussbaum became increasingly engaged in political questions: "During the past twelve years, I have drawn on Aristotle to develop a political theory and a theory of the ethical bases for international development that is a form of social-democratic liberalism. . . . Although at times I have been interested in close textual interpretation of Aristotle's views, I have primarily aimed to develop a view of my own that, though in some sense Aristotelian in spirit, departs from Aristotle in many ways, both in the direction of liberalism and in the direction of feminism."[35]

Nussbaum's view combines an Aristotelian understanding of human beings with a liberal respect for pluralism: "Over the years I have increasingly stressed the importance of respect for pluralism and reasonable disagreement about the ultimate worth and meaning of life. In a deliberate departure from Aristotle, who surely believed that politics ought to foster functioning in accordance with a single comprehensive conception of the good human life, I argue that politics should restrict itself to promoting capabilities, not actual functionings, in order to make room for choices about whether to pursue a given function or not to pursue it."[36] This focus on developing people's capabilities—the things that they are able to do and to be—and leaving people free to exercise their capabilities as they choose is a constant in Nussbaum's thinking.

Fourth, Nussbaum brings a critical perspective to bear on the emergence of virtue ethics. The 1980s and 1990s witnessed a new interest in virtue and the virtues, to the point that people began to speak of "virtue ethics" as an alternative to teleological ethics and deontological ethics. She criticizes this new taxonomy: "Kant and the major Utilitarian thinkers have theories of virtue; so in an obvious sense the suggestion that 'virtue ethics' is an approach distinct from these two involves a category mistake."[37]

Further, Nussbaum sees two different motivations at work in the turn to the virtues:

One group of modern virtue theorists turns to Aristotle and other Greek thinkers primarily out of a dissatisfaction with Utilitarianism. They believe that Utilitarians neglect the plurality and heterogeneity of values, the possibility of intelligent deliberation about ends as well as means, and the susceptibility of the passions to social cultivation. . . . Such thinkers are typically quite happy with the enterprise of theory-making in ethics; they simply want to build an ethical theory of a non-Utilitarian type, and they find Aristotle a helpful guide in the pursuit of that project. And they typically wish to expand, not to reduce, the role of reason in our ethical lives.[38]

Nussbaum sides with these theorists.

The second motivation is quite different, and Nussbaum criticizes it vigorously: "Another group of virtue theorists are primarily anti-Kantians. They believe that reason has come to play too dominant a role in most philosophical accounts of ethics, and that a larger place should be given to sentiments and passions—which they typically construe in a less reason-based way than does the first group."[39] Here Nussbaum is thinking especially of Alasdair MacIntyre and Annette Baier.[40] She is particularly critical of Baier's preference for sentiment over reason and MacIntyre's preference, as she sees it, for political or ecclesiastical authority over reason. She is critical of any attempt to use the Greek philosophers in such a way as to undermine the very enterprise of ethical theory: "It is extremely odd, it seems to me, for modern-day philosophers to invoke the Greek philosophers as allies in an enterprise of theory-bashing, when those very figures self-consciously commended philosophy to their cultures and their cultures to philosophy, as an alternative to the modes of social interaction promoted by rhetoric, astrology, poetry, and unexamined self-interest."[41]

The Discernment of Perception

In the fifteen years between the publication of *Fragility of Goodness* and her 2001 preface to it, Nussbaum elaborated her Aristotelian position in a series of major essays, only a few of which can be considered here. Some of these essays appeared in print more than once, and several of them make reference to others. Each makes its own contribution, but the result is a body of work united by three common features: adaptation and development of central insights from Aristotle, a nuanced appreciation of the strengths and limitations of Stoicism, and increased attention to central questions in political philosophy.

Chapter 2 of *Love's Knowledge*, "The Discernment of Perception," expands on the picture of Aristotelian practical reasoning in chapter 10 of *Fragility of Goodness*.[42] It presents Aristotle as attacking a pseudo-scientific conception of practical rationality found in classical utilitarianism and in contemporary rational choice theory. This attack has three dimensions: "an attack on the claim that all valuable things are commensurable; an argument for the priority of particular judgments to universals; and a defense of the emotions and imagination as essential to rational choice."[43]

The utilitarian claim that all goods are commensurable runs up against the facts. There are multiple incommensurable goods and they can conflict in ways that cannot be resolved by measurement. Nussbaum instances the conflict that Agamemnon faced between letting his expedition sail to Troy and saving his daughter's life.[44]

The argument for the priority of particular judgments to universals is an attack on any ethics, such as Kant's, that considers rules to be basic to ethics: "'The discernment rests with perception.' This phrase, from which my title is taken, is used by Aristotle in connection with his attack on another feature of pseudo-scientific pictures of rationality: the insistence that rational choice can be captured in a system of general rules or principles which can then simply be applied to each new case."[45]

The defense of the emotions and imagination as essential to rational choice is in opposition to any ethics that treats them as irrelevant or problematic for ethics, views that Nussbaum finds both in Kantianism and in classical utilitarianism: "The two dominant moral theories of our own time, Kantianism and Utilitarianism, have been no less suspicious of the passions [than Plato]; indeed, this is one of the few things on which they (regularly) agree. For Kant, the passions are invariably selfish and aimed at one's own states of satisfaction. . . . The Utilitarian believes that a passion like personal love frequently impedes rationality by being too parochial: it leads us to emphasize personal ties and to rank the nearer above the further, obstructing that fully impartial attitude toward the world that is the hallmark of Utilitarian rationality."[46]

Nussbaum then suggests that the three elements of Aristotle's position—the incommensurability of goods, the priority of particular judgments to universal judgments, and the necessity of the emotions and imagination for rational choice—together "form a coherent picture of practical choice."[47] There can be no question of capturing all the detail in the remainder of "Discernment of Perception" in this brief summary, but one element deserves mention here. The position that Nussbaum ascribes to Aristotle does not entail relativism or subjectivism: "The insistence that deliberation must take contextual features into account does not imply that the deliberated choice is correct only relative to local norms. Aristotelian particularism is fully compatible with the view that what perception aims to see is (in some sense) the way things are; it requires further argument to decide on the best interpretation of the position here. And surely the use of the concept 'human being' will play an important role in suiting the [Aristotelian] conception to make cross-cultural judgments and to ground a cross-cultural debate."[48] These claims will be important in several of the essays that follow. Nussbaum refers the reader to her "Aristotle on Human Nature" and "Non-Relative Virtues," both discussed below. I will return to the educational program that is outlined in the latter part of "Discernment of Perception."

Human Nature

Nussbaum wrote "Aristotle on Human Nature and the Foundations of Ethics" for a collection of essays on the philosophy of Bernard Williams. Its focus is on "how the idea of human nature works inside Aristotle's ethical arguments."[49] Williams takes it that the concept of human nature is foundational to Aristotle's ethics but is not itself an ethical concept; it is a natural-scientific concept, and one drawn from a biology that we can no longer accept.[50] Nussbaum disagrees with this "external" account of the foundations of Aristotle's ethics and proposes an alternative reading of Aristotle's position, a position that she herself also endorses. Her response to Williams picks up on a number of themes from *Fragility of Goodness* and sounds a number of themes that will be important in her later Aristotelian work.

First is the rejection of any sharp distinction between fact and value: "Williams claims that Aristotle's view of human nature, appealing as it does to a natural teleology, attempts to take up an extra-ethical, and even an extra-human perspective on the human situation. We can begin to respond to this claim by pointing out that Aristotle's metaphysics of nature, and his biology, are neither value-free nor external. There is nothing anywhere in Aristotle's work precisely corresponding to a modern distinction between fact and value."[51]

The argument in *Nicomachean Ethics* 1.7 from the specifically human function of reason to the definition of happiness has been read as arguing

from natural or natural-scientific fact to ethical value. Nussbaum maintains that it does no such thing. She distinguishes two readings of the passage: one on which Aristotle's phrase "the life of" this or that (nutrition,
growth, perception, reason) means simply this or that aspect of a whole
complex life, and a second on which "the life of" means "the distinctive
and guiding feature that gives the [whole] life its characteristic overall
shape." She then argues on several grounds that Aristotle's claim about the
life of reason should be read in the second way. The point of the function
argument is to establish the centrality of practical reason in a worthwhile
human life, as distinct from establishing some fact about prehuman or
extrahuman nature.[52]

A second theme is the relevance of Aristotle's ethics to politics. If
practical reason is central to human life, then so are deliberation and
choice: "Aristotle's ethical writing aims to provide instruction for the future legislator. The job of such a legislator is to give to the people in his
city the necessary conditions for choosing a flourishing human life. The
city aims at making people capable of such choices. A life that is not even
human at all is, *a fortiori*, not a *good* human life. And it is Aristotle's claim
that many conceivable political and economic arrangements do, either
wholly or in part, remove the humanity from political life by removing
choice from people—either in a single sphere or across the board."[53]

Applied to politics, Aristotle's ethics introduces a third theme. If practical reason, deliberation, and choice are central to human life, that counts
against any politics that focuses primarily on economic goods: "The focus
on practical reason as an essential necessary condition of humanness, and,
therefore, a basis for political assessment, provides political thought with
a direction strikingly different from that provided by a focus on wealth
and commodities as primary objects of the legislator's concern. For it tells
the legislator that these commodities have their place in a human life as
means to the activities of practical reason."[54] Here Nussbaum sees an important parallel between Aristotle and Marx: "They agree in condemning
societies that promote money and commodities to the status of ends in
themselves, on the grounds that this confuses and inverts values, debasing
humanity to the status of a mere means, and alienates individuals from the
truly human understanding of goods."[55]

Non-Relative Virtues

"Aristotle on Human Nature" made the point that the foundations of ethics are internal, that is, themselves ethical, rather than metaphysical or natural-scientific. "Non-Relative Virtues: An Aristotelian Approach" makes the complementary point that this approach does not entail ethical relativism:[56] "The purpose of this paper is to establish that Aristotle did indeed have an interesting way of connecting the virtues with a search for ethical objectivity and with the criticism of existing local norms, a way that deserves our serious consideration as we work on these questions."[57]

Philosophers looking for an alternative to Kantian and utilitarian ethics have focused on the concept of virtue and on Aristotle, whose ethics of the virtues would seem to be such an attractive alternative. There is, however, a problem in the turn to virtue: "The return to the virtues is connected with a turn towards relativism, towards, that is, the view that the only appropriate criteria of ethical goodness are local ones, internal to the traditions of each local society or group that asks itself questions about the good."[58] Nussbaum cites Bernard Williams, Alasdair MacIntyre, and Philippa Foot. None of these authors is an out and out relativist, but she says that they "all connect virtue ethics with a relativist denial that ethics, correctly understood, offers any transcultural norms, justifiable by reference to reasons of universal human validity, by reference to which we may appropriately criticize different local conceptions of the good. And all suggest that the insights we gain by pursuing ethical questions in the Aristotelian virtue-based way lend support to relativism."[59]

This is not just a theoretical problem. If Aristotle's scheme of the virtues was relative to his time and place and society, then his ethics of the virtues does not provide an adequate standpoint for criticizing societies today. Nussbaum's aim in "Non-Relative Virtues" is to establish that something like an Aristotelian account of the virtues applies across different human societies and that his ethics of the virtues leaves open the possibility of criticizing existing societies.[60] The core of her proposal can be captured in two distinctions: the distinction between spheres of human experience (what she calls "grounding experiences") and the virtues appropriate to those spheres; and the distinction between a "thin" description of a virtue and a "thick" description of that same virtue.[61]

Relativists may think that Aristotle's account of the virtues simply describes the virtues that were admired in his own society. This is not the case: "What *is* going on becomes clearer when we examine the way in which he does, in fact, introduce his list [of the virtues]. . . . What he does, in each case, is to isolate a sphere of experience that figures in more or less any human life, and in which more or less any human being will have to make *some* choices rather than others, and act in *some* way rather than some other."[62] Here are the spheres that Aristotle identifies and their corresponding virtues:

> Fear of important damages (courage)
> Bodily appetites and their pleasures (moderation)
> Distribution of limited resources (justice)
> Management of one's personal property, where others are concerned (generosity)
> Management of one's personal property, where hospitality is concerned (expansive hospitality)
> Attitudes and actions with respect to one's own worth (greatness of soul)
> Attitude to slights and damages (mildness of temper)
> Association and living together (truthfulness, easy grace, friendliness)
> Attitude to the good and ill fortune of others (proper judgement)
> Intellectual life (intellectual virtues: perceptiveness, knowledge, etc.)
> Planning of one's life and conduct (practical wisdom).[63]

These grounding experiences are not peculiar to ancient Greece. They occur in every age and in every culture: "On this approach, it does not seem possible to say, as the relativist wishes to, that a given society does not contain anything that corresponds to a given virtue. . . . The point is that everyone makes some choices and acts somehow or other in these spheres: if not properly, then improperly. . . . No matter where one lives one cannot escape these questions, so long as one is living a human life."[64] Thus it is possible to frame "thin" or nominal definitions of the virtues that correspond to these grounding experiences: "The thin or nominal definition of the virtue will be, in each case, that it is whatever being disposed to choose and respond well consists in, in that sphere. The job of ethical theory will be to search for the best further specification corresponding to this nominal definition, and to produce a full definition."[65]

Nussbaum goes on to outline three possible objections to her view. For present purposes the most important is the second: "The second objection goes deeper. For it questions the notion of spheres of shared human experience that lies at the heart of the Aristotelian approach. The approach, says this objector, seems to treat the experiences that ground the virtues as in some way primitive, given, and free from the cultural variation that we find in the plurality of normative conceptions of virtue."[66]

Nussbaum's reply gives important evidence about her response to the challenge of relativism. It does not commit her to any external (metaphysical or natural-scientific) basis for ethics: "The Aristotelian should begin, it seems to me, by granting that with respect to any complex matter of deep human importance there is no 'innocent eye,' no way of seeing the world that is entirely neutral and free of cultural shaping."[67] However, it is only fair to insist that different cultures still have much in common: "Relativists tend, furthermore, to understate the amount of attunement, recognition, and overlap that actually obtains across cultures, particularly in the areas of the grounding experiences. The Aristotelian, in developing her conception in a culturally sensitive way, should insist, as Aristotle himself does, upon the evidence of such attunement and recognition."[68] And, for all their differences, cultures do not exist in isolation from one another: "Furthermore, it is necessary to stress that hardly any cultural group today is as focused upon its own internal traditions and as isolated from other cultures as the relativist argument presupposes."[69]

Nussbaum then goes on to identify "certain features of our common humanity, closely related to Aristotle's original list, from which our debate might proceed."[70] These are the following:

1. Mortality.
2. The body.
3. Pleasure and pain.
4. Cognitive capability.

5. Practical reason.

6. Early infant development.

7. Affiliation.

8. Humour.[71]

"Non-Relative Virtues" does not itself provide full or thick definitions of the virtues. It offers a context within which people can carry on arguments about those definitions: "But it seems plausible to claim that in all these areas we have a basis for further work on the human good. We do not have a 'bedrock' of completely uninterpreted, 'given' data, but we do have nuclei of experience around which the constructions of different societies proceed. There is no Archimedean point here, no pure access to unsullied 'nature'—even, here, human nature—as it is in and of itself. There is just human life as it is lived."[72]

Distributive Justice

The next two essays to be considered spell out Nussbaum's view of distributive justice. Before going into them, it may be helpful to say a few words about the Harvard philosopher and political theorist John Rawls (1921–2002). Rawls and Nussbaum were in contact for decades. She is a well-informed and insightful commentator on his work.[73] Her book *Frontiers of Justice* is an attempt to address three problems of social justice that she finds his theory was unable to handle: justice with respect to people with disabilities, people of other nations, and nonhuman animals.[74] The acknowledgments and introduction to this volume state Nussbaum's relationship to Rawls's thought clearly and concisely: "My project is critical of John Rawls. I have singled out Rawls's theory for critical examination because it is the strongest political theory in the social contract tradition that we have, and, indeed, one of the most distinguished theories in the Western tradition of political philosophy."[75] Rawls's version of social contract theory is the best that we have, but Nussbaum maintains that social contract theory is unable to solve the three problems just mentioned. She argues "that, with respect to all three of the problems under consideration, the version of the 'capabilities approach' that I have been developing suggests promising insights, and insights superior to those suggested, for those particular problems, by the social contract tradition."[76] By the "capabilities approach" Nussbaum means an approach to issues of justice and human development that focuses on developing people's capabilities—the things that they are able to do and to be—while leaving people free to choose whether and how to exercise those capabilities. It will be discussed below.

Despite this fundamental difference with Rawls over social contract theory, and despite some other differences that we will see in due course, Nussbaum remains indebted to him for two important points: "the idea of political liberalism (a form of liberalism not grounded in divisive religious or metaphysical principles) and the idea of overlapping consensus (the idea that people with different metaphysical and religious conceptions can accept the core of the political conception)."[77]

In "Nature, Function, and Capability: Aristotle on Political Distribution," Nussbaum presents an interpretation of Aristotle's view of just political distribution, a view that she also endorses.[78] On this view the purpose of political arrangements is to provide people with the conditions necessary for them to lead good human lives: "A political arrangement has as its task the securing to its people . . . of the necessary conditions for a full good human life. It is to create a context in which anyone at all may choose to function in the ways that are constitutive of a good human life."[79]

The point of political arrangements is to give people the concrete possibility of making choices about the ways in which they will function. This may sound like a platitude, but it is not. Nussbaum's formulation is carefully framed in opposition to two other views. One is Rawls's view in *A Theory of Justice*, in which he holds that we need to have a "thin" theory of the good before settling on arrangements for just distribution of goods. His thin theory includes what he thinks of as bare essentials: more freedom and opportunity rather than less, more wealth rather than less.[80] Aristotle, and Nussbaum, would criticize the inclusion of wealth, which they see as an instrumental good. More importantly, they would insist that a fuller list of goods is required: "There is no way around taking some stand about what functions are constitutive of human good living—*if* we are to produce an account of distribution that offers a coherent account of the ways in which the city can actually promote people's good."[81]

The second competing view is the utilitarian view that the purpose of political arrangements is to maximize utility, understood as giving people whatever they may happen to desire:

> Aristotle would agree with the utilitarian that distributable goods are valuable because of what they do for people, and not as things of worth in their own right. This area of agreement is significant and should not be ignored. But Aristotle would of course object strenuously to the idea that the criterion the lawgiver needs is to be found in people's subjective preferences or in the satisfaction of the desires they happen, as things are, to have. For he stresses throughout his ethical and political writings that many people are badly educated and therefore want the wrong things, or in the wrong amount. They are not at all reliable judges of what functions the good human life contains.[82]

People's conscious desires or preferences may be quite different from, and more limited than, the desires and preferences that they would have if they were educated in certain ways: "Desire, the contemporary Aristotelian holds, is an easily corrupted, unstable, and unreliable guide to genuine human flourishing."[83]

Supposing that we need a fuller list of basic goods than Rawls provides, that people's conscious preferences are not in themselves sufficient to give us that list, and that the list should include certain human functionings, which functionings should political distribution try to make possible for people? "We want, I believe, a list of functionings that is, on the one hand, non-detached but, on the other, objective. . . . By non-detached, I mean that it should not be discovered by looking at human lives and actions from a totally alien point of view, outside of the conditions and experience of those lives—as if we were discovering some sort of value-neutral scientific fact about ourselves. . . . By objective, I mean that we do not want simply to take each culture's or group's word for it, when they tell us what they think the relevant human functionings are— even when they are talking about themselves."[84]

Nussbaum will go on to elaborate her list of the most important functionings in detail in "Human Functioning and Social Justice: In Defense of Aristotelian Essentialism," *Creating Capabilities*, and elsewhere. For the moment, however, we need to notice once again how she sees the relationship of fact and value. She is criticizing a reading of Aristotle that she finds in MacIntyre and Williams:

> The project of elaborating and defending Aristotle's approach to ethical objectivity needs to begin, I believe, by establishing that Aristotle's account of human nature and human functioning is not vulnerable to a criticism that recently has been made against it by several philosophers, including Alasdair MacIntyre and Bernard Williams. These writers charge that Aristotle imposes on ethics an account of human functioning derived from "metaphysical biology," basing judgements of ethical value on value-neutral scientific fact, rather than on the human experience of life and value. . . . It is possible, I believe, to answer these charges. In doing so one would begin by establishing that the fact/value distinction is not really present at all in Aristotle, even where science is concerned. Having done this, one could then, I believe, go on to show that for Aristotle . . . the question as to whether a certain function is or is not a part of our human nature is a certain special sort of evaluative question, namely, a question about whether that function is so important that a creature who lacked it would not be judged to be properly human at all.[85]

The issue for Aristotle is not one of biology, metaphysical or natural-scientific, but of how we understand and evaluate human life.

In the concluding section, Nussbaum argues that the common link among the functions and capabilities required for a good human life is practical reasoning. She cites the argument from the distinctive human function of reason in *Nicomachean Ethics* 1.7. That chapter considers and rejects the idea that a worthwhile human life could be exclusively or even primarily organized around the activities of nutrition, growth, and sense-perception: "The truly human life, by contrast, is a life organized by the activity of practical reasoning (1098a3–4: *praktikê tis tou logon echontos*), in which it is that activity that gives the life as a whole its distinctive shape and tone. (The role of reason would, here, be twofold: it would have an architectonic role, as what organizes the whole life, providing for its many activities, and it would infuse each activity, causing it to become human, rather than merely vegetative or animal)."[86]

Once again, Nussbaum sees a link between Aristotle and Marx. She cites a passage from Marx's 1844 manuscripts: "It is obvious that the *human* eye gratifies itself in a way different from the crude, non-human eye, the human *ear* from the crude ear, etc. . . . . The *sense* caught up in crude practical need has only a *restricted* sense. For the starving man, it is not the human form of food that exists, but only its abstract being as food; it could just as well be there in its crudest form, and it would be impossible to say wherein this feeding-activity differs from that of animals."[87]

She then comments: "This passage develops, I think, two points that are Aristotle's: that truly human living requires performing all one's natural activities in a way infused by human choice and rationality; and that the capability to function in this human way is not automatically open to all humans, but must be created for them (brought forward from more rudimentary capabilities) by material and social conditions."[88]

Her "Aristotelian Social Democracy" starts with Aristotle's claim that the state should ensure that no citizen is lacking in sustenance (*trophê*) (*Politics* 7.10, 1330a2) and explores what sustenance might mean today.[89] It brings together two lines of thought that we have seen in other essays: the idea that certain grounding experiences and the potential for certain human ways of functioning are common across the human species, and the idea that the aim of politics is to enable people to make choices about which of those ways of functioning they will in fact actualize. The essay is complex; no brief summary can do it justice. For present purposes I will first outline its constructive argument, and then indicate how Nussbaum's Aristotelian social democracy differs from liberalism, especially Rawlsian liberalism.

The task of political planning, as Aristotle saw it, is "to make available to each and every citizen the material, institutional, and educational circumstances in which good human functioning may be chosen; to move each and every one of them across a threshold of capability into circumstances in which they may choose to live and function well."[90] To spell out what good human functioning means, Nussbaum introduces what she calls the "thick vague conception of the good."[91] Though not a fully determinate description of the human good, the "thick vague conception of the good" is significantly more determinate than the thin descriptions of the good favored by classical liberal theories: "By this name I mean to suggest that it provides a (partially) comprehensive conception of good human functioning (in contrast to Rawls's 'thin' theory), but at a high level of generality, admitting of multiple specifications."[92]

Nussbaum explains that "the task of political arrangement is both *broad* and *deep*. *Broad*, in that it is concerned with the good living not of an elite few, but of each and every member of the polity. . . . It is *deep* in that it is concerned not simply with money, land, opportunities, and offices, the traditional political distributables, but with the totality of the functionings that constitute the good human life."[93]

The thick vague conception of the good has two levels. The first is a list of what Nussbaum calls the constitutive circumstances of the human being, or the main features of the shape of the human form of life. Human life is characterized by mortality; by the human body with its hunger and thirst, need for shelter, sexual desire, and mobility; by the capacity for pleasure and pain; by the cognitive capabilities of perceiving, imagining, and thinking; by the stage of early infant development; by practical reason, the planning and managing of one's life; by affiliation with other human beings; by relatedness to other species and to nature; by humor and play; by separateness, that is, our basic and ineliminable individuality; and by what Nussbaum calls "strong separateness," that is, the fact that each of us has a context, history, and set of relationships that are different from anyone else's.[94]

The second level of the thick vague conception is a list of ten basic human functional capabilities. Capabilities, not actual functionings: the legislator should be interested not in what people actually choose to do or how they choose to live—about this people should be free—but in what they are capable of doing.[95] Here is the list:

> 1. Being able to live to the end of a complete human life, as far as is possible; not dying prematurely, or before one's life is so reduced as to be not worth living.
> 2. Being able to have good health; to be adequately nourished; to have adequate shelter; having opportunities for sexual satisfaction; being able to move about from place to place.

3. Being able to avoid unnecessary and non-useful pain, and to have pleasurable experiences.

4. Being able to use the five senses; being able to imagine, to think and reason.

5. Being able to have attachments to things and persons outside ourselves; to love those who love and care for us, to grieve at their absence; in general, to love, grieve, to feel longing and gratitude.

6. Being able to form a conception of the good and to engage in critical reflection about the planning of one's own life.

7. Being able to live for and to others, to recognize and show concern for other human beings, to engage in various forms of familial and social interaction.

8. Being able to live with concern for and in relation to animals, plants, the world of nature.

9. Being able to laugh, to play, to enjoy recreational activities.

10. Being able to live one's own life and nobody else's.

10a. Being able to live one's own life in one's very own surroundings and context.[96]

These capabilities enable Nussbaum to spell out what Aristotelian sustenance means for politics today: "With respect to each of the functionings mentioned in the thick vague conception, citizens are to receive the institutional, material, and educational support that is required if they are to become capable of functioning in that sphere according to their own practical reason—and functioning not just minimally, but well, insofar as natural circumstances permit."[97]

Nussbaum uses the term "threshold" to indicate the condition in which people have a real choice about whether and how to exercise their capabilities: "The Aristotelian uses the available resources to bring all citizens across a threshold into a condition in which good human functioning, at least a minimal level, can be chosen."[98]

Liberals are likely to have reservations about such an Aristotelian politics:

The liberal's central motivation for operating without a "thick" conception of the good is to leave room for a pluralistic society, and to respect the equality of citizens as choosers of their own conception of the good, favoring no conception over any other. . . . The liberal view about Aristotelianism is that it always involves opting for a single conception of good rather than a plurality; and that in the process it tells people what they should be, asking them . . . to live the life that a supremely wise man thinks would be best for them. This is actually to remove their moral autonomy, and thus, from the liberal's point of view, to treat them *unequally*.[99]

Nussbaum takes these reservations seriously. The first part of her reply is a reminder that the thick vague conception of the good is vague. It has room for a great deal of plurality in the forms of plural specification and local specification: "Plural specification means just what its name implies: that the political plan, while operating with a definite conception of the good at a vague level, operates with a sufficiently vague conception that, while much is ruled out as inappropriate to full humanity, there is a great deal of latitude left for citizens to specify each of the components more concretely, and with much variety, in their lives as they plan them. Some conceptions of the good are indeed ruled out by the insistence on our list of functions. But many alternatives are left in."[100] As for local specification, "Aristotelian practical reasoning is always done, when well done, with a rich sensitivity to the concrete context, to the characters of the agents and their historical and social circumstances."[101]

Still, the thick vague conception of the good does rule out certain conceptions of the good. Plural and local specifications have some limits. People with certain conceptions of the good will recognize that Nussbaum's Aristotelian politics is incompatible with those conceptions: "A society whose entire way of life rests upon adherence to policies that deprive members of a certain race, or class, or gender of the good human life will not be eager to endorse either the contents or the procedures of the Aristotelian list as essential for all human beings."[102] Thus, although Nussbaum has formulated an Aristotelian politics in such a way as to allay liberal suspicions, she has reserved the possibility of criticizing cultures or societies that do not accept the equal dignity of all human beings. She will explore this point further in her defense of Aristotelian essentialism.

The second part of Nussbaum's reply to the liberal is to argue that the thick vague conception "provides a richer and more promising starting point for further work on divisive social issues than do the thinner conceptions used by many liberalisms—and also than the fully determinate conceptions used by many forms of conservatism and communitarianism."[103] She then confronts an objection: "It is frequently charged that there is, in the kind of social democracy imagined in the Aristotelian conception, a deep tension between the value of well-being (and of public care for well-being) and the value of choice. As government more and more supports well-being, with a more and more comprehensive (if vague) conception of the good, it more and more removes from citizens the choice to live by their own lights."[104]

Nussbaum finds the objection to be misconceived:

> The Aristotelian conception insists that this tension is, to a great extent, illusory. Human choice is not pure spontaneity, flourishing in spite of the accidents of nature. The Aristotelian uses (and defends with argument) a more naturalistic and worldly conception of choice, according to which, as we have said, both the capability to choose good functioning within each sphere and the capability of choosing at all, quite generally, have complex social and material necessary conditions, conditions that are not likely to exist without strong government intervention. . . . Choice is not only not incompatible with, but actually requires, the kind of governmental reflection about the good, and the kind of intervention with laissez-faire, that we find in Aristotelian social democracy.[105]

In her 2001 postscript, Nussbaum notes four developments in her thought since the publication of "Aristotelian Social Democracy" in 1990. She endorses a form of Rawlsian political liberalism, that is, she sees the list of central human capabilities as a list that people who otherwise differ about comprehensive conceptions of the good can endorse for political purposes. She would combine the Aristotelian conception of the human good with the Kantian conceptions of human dignity and respect for persons. She would argue, however, against certain Kantian-inspired theories that take citizens as roughly equal in need and capacity and relatively independent; these theories fail to do justice to such realities as infancy, old age, and disabilities. Finally, she believes that the capabilities approach can be extended from the human case to the ethical claims of nonhuman animals.[106]

Essentialism versus Relativism

"Human Functioning and Social Justice: In Defense of Aristotelian Essentialism" offers another statement of Nussbaum's capabilities approach.[107] For present purposes, however, the central point of the essay is her defense of Aristotelian essentialism in opposition to a kind of local tradition relativism that exempts particular cultures and traditions from critical questioning.

Nussbaum begins by recounting three "anti-essentialist conversations" that she witnessed at two international conferences held in Helsinki. Certain speakers defended the preservation of certain traditional ways of life, such as barring menstruating women from kitchens and workplaces; or they regretted that the practice of smallpox inoculation had eradicated the cult of the goddess Sittala Devi; or they claimed that "contemporary anthropology has shown that non-Western people are not especially attached to freedom of choice."[108] When other participants criticized these views, the speakers responded by charging the critics with Western essentialism. Nussbaum sees a common pattern in the three conversations: an attempt to defend local traditions, even traditions that are abusive, by appealing to relativism: "Highly intelligent people, people deeply committed to the good of women and men in developing countries, people who think of themselves as progressive and feminist and antiracist, are taking up positions that converge . . . with the positions of reaction, oppression, and sexism. Under the banner of their radical and politically correct 'antiessentialism' march ancient religious taboos, the luxury of the pampered husband, ill health, ignorance, and death."[109]

Nussbaum recognizes that "essentialism—which . . . I shall understand as the view that human life has certain central defining features—is linked by its opponents with an ignorance of history, with lack of sensitivity to the voices of women and minorities. It is taken, usually without extended argument, to be in league with racism and sexism, with 'patriarchal' thinking generally, whereas extreme relativism is taken to be a recipe for social progress."[110]

Nussbaum responds by distinguishing two kinds of essentialism: metaphysical-realist essentialism and internalist essentialism: *"Metaphysical realism* claims that there is some determinate way that the world is apart from the interpretive workings of the cognitive faculties of living beings."[111] She rejects this metaphysical realism. "To cling to it as a goal is to pretend that it is possible for us to be told from outside what to be and what to do, when in reality the only answers we can ever hope to have must come, in some manner, from ourselves."[112]

Rejection of metaphysical realism requires the rejection of metaphysical essentialism. It leaves the door open, however, for what Nussbaum calls internalist essentialism: "One might . . . believe that the deepest examination of human history and human cognition *from within* still reveals a more or less determinate account of the human being, one that divides its essential from its accidental properties."[113] And rejection of metaphysical realism and metaphysical essentialism by no means entails that relativism is true: "When we get rid of the hope of a transcendent metaphysical grounding for our evaluative judgments—about the human being as about anything else—we are not left with the abyss. We have everything that we always had all along: the exchange of reasons and arguments by human beings within history, in which, for reasons that are historical and human but not the worse for that, we hold some things to be good and others bad, some arguments to be sound and others not sound."[114] "In fact, the collapse into extreme relativism or subjectivism seems to me to betray a deep attachment to metaphysical realism itself. For it is only to one who has pinned everything to that hope that its collapse will seem to entail the collapse of all evaluation—just as it is only to a deeply believing religious person, as Nietzsche saw, that the news of the death of God brings the threat of nihilism."[115]

Nussbaum addresses three objections to internalist essentialism. The first is that it neglects historical and cultural differences. Her answer is that the Aristotelian essentialist conception of human functioning, though thick, is still a vague conception, precisely in order to accommodate a wide range of historical and cultural differences.[116] This is the point about plural and local specification that she made in "Aristotelian Social Democracy."

The second objection is that Aristotelian essentialism gives insufficient weight to personal autonomy: "The liberal charges the Aristotelian with *neglect of autonomy*, arguing that any such determinate conception removes from the citizens the chance to make their own choices about the good life." Nussbaum admits that this is a complicated issue and offers four points in response: "First, the list is a list of capabilities, and not actual functions, precisely because the conception is designed to leave room for choice. . . . Second, this respect for choice is built deeply into the list itself in the architectonic role it gives to practical reasoning. . . . Third, we should note that the major liberal view in this area, the view of John Rawls, does not shrink from essentialism of our internal sort in just this area. . . . Finally, the Aristotelian insists that choice is not pure spontaneity, flourishing independently of material and social conditions."[117]

The third objection is that the essentialist conception of human functioning can be prejudicially applied, that is, someone can have a conception of what it means to be human, but then for whatever reason deny that one or other group is truly human. Nussbaum responds that someone's refusal to recognize someone else as human counts not against the conception of a human being but against the person refusing recognition. Further, the practice of refusing recognition as human witnesses to the power of the conception of humanity itself: "Acknowledging this other person as a member of the very same kind would have generated a sense of affiliation and responsibility; this was why the self-deceptive stratagem of splitting the other off from one's species seemed so urgent and so seductive." If the person refusing recognition were to recognize the other as human, he or she would have to treat them in a very different way.[118]

Nussbaum then considers the proposal that ethics should begin not with the concept of human being but with the concept of person. She argues that the concept of human being is a better starting point than the concept of person because recognition of someone as a human being is more difficult to withhold. I will quote her at length, to bring out her view that human needs, especially in the form of unrealized capabilities, exert moral claims on human beings.

"The notion of the 'person,' for example, has sometimes been pre-
ferred to the notion of the human being as a basis for ethics, on the
grounds that it is clearly a normative conception, whose connection with
certain sorts of ethical obligations is especially evident. I have argued that
the conception of the human being is itself, in a certain way, a normative
conception, in that it involves singling out certain functions as more basic
than others."[119]

"With 'person,' the defender of equality is on uncertain ground,
ground that the opponent can at any moment shift under her feet. With
'human being,' on the other hand, it is always open to her to say to the
opponent, 'Look at these beings: you cannot fail to grant that they use
their senses, that they think about the future, that they engage in ethical
conversation, that they have needs and vulnerabilities similar to your own.
Grant this, and you grant that they are human. Grant that they are human,
and you grant that they have *needs for flourishing that exert a moral pull on
anyone who would deny them.*'"[120]

"The basis [for counting someone as a human being] cannot . . . be
the presence of the higher-level capabilities on my list, for one of the main
points of the list is to enable us to say, of some being before us, that this
being might possibly come to have these higher-level capabilities but does
not now have them. *It is that gap between basic (potential) humanness and
its full realization that exerts a claim on society and government.*"[121]

"Concerning individuals who can profit from education, care, and resources . . . the Aristotelian view observes that *these basic capabilities exert
a claim on society that they should be developed.*"[122]

"This basic intuition underlies the recommendations that the Aristotelian view will make for public action: *certain basic and central human
powers have a claim to be developed and will exert that claim on others*—and
especially, as Aristotle claimed, on government."[123]

In the remainder of "Human Functioning," Nussbaum argues that
we need some version of essentialism to guide our decisions on public
policy and especially on development. In this context she criticizes the
crude measures that guide many analyses of the quality of life: gross national product and utility understood in terms of satisfaction. At this
point she criticizes utilitarianism on three grounds.

First, "desires and subjective preference are not always reliable indices of what a person really needs, of what would really be required to make that life a flourishing one."[124] Depending on their circumstances, people may not recognize what they really need: "Thus, if we rely on utility as our measure of life quality, we most often will get results that support the status quo and oppose radical change."[125]

Second, the concept of utility as a single thing to be measured is problematic: "If utility is understood as a single thing, as in some vague sense it usually is, then the theory is implicitly committed to the commensurability of values and to the idea that for any two distinct ends, we can always imagine trade-offs in purely quantitative terms. The Aristotelian is profoundly opposed to this idea. . . . Furthermore, the usual pretense of economic utilitarianism—that all this can be modeled by attaching a monetary value to the relevant human functionings—is, to the Aristotelian, especially repellant."[126]

Third, utilitarianism lumps people together, disregarding what Nussbaum has called separateness: "Finally, utilitarianism, neglecting as it does the inalienability of certain elements of the self, neglects also the ethical salience of the boundaries between persons. As a theory of public measurement, utilitarianism is committed to the aggregation of satisfactions. Individuals are treated as centers of pleasure or pain, satisfaction or dissatisfaction, and the fact of their separateness one from another is not given special weight in the theory, which proceeds by summing. But in the world we actually inhabit, it is a highly relevant fact that my pain is not yours, nor yours mine."[127]

Then, returning to the antiessentialist conversations with which she began, Nussbaum charges that "local tradition relativism" is closer to utilitarianism than its proponents realize: "The local tradition relativism endorsed in my Helsinki examples claims to be different from prevailing economic-utilitarian views, on account of its close attention to the fabric of daily life in traditional societies. But it actually shares many of the defects of the utilitarian view, for it refuses to subject preferences, as formed in traditional societies, to any sort of critical scrutiny."[128]

Having criticized utilitarianism, Nussbaum takes on a worthier foe: liberalism.

One more anti-essentialist approach to questions of distributive justice must now be considered. It is by far the most powerful alternative to the Aristotelian approach, and its differences from it are subtle and complex. This is the liberal idea, defended in different forms by John Rawls and Ronald Dworkin, that distribution should aim at an equal allotment of certain basic resources (or, in the case of Rawls, should tolerate inequalities only where this would improve the situation of the worst off). The Rawlsian liberal insists on distributing basic resources without taking a stand on the human good, even in the vague way in which the "thick vague theory" has done so. The aim is to leave each citizen a choice of the conception of the good by which he or she will live.[129]

Nussbaum makes three replies to this egalitarian liberalism. "First . . . wealth and income are not good in their own right; they are good only insofar as they promote human functioning." Second, liberalism fails to deal with the fact that different people have different needs: "These [differing needs for resources] are not just rare exceptions; they are pervasive facts of life. Thus the failure of the liberal theory to deal with them is a serious defect. And yet, to deal with them, we need a general conception of what functions we are trying to support." "Third, the liberal, by defining being well-off in terms of possessions alone, fails to go deep enough in imagining the impediments to functioning that are actually present in many human lives." Here Nussbaum once again takes a leaf from Marx: "The structure of labor relations, of class relations, and of race and gender relations in a society can alienate its members from the fully human use of their faculties even when their material needs are met."[130] As she sees it, Rawls ought to have listed not just resources and commodities but also basic capabilities among the primary goods.

In the endnote to the final chapter, "Transcending Humanity," of *Love's Knowledge* (1990), Nussbaum looks back on four of the essays that I have tried to summarize above:

In a series of papers on Aristotelian political thought ["Nature, Function, and Capability," "Non-Relative Virtues," "Aristotle on Human Nature," and "Aristotelian Social Democracy"], I have stressed, with approval, Aristotle's use of the general notion of the human being and the human form of life to provide a direction for ethical and political thinking. I have defended this emphasis against various forms of subjectivism and cultural relativism, and also against liberalisms that attempt to choose principles of justice without relying on any theory of the good. And yet, at the same time I insist on the importance of particularity for good ethical judgment. "Non-Relative Virtues: An Aristotelian Approach" . . . said something about how these two ideas fit together. In asking how the good of a human being is to be promoted in a certain context, one must always be very sensitive to the historically concrete circumstances of that context. Yet, since it was always for the person *as a human being* that the good was sought, one must not lose hold of general notions of human functioning and human capability, which can frequently be used to criticize local traditions as inimical to human flourishing.[131]

A Feminist Liberalism

Despite her criticisms of Rawlsian liberalism, it would be a serious mistake to think that Nussbaum rejects liberalism across the board. "The Future of Feminist Liberalism," her 2000 presidential address to the Central Division of the American Philosophical Association, begins by posing a problem.[132] Political liberalism is very much alive in the work of such thinkers as Rawls and Jürgen Habermas. But many serious feminists doubt that liberalism can do the work that needs to be done to address feminist concerns. They think that liberalism has "insufficient radical potential to expose the roots of women's subordination or to articulate principles for a society of gender justice."[133] Nussbaum examines two areas of special concern to feminists, two areas where contemporary liberalism is weak and needs to be strengthened: the need that people have for care in times of extreme dependency and the political role of the family.

Nussbaum remarks that one weakness of contract theories of justice and morality is their reliance on what she calls "the fiction of competent adulthood," that is, the assumption they make that everyone in the state of nature is free, equal, and independent.[134] This is not at all true of the humanity that we know from experience. People are heavily dependent on others for perhaps the first twenty years of life. Many are heavily dependent on others during their final years. And even in the middle years, significant numbers of human beings are dependent on others to meet their physical needs, mental needs, or both. Thus, instead of being made up of free and equal members, every society is really a caregiving society, which raises questions both about the status of those needy and dependent individuals receiving care and about the status of the members of society who are giving the care.[135]

What would an Aristotelian liberal approach to care and dependency involve? One step, in line with the capabilities approach, would be to recognize that the labor involved in caregiving can limit one's capabilities. Recognizing this would provide a justification for government intervention in favor of caregivers to restore or protect their capabilities. Another step would be to add the capabilities to the list of primary goods already recognized by liberals such as Rawls. The most important Aristotelian step, however, would be to modify the liberal conception of the person by bringing the animal dimension and the rational dimension of humanity closer together: "So I believe that we need to delve deeper, redesigning the political conception of the person, bringing the rational and the animal into a more intimate relation with one another, and acknowledging that there are many types of dignity in the world, including the dignity of mentally disabled children and adults, the dignity of the senile demented elderly, and the dignity of babies at the breast. We want the picture of the parties who design political institutions to build these facts in from the start."[136]

Nussbaum criticizes the liberal tradition found in Kant and Rawls for splitting the human being into two parts, one natural and the other rational, with the claim to respect resting entirely on the rational side. Aristotle makes no such split. For him it is the whole human being, in its rationality and its needy animality, that is the object of respect. An Aristotelian account of the person will enable liberalism to address feminist concerns about caregiving better than a Kantian account: "So I believe we need to adopt a political conception of the person that is more Aristotelian than Kantian, one that sees the person from the start as both capable and needy—'in need of a rich plurality of life-activities,' to use Marx's phrase, whose availability will be the measure of well-being."[137] "So I believe that the problem we have investigated shows us that liberal theory needs to question some of its most traditional starting points—questioning, in the process, the Kantian notion of the person. But that does not disable liberalism; it just challenges us all to produce a new form of liberalism, more attentive to need and its material and institutional conditions."[138]

"The Future of Feminist Liberalism" has much to say about justice in the family. The family is the locus and condition for many good things, but it is also, as many feminists have asserted, and as Nussbaum agrees, "one of the most notorious homes of sex hierarchy, denial of equal opportunity, and sex-based violence and humiliation."[139] Liberal theories of justice have a hard time addressing the negative aspects of the family, because they tend to treat the family as a private sphere into which the state should not intrude. Even Rawls, who recognizes that the claims of justice do apply to the family, thinks that they apply to the family in something like the way that they apply to voluntary associations, such as churches and universities. But this will not do, because families are not voluntary associations. Membership in a given family is not something that one chooses. And the family, Nussbaum continues, is not some sort of natural entity, but rather a political and legal construct. It is the state that determines the conditions under which people are married and recognized as members of families. There is no reason why the family should be considered as a sphere independent of justice and of state regulation in the name of justice:[140] "The only thing that stops state intervention is the person and the various liberties and rights of the person."[141]

Nussbaum's capabilities approach and Rawls's contractarian approach will agree on many of the practical measures to be taken with regard to the family, but for different reasons. Rawls sees laws as external to the family. Nussbaum sees laws as entering into the very constitution of the family. Her approach can accept laws in favor of the family, not because the family as such has any claim to favor, but because the central capabilities of individuals deserve to be protected. Her approach would also and for the same reasons justify protecting nontraditional affective groupings, such as women's collectives in India, to the extent and only to the extent that these groupings promote the central capabilities. And on the same ground her approach can justify significant modifications in the legal arrangements for marriage, such as the abolition of the dowry system in India, the making of special provisions to give women access to credit, and the like. As Nussbaum sees it, Rawls rejects the older liberal distinction of public and private, but not in a sufficiently thoroughgoing way. Her approach, by contrast, sets the distinction aside and concentrates exclusively on the protection and development of human capabilities.[142]

Nussbaum acknowledges that her proposal will run into opposition: "There is no doubt that some of the major comprehensive views of what gives life meaning are dead set against the kind of revisionary treatment of family structure that my approach sees as required by political justice. . . . It is no accident that in a sphere that is the home both of intimate self-definition and also of egregious wrongdoing the search for liberal justice should encounter difficulties: for liberal justice is committed both to protecting spheres of self-definition and to ending the wrongful tyranny of some people over others."[143]

I would not wish to leave the impression that the above reflections on feminist liberalism represent the sum total of Nussbaum's feminism. Her *Women and Human Development* gives an extremely detailed analysis of the situation of poor women in India, an analysis that played an important role in the development of Nussbaum's capabilities approach to human development.[144] More about this approach below. The situation of women is also central to her *Sex and Social Justice*, along with the situations of lesbians and gay men.[145]

Educational Agenda

Deep concern for liberal education has been an abiding theme in Nussbaum's work. In the concluding section of "The Discernment of Perception," she outlines the educational implications of her Aristotelian concept of rationality.[146] As she sees it, education, even to the college or university level, is fundamental for citizenship. Providing an education that enables people to function well is a major task, even the primary task, of politics. The education to be provided needs to be centered on the humanities, which are not to be replaced by "technical and quantitative analyses of social reality."[147] It should include the study of moral reasoning, which is not to be identified with formal decision theory or with the principles of economic rationality: "In short: the acceptance of an Aristotelian conception should lead to the recognition that the humanities are the core of our public culture, and that other techniques of reasoning are tools whose place is to assist them in their task of revealing and enacting a full and rich sense of human life and its public requirements."[148]

This concern for the ethical and political dimensions of education pervades *Cultivating Humanity*.[149] The book considers the meaning of a liberal education under such headings as Socratic self-examination, narrative imagination, non-Western, African American, and women's studies, and the study of human sexuality. A passage from chapter 2, "Citizens of the World," captures the general direction of Nussbaum's approach: "It is up to us, as educators, to show our students the beauty and interest of a life that is open to the whole world, to show them that there is after all more joy in the kind of citizenship that questions than in the kind that simply applauds, more fascination in the study of human beings in all their variety and complexity than in the zealous pursuit of superficial stereotypes, more genuine love and friendship in the life of questioning and self-government than in submission to authority. We had better show them this, or the future of democracy in this nation and in the world is bleak."[150] The same concern also pervades *Not for Profit*,[151] which covers much of the same ground as *Cultivating Humanity*, but with more attention to the state of liberal education around the world and to various threats besetting it, especially in chapter 1, "The Silent Crisis," and chapter 7, "Democratic Education on the Ropes."

Passions and Politics

In 1986, the year that she published *Fragility of Goodness*, Nussbaum delivered the Martin Classical Lectures at Oberlin College. In time, these lectures gave rise to *The Therapy of Desire*.[152] The book signaled a major shift in the focus of her research, from Aristotle to the Hellenistic and Roman Epicureans, Stoics, and Skeptics, and a major shift in her philosophical interests, to the passions or emotions, with which the Hellenistic philosophers were so largely concerned:

> One thing, I think, is indisputable: that the analyses of emotions offered by Stoic and Epicurean texts have a subtlety and cogency

unsurpassed by anything on the topic in the history of Western philosophy. Aristotle's accounts were valuable predecessors, clearly. But the Hellenistic thinkers go beyond Aristotle, I believe, in the detail and power of their analyses of the relation between emotion and belief, in their accounts of the evaluative element in emotion, in their suggestions concerning the interrelationships among the emotions, and, finally, in their connection of the emotional life with a very general view of the world, one in which we have hostages to fortune. Whatever one thinks of their arguments against the passions, and whatever one finally decides about the Stoic identification of passion with belief or judgment, these accounts are indispensable starting points for any future work.[153]

Therapy of Desire was by no means a complete rejection of Nussbaum's earlier Aristotelianism, but it did criticize Aristotle in two important respects. The Hellenistic philosophers were concerned with therapy, with helping people deal with their passions. Aristotle's contributions in this area—a dialectical approach to education and a reflection on the best form of political society—were real but also limited:

> In short: if one agrees with Aristotle, then philosophy can do little for the real misery of the world. It can refine already refined and lucky young gentlemen. It can point the way toward an ideal that may or may not have any chance of being realized in any place at any time. These are the limits of its practical efficacy. If, however one conceives of philosophy [as the Hellenistic philosophers did] as a medical art for the human soul, one is unlikely to accept this as the last word. For medicine would be no good as medicine if it simply gave vitamins to the healthy and designed impracticable schemes for ideal health insurance. Its job is here and now, with this patient's actual sufferings. If it does nothing for these sufferings, it does nothing at all. The Hellenistic philosophers think this way about philosophy. That is why they feel they must leave Aristotle behind.[154]

Study of the Hellenistic philosophers also led Nussbaum to articulate and criticize the presuppositions of Aristotle's method of appearances:

Aristotelian dialectic . . . makes several controversial assumptions about the nature of the ordinary person's ethical beliefs. It assumes that these beliefs are essentially healthy: truth is in there, along with whatever is false, and in such a way that, in the process of scrutiny, the true beliefs will turn out to be the "greatest number and the most basic." Since the beliefs in question are for the most part socially taught, the procedure also assumes the relative health of the surrounding society. Moreover, the method assumes that the most important beliefs lie close to the surface of the interlocutor's reason in such a way that they can be elicited by calm dialectical questioning. And finally, the method appears to assume that everyone who *ought* to be helped by the dialectical process *can* be so helped: it points to no troublesome gap between the availability of rational "therapy" and the needs of its intended recipients.[155]

Therapy of Desire set the agenda for a series of major books that explore the emotions and their relevance for social and political life.[156] In these books, Nussbaum has moved on from the Aristotelian position that I find in her earlier work and that is the focus of this chapter. I mention them here simply to give some idea of her concerns in this latter period: *Upheavals of Thought: The Intelligence of Emotions* (2001), *Hiding from Humanity: Disgust, Shame, and the Law* (2004), *Liberty of Conscience: In Defense of America's Tradition of Religious Equality* (2008), *From Disgust to Humanity: Sexual Orientation and Constitutional Law* (2010), *The New Religious Intolerance: Overcoming the Politics of Fear in an Anxious Age* (2012), *Political Emotions: Why Love Matters for Justice* (2013), *Anger and Forgiveness: Resentment, Generosity, Justice* (2016), and *The Monarchy of Fear: A Philosopher Looks at Our Political Crisis* (2018).

CREATING CAPABILITIES

Creating Capabilities is a book-length introduction to Nussbaum's version of the capabilities approach. This is first of all an approach to issues of development. In opposition to a hitherto dominant approach that takes gross domestic product to be the measure of progress in development, it asks, "What are people actually able to do and to be? What real opportunities for activity and choice has society given them?"[157] My treatment of the book will be selective, focusing on the philosophical roots of Nussbaum's approach, her view of the minimum requirements of justice, her commitment to political liberalism, and her position on justice in the family. I do not suggest that *Creating Capabilities* is on the whole an Aristotelian book, only that the capabilities approach has important Aristotelian roots and embodies Aristotelian insights. Much of the interest of the book lies in the way it combines these insights with other elements, especially with political liberalism.

Philosophical Roots

Chapter 7 of *Creating Capabilities* is Nussbaum's account of the philosophical roots of her approach. First and foremost is Aristotle. Aristotle anticipates the approach in many ways: by his emphasis on people making choices for themselves, as distinct from society or the state making people perform desirable activities; by his insistence that "the pursuit of wealth is not an appropriate overall goal for a decent society"; by his arguments against hedonism, which, Nussbaum says, "are good arguments today against Benthamite forms of utilitarianism"; by his recognition that "pleasure and the satisfaction of desire are utterly unreliable as guides to what is to be promoted in society"; and by his recognition of diverse and incommensurable goods.[158] "What makes Aristotle of continuing centrality for political thought is the way in which he coupled an understanding of choice and its importance with an understanding of human vulnerability," states Nussbaum.[159] Where Aristotle's position suffers from deficiencies, such as an overly restrictive view of who count as citizens and an apparent lack of "the basic idea of human equality, of a worth all humans share across differences of gender, class, and ethnicity," the Stoics remedied these deficiencies.[160]

The insights of Aristotle and the Stoics are basic to Nussbaum's approach, but they are by no means her only sources: "Among Euro-American antecedents, the most important sources of my version of the Capabilities Approach are works from ancient Greece and Rome, although Adam Smith, Kant, Mill, and Marx have also greatly influenced my formulations. John Rawls's work has been of the utmost importance, particularly in convincing me that the view ought to be expressed as a type of political liberalism."[161]

Nussbaum also acknowledges a debt to classical modern natural law theory: "Typically, thought about 'natural law' in the seventeenth and eighteenth centuries—and thus the core of the classical education given to people bound for politics and government—melded Aristotelian with Stoic elements. Although different combinations of ideas could be made, one attractive and enduring marriage, compatible with mainstream Christian beliefs, was that between Stoic ideas of the equal worth of all human beings and Aristotelian ideas about human vulnerability."[162]

Nussbaum is particularly concerned to rebut the idea that the capabilities approach is foreign to European and Anglo-American traditions: "Studying this history [Adam Smith's and Thomas Paine's support for government intervention to provide education and other benefits] we learn that the basic ideas of the Capabilities Approach, including the importance of government support for basic human welfare, are no recent invention; nor are they associated only with European-style social democracy. They are a deep part of mainstream liberal Enlightenment thought, in both Europe and North America."[163]

The capabilities approach witnesses to a number of Nussbaum's philosophical commitments, but it is by no means an adequate statement of her own comprehensive ethical doctrine. More about this point below.

The Minimum Requirements of Justice

Chapter 2 of *Creating Capabilities* lists and explains the ten basic capabilities. The list differs in some respects from the list in "Aristotelian Social Democracy," and so I give it here:

> 1. *Life.* Being able to live to the end of a human life of normal length; not dying prematurely, or before one's life is so reduced as to be not worth living.
> 2. *Bodily health.* Being able to have good health, including reproductive health; to be adequately nourished; to have adequate shelter.

3. *Bodily integrity*. Being able to move freely from place to place; to be secure against violent assault, including sexual assault and domestic violence; having opportunities for sexual satisfaction and for choice in matters of reproduction.

4. *Senses, imagination, and thought*. Being able to use the senses, to imagine, think, and reason—and to do these things in a "truly human" way.

5. *Emotions*. Being able to have attachments to things and people outside ourselves, to love those who love and care for us, to grieve at their absence; in general, to love, to grieve, to experience longing, gratitude, and justified anger.

6. *Practical reason*. Being able to form a conception of the good and to engage in critical reflection about the planning of one's life.

7. *Affiliation*. (A) Being able to live with and toward others, to recognize and show concern for other human beings, to engage in various forms of social interaction; to be able to imagine the situation of another. . . . (B) Having the social bases of self-respect and non-humiliation; being able to be treated as a dignified being whose worth is equal to that of others.

8. *Other species*. Being able to live with concern for and in relation to animals, plants, and the world of nature.

9. *Play*. Being able to laugh, to play, to enjoy recreational activities.

10. *Control over one's environment. (A) Political*. Being able to participate effectively in political choices that govern one's life; having the right of political participation, protections of free speech and association. *(B) Material*. Being able to hold property (both land and movable goods) and having property rights on an equal basis with others; having the right to seek employment on an equal basis with others; having the freedom from unwarranted search and seizure. In work, being able to work as a human being, exercising practical reason and entering into meaningful relationship of mutual recognition with other workers.[164]

The list is a statement of the minimum that any society must do in order to be just: bring each and every individual to the threshold where he or she has a real choice about whether and how to actualize the ten basic capabilities. This is partly a matter of education, in a broad sense of that term, and partly a matter of ensuring that economic and social conditions are such that individuals can actually implement their choices. This is what a society must do if it is to respect human dignity: "Part of the conception of the capabilities list, as we have already seen, is the idea of a *threshold*. The approach, in my version, is a partial theory of social justice: it does not purport to solve all distributional problems; it just specifies a rather ample social minimum. Delivering these ten capabilities to all citizens is a necessary condition of social justice. Justice may well require more."[165]

Nussbaum clarifies the minimum requirements of justice in a number of different ways. Here are two of the more important. First, Nussbaum proposes these requirements not just as desirable goals to be achieved through the normal political process, but as fundamental entitlements that should be entrenched in the constitution so as to structure and condition the political process.[166] Second, her focus on people's capabilities and choices is designedly liberal. It should be up to individuals themselves to choose whether and how to actualize their capabilities.[167] This brings us to Nussbaum's political conception of justice.

A Political Conception of Justice

The starting point of Rawls's *Political Liberalism* is, "How is it possible for there to exist over time a just and stable society of free and equal citizens, who remain profoundly divided by reasonable religious, philosophical, and moral doctrines?"[168] The core of his answer is that they should accept the principles of justice as a specifically political conception that people holding different comprehensive doctrines can share.

Here Nussbaum follows Rawls. She proposes the understanding of justice embodied in the capabilities approach not as a comprehensive ethical doctrine, but as a political conception that is compatible with a wide range of comprehensive ethical doctrines. The minimum requirements of justice should become the object of an overlapping consensus, a module on which individuals who hold different and incompatible comprehensive ethical, religious, and metaphysical doctrines can agree:

If we are convinced that the political principles of a decent society ought to be respectful of a wide range of different comprehensive doctrines and should seek to become the object of an overlapping consensus among them, then we will not want to propose principles that use the idea of capability as a comprehensive theory of the value or quality of life. Theorizing about the overall quality of life should be left to each comprehensive doctrine, using whatever terms and concepts it uses. What it is reasonable to ask citizens to affirm is the political importance of a relatively short and circumscribed list of fundamental entitlements—in the form of the capabilities list—that could be attached to the rest of their comprehensive doctrine in each case.[169]

The capabilities approach differs from Rawls's approach in significant respects, but agrees with his political liberalism:

If the Capabilities Approach takes issue with Rawls in some areas, it also endorses and develops another prominent aspect of his approach to political justice: the idea of *political liberalism*. Given that all societies contain a plurality of religious and secular views of the meaning and purpose of human life, it seems strategically unwise to adopt a political view that opts for one of these against the others: such a political regime is likely to prove unstable, at least under conditions of freedom. But that is not the only or even the primary objection to that sort of political doctrine. The deeper moral problem is that any such doctrine is insufficiently respectful of citizens who hold a different view.[170]

As an account of the minimum requirements of justice, the capabilities approach is deliberately "thin," that is, it does not presuppose or depend on any particular comprehensive ethical view, or on metaphysical or religious views. As a political conception, it is not, and does not pretend to be, an adequate account of the human good or of what makes a human life worthwhile:

Of course a political view must take a moral stand, basing political principles on some definite values, such as impartiality and equal respect for human dignity. Such values, however, either are or can become a part of the many comprehensive doctrines that citizens reasonably hold. If they are articulated in a calculatedly "thin" way, without grounding in controversial metaphysical notions (such as the idea of the immortal soul), epistemological notions (such as the idea of self-evident truth), or thicker ethical doctrines (such as Kantianism or Aristotelianism), they can potentially command the approval of a wide range of citizens subscribing to different religious and secular positions. What is asked of them is that they endorse the basic ideas of the Capabilities Approach *for political purposes only*, not as a comprehensive guide to life, and that they view them as operative within a distinctive domain, namely, that of the political.[171]

The capabilities approach witnesses to a number of Nussbaum's philosophical commitments, but it is not a statement of her own comprehensive ethical doctrine, or, for that matter, of any comprehensive doctrine. In particular, the approach is not committed to the comprehensive doctrine called cosmopolitanism, "which is usually defined as the view that one's first loyalty should be to humanity as a whole rather than to one's nation, region, religion, or family."[172]

Justice and the Family

Creating Capabilities forcefully restates the view of the family that we met in "The Future of Feminist Liberalism": "Capabilities belong first and foremost to individual persons, and only derivatively to groups. The approach espouses a principle of *each person as an end*. It stipulates that the goal is to produce capabilities for each and every person, and not to use some people as a means to the capabilities of others or of the whole. This focus on the person makes a huge difference for policy, since many nations have thought of the family, for example, as a homogeneous unit to be supported by policy, rather than examining and promoting the separate capabilities of each of its members."[173]

As in "The Future of Feminist Liberalism," Nussbaum argues that classical liberalism has not faced up to the problems of the family:

> One place where ideas of state inaction and "negative liberty" have been especially pernicious is in the state's relationship to the household or family. The classic liberal distinction between the public and the private spheres aids the natural standoffishness that many liberal thinkers have had about state action: even if it's fine in some areas for the state to act to secure people's rights, there is one privileged sphere that it should not touch, that of the home. Women have rightly complained that some traditional human rights models have wrongly neglected abuses that women suffer in the home. The Capabilities Approach corrects this error, insisting that intervention in the home is justified whenever the rights of its members are violated.[174]

This concludes our survey of Nussbaum's Aristotelian ethics and politics. Now it is time to consider how she addresses the problems that we have identified in Anglo-American moral philosophy and how she appropriates Aristotle.

REVISITING ANGLO-AMERICAN MORAL PHILOSOPHY

Anglo-American moral philosophy in the period 1950 to 1990 found itself grappling with five sets of problems: (1) the competing claims of deontological and teleological ethics, especially Kantian and utilitarian ethics; (2) the claims of egoism and altruism; (3) the claims of naturalism, intuitionism, and noncognitivism in metaethics; (4) the relations between fact and value, is and ought; and (5) the challenges of relativism and skepticism. Without suggesting that Nussbaum made it her project to solve these problems precisely as posed, I find that her Aristotelian work addresses them in a number of different ways.

Nussbaum's position combines teleological and deontological elements, but her versions of teleology and deontology are significantly different from those we met in Anglo-American moral philosophy. She takes her teleology not from Bentham and Mill but from Aristotle. She rejects hedonism and utility, the satisfaction of people's de facto preferences, as accounts of the good, and insists on the existence of multiple incommensurable goods, thus ruling out anything like the utilitarian calculus of outcomes. She also rejects the narrowly economic conceptions of human development that stem from utilitarian thinking. Her deontology draws on the Stoics and Kant, but her understanding of what respect for human beings requires is informed by her Aristotelian understanding of human beings as needy and vulnerable animals, a point muted or neglected in the Stoics and Kant.

Nussbaum accepts that there is an antithesis between egoism and altruism. She criticizes the attempts of the social contract tradition to base the claims of justice on self-interest and freely admits that her approach to politics presupposes some degree of altruism.[175] At the same time, she holds out the hope that the right kind of education can instill in people an awareness of the human dignity of other people, an appreciation of the claims that other human beings make to be respected, for their needs to be met, and their potentialities to be realized. Such an education would seem to be a way of cultivating altruism.

Nussbaum does not hesitate to use the word "intuition," but her position is not "intuitionist" as that term is commonly understood. Instead of understanding goodness as a nonnatural property to be known by intuition, she talks of many and various goods, all of them natural. Her position is realist or cognitivist, but her realism is an internal or internalist realism, not a metaphysical realism, which she rejects. Yes, there are moral truths, but they are not Baconian hard facts, prior to and independent of human language and interpretation. Rather they are, like everything else, within the circle of appearances. Nussbaum rejects any attempt to reason from supposedly scientific or neutral facts about human nature to conclusions about value or obligation. On the contrary, she understands humanity to be an ethical and evaluative concept from the start. She reads Aristotle as rejecting any clear line between fact and value, and she concurs. And she regards unfulfilled human capabilities as exerting moral claims. Her metaethics is, then, a sophisticated form of naturalism, one situated within an internal realist theory of knowledge.

Nussbaum offers a vigorous critique of relativism and of the use of relativism to defend various local and traditional customs and practices that fail to respect the equal dignity of human beings. She is also critical of positions that she sees as diminishing the role of reason in ethics or undermining the importance of ethical theory. In *Fragility of Goodness*, Nussbaum discusses Aristotle's response in *Metaphysics* 4 to a skeptical denial of the principle of noncontradiction. That discussion suggests a possible response to generalized ethical skepticism: someone who doubts the force of any and every ethical claim is simply placing himself or herself outside the context of discussion.[176]

NUSSBAUM'S APPROPRIATION OF ARISTOTLE

Nussbaum is a recognized scholar of Aristotle. But even when she identified herself as an Aristotelian, she was careful to note where she disagreed with Aristotle, dismissing, for instance, his views about women and natural slavery. She treated *Nicomachean Ethics* 10.6–8, which asserts the primacy of contemplation, as stating a Platonic position that is incompatible with the rest of Aristotle's ethics.[177] She supplemented Aristotle's account of feeling with the Stoic view that feelings are states of mind. She supplemented his ethics with notions of dignity and respect that she finds in the Stoics and Kant. She saw important parallels between Aristotle and Marx. She rejected utilitarianism in its classical form and many of its contemporary forms, but she sympathized with Mill's liberalism and egalitarianism. She rejected the social contract tradition, but she took Rawls's theory seriously as the strongest form of that tradition. She criticized Rawls's thin theory of the good and moved to strengthen it with what she called a "thick but vague" account of the good. At the same time, she used Rawls's political conception of justice to develop an Aristotelian form of social democracy that she argued could be accepted within a liberal approach to politics. She used a form of Aristotelian essentialism to counter what she called "local tradition relativism." Altogether this was a remarkable fusion of Aristotelian insights with insights drawn from other sources.

At the same time, not everyone who studies Aristotle, or who draws on Aristotle for ethical and political insight, would go along with Nussbaum's readings of Aristotle. Some would question her interpretation of Aristotle's "method of appearances" and her reading of Aristotle as an internal realist along the lines developed by Hilary Putnam.[178] Some would question her attempt to synthesize Aristotle with the liberal tradition that comes from the Enlightenment. Some would question whether her liberal focus on individuals and their rights is compatible with Aristotle's emphasis on communities and their common goods. Some would question whether an Aristotelian eudaimonism can bear the weight of moral obligation that the capabilities approach would seem to require, even if that approach is proposed as part of a political conception of justice. But here questions about Nussbaum's reading of Aristotle shade into questions about her earlier philosophical position as such. My aim in the next section will be to pose a few such questions.

SOME QUESTIONS

Nussbaum's interests have shifted and her philosophical position has changed since *Fragility of Goodness*. The questions that I will raise here are questions about the views that she expressed in her Aristotelian period, not about her current position.

A first question concerns the philosophical method of appearances set forth in chapter 8 of *Fragility of Goodness*. Nussbaum herself, in *Therapy of Desire*, criticized some of the assumptions behind that method. It is no longer her own method, and criticism of it does not touch her current position. At the same time, I think, we should question another assumption behind the method. As presented in *Fragility of Goodness*, the method assumes that the appearances—the things that we, the many and the wise, think and say—are largely consistent with one another. This need not, of course, be clear at the outset. We may have to work through many puzzles and contradictions. But the method holds out the hope that if we do the hard work of going through the puzzles, eliminating inconsistencies, discarding appearances that clash with deeper or more important appearances, we may save the greatest number of the appearances and the most authoritative. We would then be entitled to use the first-person plural "we" ("we think," "we say") with confidence.

But is this really the case? If, as MacIntyre has argued, we are living in a situation of unsettleable moral disagreements, people on different sides of those disagreements would seem to have (in Nussbaum's Aristotelian terms) radically different sets of appearances, and it is difficult to see how her method of appearances could lead to consensus. Nussbaum might, of course, challenge the accuracy of MacIntyre's portrayal, as she has challenged his views on various other points.[179] Alternatively, she might grant that we are facing what currently look like unsettleable disagreements, but then argue that this is because people have not yet done the hard work of going through the puzzles, eliminating inconsistencies, and discarding appearances that clash with deeper or more important appearances.[180]

But is this hope realistic? Consider the range of opponents whom Nussbaum herself has, in her Aristotelian work, taken on: utilitarians, insofar as they focus on the satisfaction of people's de facto desires and aggregate satisfactions across individuals; economists who treat gross domestic product as the principal measure of development; benighted followers of local customs and traditions, and theorists who invoke relativism to defend those customs and traditions; those liberals who think that the nuclear family should be exempt from government intervention; proponents of negative liberty and small government; philosophers whom she takes to be hostile to reason and the enterprise of ethical theory; and there are others. This list of confrontations suggests that we are faced with many serious, if not unsettleable, disagreements.[181] How far can the method of appearances help us to resolve these disagreements?

This point about the range of disagreement prompts a second question, about the political conception of justice that is central to the capabilities approach. Nussbaum claims that minimal justice requires bringing each and every individual to the threshold where they have real choices about whether and how to exercise the ten basic capabilities. She proposes this as a political conception on which adherents of many different comprehensive doctrines should be able to agree, a module that they should be able to attach to their various comprehensive doctrines and to agree that it should be entrenched in the constitution.

Let us grant for the sake of discussion that in a pluralistic society, whose citizens hold many different comprehensive doctrines, the basic idea of a minimum conception of justice that can be the object of a political consensus is attractive. But is Nussbaum's conception any such thing? In philosophy, libertarians generally and Randians in particular would reject Nussbaum's conception of justice as incompatible with their understandings of human freedom and autonomy. If they chose to speak in Nussbaum's language, they might reject the capabilities approach as incompatible with their comprehensive doctrines. I would expect many members of (for instance) the Federalist Society to express comparable reservations about entrenching a wide range of entitlements in the U.S. Constitution. In practical politics—in, for instance, the recent debate in the United States over health care—there are plenty of voices speaking not for an expansion of entitlements but for a limitation or even a reduction of entitlements.[182] There is, then, a prima facie case that Nussbaum's view of the minimum requirements of justice is not, at least under present circumstances in the United States, a viable candidate to be the object of a political consensus. It is not hard to imagine opponents charging that her political conception of justice only pretends to be neutral with respect to different comprehensive doctrines—that under the guise of political neutrality it incorporates important and controversial elements of her own comprehensive doctrine.

The Aristotelian Nussbaum could, I think, admit that as things stand, considerable numbers of people are unwilling to endorse her claims about minimal justice, because they see them as conflicting with their own comprehensive doctrines. She might then suggest, in line with the method of appearances, that a searching examination of their own positions should eventually show them either that they are mistaken about the conflict or that the conflict, though real, arises from elements in their positions that they should, on reflection, abandon. A hypothetical example: libertarians might come to see that respect for human freedom and autonomy actually requires them to endorse Nussbaum's political conception of minimal justice. They might shift from thinking that her political conception was a threat to their freedom and autonomy. They might then join her overlapping consensus.

What if this approach did not succeed? It seems to me that the Nussbaum might then shift to a second line of reply. This would be to argue that the dissenting comprehensive doctrines are unreasonable, that disagreements with the minimum requirements of justice arising from those comprehensive doctrines are not reasonable disagreements, and that there is no need to take those unreasonable doctrines into account in formulating political arrangements.[183] That would, of course, open up the large question about the grounds for evaluating different comprehensive doctrines. Is there a neutral and impartial standpoint from which they can be evaluated? Or is all such evaluation necessarily carried on from a particular standpoint, as MacIntyre has argued, whether the adherents of that particular standpoint recognize it or not?

A third question concerns the place of communities in Nussbaum's thought. Her position, even in her Aristotelian period, would seem to be a form of individualism or social atomism.[184] That is, she seems to understand society to be essentially or fundamentally a collection of distinct individuals. Her insistence that separateness and strong separateness are basic features of human life points in this direction. So does her criticism of utilitarians for aggregating satisfactions without consideration for distinct individuals. So does her insistence that individuals, once brought to the thresholds of the various capabilities, should be left free to decide whether and how to actualize those capabilities. So too do the passages where she argues against any sort of natural or specially privileged status for the nuclear family: "The only thing that stops state intervention is the person and the various liberties and rights of the person."[185] It would appear that individuals are basic, that the state exists for the protection and sustenance of individuals, and that other social groupings are subordinate to the rights of the individual as protected by the power of the state. One does not have to be a communitarian to wonder whether the individualism of Nussbaum's position needs to be tempered by more attention to the positive significance that groups, including families, can have in human life.[186]

Individualism, or social atomism, has a long history in modernity. This is not the place to argue that it is mistaken. There is, however, a practical political question about how to foster social solidarity or promote cooperative action, given an individualist or atomist understanding of society. And that practical question is relevant to Nussbaum's capabilities approach. Implementing Nussbaum's conception of minimal justice in a democratic context would seem to presuppose a fairly high degree of solidarity among citizens—at the least a readiness to be taxed and regulated at the level necessary to ensure that each and every individual is brought to the threshold of the ten capabilities and to trust that the powers of the state will for the most part be well used. What are the roots, the social and political conditions of possibility, for this solidarity?[187]

I hope this chapter has established that a close study of Nussbaum's Aristotelian work is worthwhile and rewarding, despite the fact that she herself has moved on in her scholarship from her earlier focus on Aristotle. But is there anything important to be learned from that fact? It is no surprise if a vigorous and probing thinker discovers new interests and moves in new directions. But perhaps more is involved. Perhaps there is something inherently unstable about the synthesis of Aristotelianism and liberalism that Nussbaum developed during her Aristotelian period. The more strongly someone is committed to liberalism, with its attendant individualism or social atomism, the less attractive, it seems to me, they will find Aristotle's ethics and politics of communities with shared or common goods. The moral of the story may be that Nussbaum's individualism won out, and had to win out, over her Aristotelianism.

Nussbaum's Aristotelian position, then, invites the following questions. How much can we expect from her method of appearances? How well can it serve us in situations of deep disagreement? Can her version of the minimum requirements of justice really be the object of an overlapping consensus among the main comprehensive doctrines in circulation today? Does she, in proposing her political conception of justice, speak from a neutral and impartial standpoint, or from a particular and controversial standpoint? How well does her focus on individual rights and entitlements promote the social solidarity that implementing the capabilities approach would require? And what are we to learn from her moving away from Aristotelianism toward her current position?

FURTHER READING

Most of these suggestions for further reading are concerned with Nussbaum's Aristotelian period. Readers seeking to learn about her more recent work may, however, find some help in the more recent interviews and internet resources mentioned below.

Apart from Nussbaum's curriculum vitae, there is no comprehensive bibliography of her published work. The preface to the 2001 edition of *Fragility of Goodness* (xxxvii–xxxix) updates the bibliography of Nussbaum's work to that point. The introduction to the 2009 edition of *Therapy of Desire* includes a specialized bibliography of work by Nussbaum on the themes of that book. The list in *Creating Capabilities* (211–21) is, as Nussbaum herself says, "highly selective and includes only works relevant to chapter discussions." *Philosophical Interventions: Reviews 1986–2011* (xiv–xvii) includes a complete list of Nussbaum's reviews down to 2010.

Nussbaum, "Aristotle (384–322 B.C.)," in *Ancient Writers: Greece and Rome*, ed. T. James Lucas (New York: Charles Scribner's Sons, 1982), 1:377–416, a considerable article—forty large double-column pages—is an excellent introduction to her reading of Aristotle in the years immediately preceding publication of *Fragility of Goodness*.

An issue of *Philosophy and Phenomenological Research* 59 (1999) includes a book symposium on *Therapy of Desire* with papers by John Martin Fischer, Robert C. Roberts, Richard Sorabji, and Brad Inwood, along with Nussbaum's précis of the book and her response to the papers. The journal *Ethics* 111 (2000) includes a symposium on Nussbaum's political philosophy, including her "Aristotle, Politics, and Human Capabilities: A Response to Antony, Arneson, Charlesworth, and Mulgan," 102–40. In the course of responding to these four authors Nussbaum comments on a number of her essays that we discussed above. An issue of *Philosophy and Phenomenological Research* 68 (2004) includes a symposium on *Upheavals of Thought* with papers by Aaron Ben-Ze'ev, Nancy Sherman, and John Deigh, along with Nussbaum's précis of the book and her response to the papers.

This chapter has done no more than mention Nussbaum's engagement with different aspects of justice, human development, and other issues of the day. To mention but one example among many, she appeared as an expert witness in *Evans v. Romer* (1996), a U.S. Supreme Court case about whether a provision of Colorado's state constitution denying official protection to persons suffering discrimination because of their sexual orientation was constitutional. She stated her position in Nussbaum, "Platonic Love and Colorado Law: The Relevance of Ancient Greek Norms to

Modern Sexual Controversies," *Virginia Law Review* 80 (1994): 1515–1651. A shorter version under the same title appeared in Robert B. Louden and Paul Schollmeier, eds., *The Greeks and Us: Essays in Honor of Arthur W. H. Adkins* (Chicago: University of Chicago Press, 1994), 168–218 (followed by a response from Richard Posner, 218–23), and later as chapter 12 of *Sex and Social Justice*, 299–331. Nussbaum's position was criticized by John Finnis, "'Shameless Acts' in Colorado: Abuse of Scholarship in Constitutional Cases," *Academic Questions* 7 (1994): 10–41, and by Robert P. George, "'Shameless Acts' Revisited: Some Questions for Martha Nussbaum," *Academic Questions* 9 (1996): 24–42.

Nussbaum has been critical of the law and economics movement associated with the economist Gary Becker, the federal appeals court judge Richard Posner, and others. See Nussbaum, "Flawed Foundations: The Philosophical Critique of (a Particular Type of) Economics," *University of Chicago Law Review* 64 (1997), 1197–1214.

Nussbaum and University of Chicago law professor Saul Levmore have collaborated on Nussbaum and Levmore, *Aging Thoughtfully: Conversations about Retirement, Romance, Wrinkles, and Regret* (Oxford: Oxford University Press, 2017). See also Nussbaum, *The Monarchy of Fear: A Philosopher Looks at Our Political Crisis* (New York: Simon and Schuster, 2018); *The Cosmopolitan Tradition: A Noble but Flawed Ideal* (Cambridge, MA: The Belknap Press of Harvard University Press, 2019); *Citadels of Pride: Sexual Abuse, Accountability, and Reconciliation* (New York: W. W. Norton, 2021); and *Justice for Animals: Our Collective Responsibility* (New York: Simon and Schuster, 2022).

Some of Nussbaum's work is both philosophical and autobiographical, for instance, Nussbaum, "'Don't Smile So Much': Philosophy and Women in the 1970s," in *Singing in the Fire: Stories of Women in Philosophy*, ed. Linda Martín Alcoff (Lanham, MD: Rowman and Littlefield, 2003), 93–108.

At the time of her marriage in 1969, Nussbaum converted to Judaism. She is committed to a form of Enlightenment Judaism, specifically a Mendelssohnian Judaism. Her most detailed statement of what her religious commitment involves is Nussbaum, "Judaism and the Love of Reason," in *Philosophy, Feminism, and Faith*, ed. Ruth E. Groenhout and Marya Bower (Bloomington: Indiana University Press, 2003), 9–39.

Nussbaum has given a number of interviews on philosophical issues, for example, the interview in *Kinesis* 23 (1996): 3–15; *Key Philosophers in Conversation: The "Cogito" Interviews*, ed. Andrew Pyle (London: Routledge, 1999), 239–56; "Martha C. Nussbaum: Morality and Moral Perception," in *Constructions of Practical Reason: Interviews on Moral and Political Philosophy*, ed. Herlinde Pauer-Studer (Stanford, CA: Stanford University Press, 2003), 113–27; and "Martha Nussbaum: Justice," in *Examined Life: Excursions with Contemporary Thinkers*, ed. Astra Taylor (New York: The New Press, 2009), 115–32. A 1997 interview with Klaus Taschwer, entitled "Liberaler Aristotelismus," appears at the end of the German translation of "Why Practice Needs Ethical Theory: Particularism, Principle, and Bad Behavior," in *Vom Nutzen der Moraltheorie für das Leben* (Vienna: Passagen Verlag, 2000), 89–96.

More than most philosophers, Nussbaum has been interviewed and reported on in the popular media. See, for instance, Robert Boynton, "Who Needs Philosophy? A Profile of Martha Nussbaum," *New York Times Sunday Magazine*, November 21, 1999; Rachel Aviv, "Captain of Her Soul: The Philosopher Martha Nussbaum's Emotions," *The New Yorker*, July 25, 2016.

Among internet resources, I would mention the 2006 six-part interview with Harry Kreisler in the University of California Berkeley's Conversations with History series, at http://globetrotter.berkeley.edu/people6/Nussbaum/nussbaum-con0.html, and the 2017 interview with Andrea Scarantino, "On Anger, Disgust, and Love," at http://emotionresearcher.com/on-anger-disgust-love/.

CHAPTER FOUR

THE PERSONALIST ARISTOTELIANISM OF ROBERT SPAEMANN

Robert Spaemann (1927–2018) was a complex figure: a philosopher, an intellectual historian, and a commentator on current events; an Aristotelian who made the post-Aristotelian concept of person central to his ethics; and a Thomist in many of his convictions but whose philosophical style was more Socratic than systematic. This chapter will attempt to present his combination of Aristotelianism, Thomism, and personalism. Because Spaemann is not as well known to Anglo-American readers as Alasdair MacIntyre and Martha Nussbaum, this introductory section will say more about his background and project than the last two chapters said about theirs.

Spaemann was born in Berlin in 1927. His parents, who had been atheists, converted to Roman Catholicism in 1930. After his mother's early death, his father was ordained a Catholic priest. The younger Spaemann thus had the unusual experience of growing up with a Catholic priest for his father. As a teenager in the closing years of World War II, he lived "on the other side," evading military service and distributing Roman Catholic literature. After training in history, philosophy, theology, and Romance literature, Spaemann taught at the Technical University in Stuttgart, the University of Heidelberg, and the University of Munich.[1]

Spaemann's first major publication was his doctoral dissertation, a study of the French traditionalist thinker the Vicomte de Bonald.[2] His next book was his habilitation, a study of Fénelon, Bossuet, and the seventeenth-century debate over the pure love of God.[3] These two books laid the foundations of his intellectual project. More about them in a moment.

In 1977, Spaemann published a volume of political essays whose unifying thread is criticism of the abstract utopia of the rule of pure reason.[4] In *Rousseau—Bürger ohne Vaterland* (*Rousseau—A Citizen without a Country*), he argued that Rousseau used a nonteleological conception of nature as a standard by which to criticize modernity.[5]

In *Die Frage Wozu?*, written in cooperation with Reinhard Löw, Spaemann surveyed the history of teleological thinking from the Greeks through the medievals and moderns down to the nineteenth century and argued for a revival of teleological thinking.[6] In *Moralische Grundbegriffe* (*Basic Moral Concepts*), originally a series of talks on Bavarian Radio, he discussed the concepts of ethical relativity, moral development, the relationship of ends and means, justice, conscience, and equanimity.[7] This slim volume spells out what Spaemann considers to be common moral consciousness, the convictions about good and evil, right and wrong, that Spaemann thinks most human beings share. It remains the most accessible introduction to his ethics.

Philosophische Essays (*Philosophical Essays*) (1983), contains seven essays on the nature of philosophy, natural teleology, natural law, and modernity. A second edition of this work (1994) included three additional essays.[8] In 1987, he published a collection of four essays on philosophical anthropology.[9]

Glück und Wohlwollen (*Happiness and Benevolence*) (1989), addressed the antithesis between the pursuit of happiness and the claims of moral obligation.[10] It will be the focus of this chapter. *Personen: Versuche über den Unterschied zwischen "etwas" und "jemand"* (*Persons: The Difference between "Someone" and "Something"*) (1996), is a series of meditations on various aspects of personhood.[11] *Grenzen* (*Limits* or *Boundaries*) (2001),[12] is a 559-page work that brings together forty-six of his articles and essays on ethical topics. The first nineteen chapters deal with basic ethical questions, and the remaining twenty-seven deal with contemporary ethical issues, such as nuclear warfare, abortion, euthanasia, the environment, and education.

In 2007, Spaemann published two books in the philosophy of religion;[13] in 2010 and 2011, two volumes of collected essays.[14] *Love and the Dignity of Human Life* (2012) is a set of three lectures delivered at the Catholic University of America in 2010.[15] *Über Gott und die Welt* (*On God and the World*) (2012) is an autobiography that includes a number of interviews in which he discusses his life and his major books.[16]

Spaemann has frequently taken stands, often controversial, on issues of ethics, politics, and theology. The essays in the latter part of *Grenzen* provide numerous examples. The bibliography in *Über Gott und die Welt* lists *Nach uns die Kernschmelze: Hybris im atomaren Zeitalter* (*After Us, Nuclear Meltdown: Hubris in the Atomic Age*) (Stuttgart: Klett-Cotta, 2011). He has published numerous short opinion pieces in the German press. He was one of the signatories of the controversial 1978 manifesto "Mut zur Erziehung" ("Courage to Educate") and "The Paris Statement: A Europe We Can Believe In" (2017).[17]

In the autobiographical introduction to *Philosophische Essays*, Spaemann cites the following as having influenced him: Thomas Aquinas, *Summa theologiae*; the lectures of Joachim Ritter (his *Doktorvater* in Münster) on the topic of past and future; Max Horkheimer and Theodor W. Adorno, *Dialektik der Aufklärung*; and C. S. Lewis, *The Abolition of Man*.[18] He remarks that Lewis's little book, first published in 1943, says more briefly and less dialectically everything that *Dialektik der Aufklärung* was trying to say. Spaemann's 2012 intellectual autobiography expands the list of influential figures to include Hans-Eduard Hengstenberg (a student of Max Scheler and a friend of Spaemann's father), the jurist and political thinker Carl Schmitt, the existentialists Kierkegaard and Sartre, John Henry Newman's *Grammar of Assent*, Karl Barth's *Letter to the Romans*, and the Thomists Jacques Maritain, Etienne Gilson, and Josef Pieper. He credits Leo Strauss's *Natural Right and History* with introducing him to the classical understanding of teleology. He was deeply influenced by Plato and Aristotle. His writings show a familiarity with Kant, Hegel, and Nietzsche. With so many different influences on Spaemann's thought, it is difficult to maintain that any one influence was decisive.

Spaemann's thought also developed in opposition to the ideology of National Socialism that dominated Germany in his youth. After World War II, he moved for a while in Marxist circles, but ended up rejecting

Marxism. His works include criticisms of Descartes, Locke, and Hume, of Nietzsche and Weber, and of Peter Singer and Derek Parfit. He was critical of the applied ethics movement, at least in its German form. Other targets include the behaviorist B. F. Skinner, the social scientists Niklas Luhmann and Ralf Dahrendorf, and the movement of discourse ethics whose most prominent exponent is Jürgen Habermas.

Spaemann's approach to philosophical ethics remained remarkably consistent over the years. He saw the task of ethics as explicating and refining a moral consciousness that most people have and defending it against misconceptions and sophistries.[19] It is not the business of ethics to try to prove that this moral consciousness is correct. It is certainly not the business of ethics to discover new ethical truths. *Happiness and Benevolence* begins, "My hope is that these thoughts on ethics contain nothing fundamentally new. In seeking answers to questions about the right kind of life, only the false could be really new."[20] But although Spaemann's ethics remained consistent over the years, it was not easily synthesized. He wrote for many different publics. His ethical writings include long and highly technical essays, books such as *Happiness and Benevolence* and *Persons* that reflect their origins in lecture courses, the popular *Basic Moral Concepts*, and short opinion pieces in the press. Even his longer and more technical pieces are written in a relaxed essayistic style that is quite different from the style of the typical Anglo-American philosophy journal article. He mixes, sometimes on a single page, historical narratives, philosophical arguments, and vivid examples. He alludes to issues in metaphysics and philosophy of religion that he sees as germane to ethics, but for the most part he does not address them directly. Most importantly, he conceives of philosophy as an essentially controversial enterprise and therefore always incomplete. He sees the arguments of ethics as largely ad hominem, directed to particular persons holding particular positions.[21] There is therefore something inauspicious about the very attempt to state Spaemann's position in a systematic way.[22]

This chapter will outline Spaemann's overall philosophical project, including his understanding of natural teleology and his conception of philosophical ethics. It will then present his argument in *Happiness and Benevolence* about how the claims of happiness and the claims of moral obligation or, as he terms it, benevolence, are to be reconciled.

SPAEMANN'S PHILOSOPHICAL PROJECT

Understanding Modernity

Spaemann's decades-long project was, first of all, an attempt to understand modernity. As we have seen, his first major publication was his dissertation on the Vicomte de Bonald (1754–1840). The period of restoration or reaction against the French Revolution would seem to have been opposed to modernity and Enlightenment. Study of Bonald, however, indicates that the restoration was not in fact opposed to modernity. On the contrary, by interpreting metaphysics (or religion or anything else) as a means to human self-preservation, Bonald brought modernity to completion in the notion of functionality. Suspicion of such functional interpretations is a constant in Spaemann's later work.

Spaemann's next book was a study of François Fénelon, Jacques-Bénigne Bossuet, and the seventeenth-century debate over the pure love of God. This was a debate about whether human beings can or should love God to the point of not caring about their own happiness, or whether they necessarily love God with a view to their own happiness. Fénelon, the archbishop of Cambrai, took the former position. Bossuet, the bishop of Meaux, took the latter: "What was it that suddenly made the thousand-year-old Platonic-Christian teaching about the love of God for God's sake something ambiguous and set 'self-realization' and 'self-transcendence' over against each other as opposites? The presupposition behind this opposition was the instrumentalization of the teleological ontology at the beginning of modernity: it inverted teleology into the preservation of existence, and reduced all the features of life to instruments of this preservation."[23] Spaemann found that the inversion of the classical teleological view of things, that is, the shift from looking on things as having ends in themselves to looking on them as means to the satisfaction of human ends, gave rise to the modern antithesis of self-fulfillment versus self-transcendence. The opposition between classical teleology and what Spaemann calls "the inverted teleology of modernity" is fundamental to his later writing.

As Spaemann sees it, modernity has tended to interpret itself as an emancipation from what preceded it. This emancipation has both a positive dimension (the recognition and expansion of freedom) and a negative dimension (a disregard for norms of good and evil), as seen in the Marquis de Sade and German National Socialism.[24] This negative side of modernity is very much alive. Contemporary civilization poses a greater threat to human dignity than any previous civilization.[25] But there is no question of returning to a premodern outlook. Modernity has made great positive contributions: enlightenment, emancipation, human rights, and modern natural science. Spaemann wants to take these achievements into a kind of protective custody. The second part of his project is an attempt to rescue modernity from its own self-interpretation by imbuing it with a teleological outlook.[26] This is no easy task.

Spaemann describes his project in the introduction to *Philosophische Essays*:

> One way to approach modernity would be to understand it strictly on its own terms, as radically liberating. In this case we understand it as advancing toward death; the inevitable result of the Enlightenment's dialectic is self-annihilation. . . . If we want to avoid this self-annihilation, then we may not understand modernity on its own terms. On the contrary, we have to defend enlightenment, emancipation, human rights, science, and the mastery of nature against themselves. We have to grasp modernity in a teleological way, as the unfolding of an original truth about man that modernity did not itself establish. Modernity will be saved in the twenty-first century only if it measures itself by this truth.[27]

Natural Teleology

A brief account of Spaemann's understanding of natural teleology will make it easier to follow his argument in *Happiness and Benevolence*. This account will draw on a number of his essays, mostly untranslated, and on *Persons*.[28]

Natural teleology, in the sense that Spaemann is arguing for it, is the idea that living beings have natural tendencies to develop in certain ways and natural drives that explain, at least in part, what those living beings do: "The basic structure of subjective experience is pursuit, or 'going out for' something, i.e. 'drive' [*Trieb*]."[29] We meet our natures in the form of drives. Those drives provide prima facie reasons for actions. If someone is hungry, that provides a reason to eat. If we ask why someone is eating, to say that they are hungry is a sufficient answer.

The natural teleology that Spaemann is talking about is, then, immanent in living things themselves. This is not the Stoic and Christian idea that the world as a whole has a purpose or has been designed for a purpose. That conception, he thinks, played an important role in the late medieval and early modern rejection of immanent natural teleology. Where Aristotle took nature to be something ultimate, Christian thinkers saw the world as designed and created by God. In the fifth of his Five Ways, Aquinas argued that just as the flight of an arrow to its target requires an archer, so there must be a God to explain the order that we find in the world. Taken by itself, this might seem to imply that things only have a *telos* because God imposes it on them. Later medievals, such as Ockham and Buridan, took this idea further, restricting teleology to conscious purpose. They saw the world as a great machine designed by God, a machine whose workings manifest God's glory. The first motivation for discarding natural teleology was thus, perhaps surprisingly, religious. A second was the apparent uselessness of final causality for science, noticed by Francis Bacon: the final cause is like a consecrated virgin who bears no children. A third and highly important factor was articulated by Thomas Hobbes: the interest in mastering the world of nature. Natural teleology was set aside in part because it did not contribute to the project of mastering the world of nature.[30]

The classical immanent teleology of beings developing toward complete realization did not simply disappear in the modern period. It was replaced by a limited and deficient conception that Spaemann calls "inverted teleology" or an "inversion of teleology." This is the idea, found in Spinoza and others, that the essence of things is their striving to preserve themselves, to keep themselves in being: *conatus sese conservandi est essentia rerum*, "the essence of things is their effort to preserve themselves."[31] Spaemann does not deny that beings try to preserve themselves— this is something that animals do—but, borrowing a phrase from Albert the Great, he calls this nature curved in upon itself (*natura semper recurva in se ipsa*).[32]

Spaemann understands persons to be living beings, animals. Their identity is that of living beings. Their continuity through time is the continuity of living beings. In chapter 12 of *Persons*, "Subjects," he explains how modern philosophy departed from this view, and how Descartes, Locke, and Hume found it difficult, indeed impossible, to make sense of persons, of their identity or continuity through time. For Descartes, organic life drops out of the picture. A human being is a thinking substance, a *res cogitans*, that possesses a body as an instrument. He understands this body not as a living thing but as a machine. Descartes's inability to make sense of organic life made it impossible for him to understand persons as beings that have, but are not identical with, their life. For Descartes, the living being and the thinking being are two different things: "And where consciousness and matter are defined independently and opposed as incommensurables, we end up with quite different criteria for the identity of human beings and of persons."[33]

For Locke, identity or continuity through time, in any literal sense of those terms, drop out of the picture. Instead of continuous time, Locke envisions a series of discrete instants. Organic life drops out of the picture too. There is no fundamental difference between animals and machines. But then, Spaemann argues, "if life is not the mode in which living things have their being, the being of the person is not identical with a human life."[34] Locke's inability to make sense of life led him to reduce personal identity to the identity of the person's consciousness, to the person's ability to claim various representations as their own.

For Hume, the subject itself drops out of the picture. There is no such thing as a *res cogitans*. All there is is a series of impressions, representations. Spaemann asks: "Is there an impression corresponding to the 'self,' that may be thought to persist alongside all our perceptions? No, Hume replies, the perceptions are all there is, and the self is not another one. . . . Identity is an impression arising from three kinds of relation: resemblance, contiguity, and causation. Now relations are not real things; there are no perceptions corresponding to them. And so there are no relations between perceptions either, only the impression of a relation that arises when we reflect on the perceptions. The person is just such a relation imagined in the mind."[35] We may try to connect our representations by treating some as causes and others as effects, but this is our doing, not something real. Causal relations are fictions. So is the person.

The net result is that these modern philosophers have made it impossible to make sense of the notion of a person. In response to the modern misunderstanding of organic life and of person, and in opposition to the Cartesian notion of soul as an independent thinking substance, connected in some obscure way with a material body, Spaemann attempts to rehabilitate the Aristotelian notion of soul as the teleological principle of life that makes a given substance distinct from other substances. In chapter 13 of *Persons*, "Souls," he argues that we need this notion of soul to make sense of animal life, including our own animal life.

In "Teleologie und Teleonomie" ("Teleology and Teleonomy"), Spaemann argues that the Aristotelian concept of teleology is indispensable to biology and that the attempt to do without it involves serious misunderstandings of biological reality in general and of the human being in particular.[36] He starts by admitting that the relationship between biology and teleology is problematic. For biology, teleology is an embarrassment. It is like a man's mistress: he cannot bear to live without her, but he does not want to be seen with her in public.[37] This is why biologists such as Colin Pittendrigh and Ernst Mayr adopted the word "teleonomy" instead. The word is used in different senses, but the core idea is to recognize that certain processes are end-directed, without that recognition involving any commitment to Aristotelian final causality. The idea is for teleonomy to do the work that the old mistress teleology used to do, but without her checkered past.[38] Spaemann argues that this move will not work and that biology needs teleology, properly understood.

Spaemann distinguishes Aristotelian teleology, in the sense that biology needs it, from other conceptions of or substitutes for teleology. The early modern period, which dismissed the idea that natural things had inner tendencies to develop and act in certain ways, thought of nature as a great machine designed by God and operating by purely mechanical laws.[39] Another conception of teleology goes back to the Stoics and reappeared in the Enlightenment: the idea that the world and all its parts form an order. This is the view in which it makes sense to say that rain falls for the sake of watering crops. This "ecological" or "universal" teleology is utterly different from Aristotle's conception of the programmed way in which an organism builds itself up (*programmierter Selbstaufbau des Organismus*). It goes against Aristotle's idea that each and every living thing exists for its own sake.[40]

The materialistic biology of the nineteenth century treated teleology as a heuristic principle, a tool of investigation by which to identify the objects that it was to study, but then it studied those objects with a view to reducing them to nonteleological causal processes. As Spaemann puts it, the goal of this kind of biology was to eliminate itself as a distinct discipline. This was precisely what Kant had argued was impossible.[41] Yet another conception of teleology grew up in the nineteenth century: the understanding of evolution as the realization of a preexisting program, an "orthogenesis." Biologists (rightly) raise serious objections against this view, but they (wrongly) confuse it with Aristotle's view. That is a mistake, because Aristotle thought that actuality had priority over potentiality. The form that sets the goal for a living substance preexists in the earlier instances of the species.[42]

Biology has passed a critical judgment on the teleology of external design, on universal teleology, and on the teleological interpretation of evolution. Does this mean that biology has rediscovered the original idea of an end or goal, a *telos*? No. Biology and teleology are not saying the same thing. Yet the difference between them is not the difference between two competing biological theories. It is the difference between a biological theory and a philosophical theory. It is not that biology is false. It is that biology is not a kind of first philosophy that tells us what life and knowledge really are.[43]

Spaemann contrasts teleology and teleonomy as follows. Teleology is the assumption that a process has a goal that is already given at the outset. Teleonomy is the coming to be of programs (*Programmen*) that have all sorts of consequences. Aristotle cannot be understood as a proponent of teleonomy, because he believes in the eternity of species. He may seem to be a proponent of teleonomy, but that is because of the way that he uses art or craft as his model of how nature operates. There is indeed a certain similarity between the model of an art or craft and the model of a program. But Aristotle does not confuse his model with the object that he is using the model to represent: "He has a teleonomic model, but his ontology is teleological" (*Er hat ein teleonomisches Modell, aber seine Ontologie ist teleologisch*).[44] He remains a proponent of teleology.

Spaemann says that there are really only two possibilities: either human purposive action is something ontologically secondary, the product of a contingent process of selection; or the categorical structure of "being out for" (*Aus-sein-auf*) is constitutive, at various levels of complexity, for natural being in general. The former is the viewpoint of the proponents of teleonomy. The latter is Spaemann's viewpoint.[45]

Teleonomy, Spaemann says, is a scientific reconstruction of teleology. But in the end, any reconstruction is something that *we* do. We may reconstruct something's development in terms of a program, but the program is a program *for us*, not for the thing that we understand in terms of the program. The structure of "being out for something" is something that we know first of all by acquaintance, from our experience of ourselves. And this is not, first of all, the experience of consciously setting goals for ourselves, but rather the experience of finding goals already set for us in the form of drives. We can only speak of setting goals because we first of all experience "being out for" things as the form of our inner unity as living beings. Teleology is an original or primordial given. Teleonomy is simulated teleology, a simulation of teleology. Teleonomy always presupposes teleology.[46]

In "Naturteleologie und Handlung" ("Natural Teleology and Action"), Spaemann says that he does not propose to prove that there is such a thing as natural teleology. This is not the kind of claim that can be proven or disproven. He proposes instead to consider what we are doing when we speak the language of natural teleology and what interests are involved in affirming or denying that there are final causes. He admits that natural teleology did not advance the modern project of mastering nature through science and technology, but he does not regard that as a decisive objection. Human beings have another interest besides their interest in mastering nature: an interest in achieving a symbiosis with nature, in being at home in nature. The ecological crisis of the late twentieth century indicated that the modern project of mastering nature was running up against limits. And the antiteleological view of nature tends to reduce human beings themselves to natural objects without a teleology of their own, objects to be mastered by science and technology just like any other object. Spaemann finds this to be explicit in the behaviorism of B. F. Skinner. We have, then, a practical interest in interpreting nature by analogy with our own action: "One may call this anthropomorphism; but to renounce the anthropomorphic view of nature leads inevitably to the point where the human being itself becomes an anthropomorphism."[47]

Spaemann is alert to the charge that such an anthropomorphism is reading onto animals the intentionality of human decision and action. He admits that natural teleology is a way of understanding what other living beings do by analogy with what we human beings do. But the word "analogy" is important here. Spaemann is not proposing that other animals do the exact same thing as humans do. He speaks of natural teleology as a hermeneutic of nature, a way of interpreting what goes on in nature by analogy with human action.[48] If a dog makes for its bowl, it is reasonable to read this as a response to hunger.[49] And to look at the same point from the other side, the hunger that leads human beings to eat is not radically different from what leads dogs to eat. We ourselves experience natural teleology at a level more basic than conscious choice.

"Die Aktualität des Naturrechts" ("The Contemporary Relevance of Natural Right") complements "Naturteleologie und Handlung" by outlining the ethical and political implications of being mindful of nature and natural teleology.[50] Modern science rejects teleology in order to master nature. The phenomena, the facts, resist this rejection of teleology, and so, to save the phenomena, we have a series of what Spaemann calls "two-world theories," theories that distinguish between a realm of causes and a realm of ends, between is and ought, between facts and values. These theories are residues of the preceding Aristotelian notion of entelechy, of a thing's having its *telos* within it. The powerful interest in mastery over nature is the source of the antithesis between humans and nature, which opposes the traditional symbiosis. So long as mastery over nature is not guided by respect for teleology, it is bound to be mastery over humans too. The slogan of emancipation, "more power over nature, no power over human beings," is naïve. It forgets that human beings too are part of nature.[51]

Spaemann's Conception of Ethics

The best short statement of Spaemann's conception of ethics is "Was ist philosophische Ethik?" ("What Is Philosophical Ethics?"), first published as the introduction to a collection of readings in ethics, and republished as the lead essay in *Grenzen*.[52] It anticipates some of the central claims of *Happiness and Benevolence*.

Philosophical ethics does not try to ground or prove moral experience. It presupposes moral experience, in particular the experience of using "good" in its absolute sense (good in itself as opposed to "good for" this or that purpose). Ethics starts with our moral convictions and tries to understand what they mean and why we take them to be unconditional. It searches for a basic unity underlying our convictions and tries to bring them into a consistent whole. This search for consistency may lead us to modify our ethical views.[53]

Bringing our moral convictions into philosophy means exposing them to questioning. The point of this questioning, however, is not to compromise our convictions but to understand why they are unconditional. Questioning leads to controversy, but the controversy is not about the existence of the moral phenomenon. It is about what the moral phenomenon is and what it means. Philosophical ethics also tries to compare and judge the experiences, feelings, and judgments of different people, ages, and cultures. This too can lead to controversy and conflict.[54]

When individuals or groups with different moral convictions clash, there are two ways of dealing with these clashes. The first is what Spaemann somewhat misleadingly calls "metaethics." By this he means an attempt to take a position above the ethical fray, to take no part in ethical argument, that amounts in practice to relativism.[55] This abstention from philosophical ethics may present itself as a position of tolerance for a variety of views. But someone who relativizes ethical convictions, including his or her own, thereby places himself or herself in opposition to all people with substantive ethical convictions. The consistent relativist has to deny the self-understanding of practically every lived ethic, that one should do certain things because it is good to do them and not do others because it would be bad to do them. Further, there are whole cultures that make universal claims. European culture, for example, makes claims about human rights. The relativist has to oppose these universal claims, and so shows himself not as tolerant of all claims but as himself also making universal claims, albeit negative ones. So much for tolerance![56]

The second way of dealing with the conflicts is to face them head on: that is, to do philosophical ethics. Philosophical ethics takes up the challenge of disagreement. It looks for the best-grounded moral conviction. In the process it discovers that the moral outlooks of different cultures are not all that different, that they agree on a great number of basic convictions. Again, philosophical ethics presupposes moral experience. It does not try to convince someone that "good" and "bad" have a meaning. It does not try to "ground" the moral dimension. Rather it tries to show that the moral dimension is the ground on which we already stand.[57]

Philosophical ethics is a practical discipline and its claims are not deductions from theoretical premises, but certain theoretical assumptions contradict our common moral intuitions. One of these, Spaemann thinks, is the assumption that acting morally is incompatible with leading a happy, successful life, with what the Greeks called *eudaimonia* and the German tradition has called *Glückseligkeit*, "blessedness." Philosophy from Plato to Kant has tried to show that this is not the case, that the good person is not a fool. To show this has meant showing that good action is an integrating component of happiness, and that the moral impulse is part of our rational nature: "Western philosophical ethics culminates in the idea of love in the sense of free and rational benevolence toward an other who is experienced as real and toward oneself."[58]

This ethics has theoretical implications, but these implications are neither first principles from which a metaphysically grounded ethics might be derived nor postulates in the Kantian sense:[59]

> Love in the sense of benevolence is the attitude in which that which for a purely theoretical attitude would only have the character of an object is changed, for the one loving, into the reality [*Wirklichkeit*] of selfhood. For one who loves, love is the becoming real of the real. From an "objective" state of affairs, just by itself, no ought ever follows. But what "being" [*Sein*] means, over and above being an object,

first reveals itself to benevolence. For being in the sense of "existence" [*Existenz*] does not have an objective "meaning." Applying these words means positing something outside of every context of meaning for myself, positing something as its own center of possible meanings. That such a being-for-itself becomes real [*wirklich*] for me is not the result of an "ought." It precedes every ought. It is that basic intuition in which theory and praxis coincide. The medieval monk Richard of St. Victor coined the beautiful phrase *ubi amor, ibi oculus* [where there is love, there is an eye].[60]

This quotation anticipates the core of *Happiness and Benevolence*, to which we now turn.

HAPPINESS AND BENEVOLENCE

In *Happiness and Benevolence*, Spaemann sets out to do justice to two very different approaches to ethics: what he calls "classical eudaimonism," the philosophical quest for the happiness or fulfillment that we want for our-selves, and what he calls "modern universalism," the philosophy of our duties and obligations to other people or, as he also puts it, the benevo-lence that we owe to other human beings. He attempts to adjudicate the claims of "happiness" and the claims of "benevolence" by analyzing these two terms. His central thesis is that the claims of happiness and the claims of benevolence can be reconciled, but only if we have a correct under-standing of happiness and a correct understanding of benevolence; that happiness, correctly understood, actually requires benevolence. This thesis and the arguments for it are at the core of his ethics. Here we will outline the main argument of *Happiness and Benevolence*, drawing on *Persons* and other writings to explain and fill out certain aspects of that argument.

Happiness and Benevolence also advances claims about metaphysics and the philosophy of religion. Perhaps most strikingly, it claims that the reason why persons owe one another recognition and unconditional re-spect is that each and every person is an image or representation of an ab-solute or unconditioned reality (*ein Bild des Unbedingten*), and that the notion that persons have a responsibility to themselves only makes sense on the assumption that they are images of an unconditioned reality. These claims, which also figure in *Persons*, are parts of Spaemann's overall position, but not premises in his arguments. To examine them would take us beyond the scope of this chapter.

Classical Eudaimonism and Modern Universalism

Classical eudaimonism (the sophists, Epicurus, the Stoics, and especially Aristotle) arises because our drives do not, on their own, integrate themselves into a life that turns out well. If our lives are to succeed, we need to think about them and plan them. Modern universalism (most of modern ethics and especially Kant) arises because our interests do not automatically or necessarily coincide with other people's interests or with the common good of society. Eudaimonism, just by itself, only takes us as far as hypothetical rules of prudence. It does not give us unconditional obligations to others. But modern universalism, with its focus on duties, obligations, and rules, cannot stand on its own. Why should anyone pay attention to duties, obligations, and rules to the possible detriment of his or her own happiness? "The difficulty for any eudaimonistic ethics consists in the grounding of a principled interest in the welfare of others. . . . On the other hand, any ethics which universalizes what 'ought' to be done faces the difficulty of explaining why anyone would have a real interest of the kind that brings an individual to will what he sees would be good if everyone else would also will it."[61]

As for combining eudaimonism and universalism, that is easier said than done. The ancients tried to integrate duties toward the other into *eudaimonia*, and Kant subordinated happiness to morality, but neither really overcame the dualism between eudaimonism and universalism. We seem, then, to be faced with an arbitrary choice between two quite different types of ethics. But if that is really the case, then philosophical ethics is at a dead end.[62]

Spaemann contends that the happy life has both a subjective dimension, happiness insofar as a person experiences it, and an objective dimension, someone's happiness insofar as it can be assessed by other people after the person's life is complete. By itself, the subjective dimension is insufficient. Spaemann introduces the thought experiment of a person experiencing euphoria through electric stimulation and says that none of us would change places with such a person. Life is not successful if the price of success is losing contact with reality, and reality cannot be defined by a purely subjective perspective. We want not just subjective states, which can be simulated, but intentional experience, experience that makes contact with reality. And apart from the subjective dimension, the objective dimension, assessed by observers apart from the experience of the person observed, is likewise insufficient.[63]

Classical eudaimonism turns into something other than eudaimonism. One may start by pursuing happiness, but the pursuit then leads beyond happiness to something else. Epicurus, as Spaemann reads him, started with a quest for happiness in the sense of subjective contentment. He found that subjective contentment depends on having good friends, and then realized that having good friends requires someone to *be* a good friend. Starting with hedonism, he ended with generosity and even self-sacrifice. As Spaemann interprets the Stoics, they began with the goal of self-preservation, but this led them to a doctrine of "appropriation" (*oikeiôsis*), or identification with the universe, to an acceptance of the roles assigned them by nature, and to the disinterested fulfillment of duty. In both cases the quest for happiness pointed the way to something beyond happiness.[64]

One might expect that Spaemann, as an Aristotelian, would represent Aristotle as solving the problem about happiness and benevolence. He does nothing of the kind. In chapter 5, "The Aristotelian Compromise," of *Happiness and Benevolence*, he argues that Aristotle's understanding of happiness, subtle as it is, nonetheless fails to resolve the problem.

Unlike Plato, Epicurus, and the Stoics, Aristotle distinguishes two different kinds of *eudaimonia*: the more-than-human happiness of theoretical contemplation and the everyday human happiness of the virtuous citizen of a *polis* (city-state). He recognizes the possibility that what someone finds satisfying may not be the same as what preserves the *polis* and makes it prosper. His solution to this problem is not theoretical but practical: to craft political arrangements that reward the virtues and actions that profit the city. So Spaemann: "Citizens of a free polis so identify themselves with it that this usefulness for the polis means at the same time their own contentment, because the welfare of the polis consists in nothing other than the welfare of its citizens, that is, in the turning out well of the lives of its citizens."[65] Aristotle's ethics thus represents a compromise between the self-interested and community-oriented aspects of happiness.

Aristotle recognizes both the subjective and the objective dimensions of human happiness. The subjective: how someone experiences his or her life. The objective: how that someone's life actually is and, ultimately, how (in the judgment of others) it turns out. This distinction is what Aristotle recognizes when he says that we cannot be certain that people have led happy lives until after they have died.[66] Aristotle's ethics thus represents a compromise between the subjective and objective dimensions of happiness. He does not resolve the problem about happiness and benevolence.

In chapter 6, arguably the most difficult chapter in *Happiness and Benevolence*, Spaemann argues that the very concept of happiness is fraught with paradoxes or, as he says, "antinomies." The most basic antinomy, he says, is that any integration of our life as a whole that is greater than time can only be one event within this whole, the whole becoming a part of itself. We cannot really see our lives as wholes.[67] By my count, chapter 6 mentions six other antinomies of happiness, or, perhaps better, six specifications of this basic antinomy. These are (1) the oppositions between the dream of perfect happiness and the limited possibilities for its realization; (2) between the subjective experiential dimension of happiness and the objective dimension (already mentioned); (3) between intentionality (focus on the other, the real) and reflexivity (focus on the self); (4) between self-preservation, self-sufficiency, the cultivation of contentment, on the one hand, and discontent and the drive for self-fulfillment, on the other hand; (5) between the preservation of freedom and the realization of freedom; and (6) between the successful life and ethical responsibility or justice. These oppositions or contradictions, Spaemann says, cannot be resolved so long as we think of happiness as an empirical concept rather than a transcendental concept.[68] Chapter 9 of *Happiness and Benevolence* will show us how Spaemann understands this Kantian language.

Spaemann's presentation of the antinomies in chapter 6 gives rise to a slew of questions that I set aside to focus on the antinomy that is central to *Happiness and Benevolence*—the apparently insurmountable opposition between the pursuit of *eudaimonia* and the duty of justice:

Justice is, on the one hand, a part of life, and its demands can be judged according to whether they are appropriate for promoting the happiness of life or for impairing it. On the other hand, every effort toward the turning out well of one's own life can be measured by its conformity with justice, whose commands inexorably relativize the individual's pursuit of happiness. If there is no possibility of grasping the dualism and thereby overcoming it, then the mutual relativization of the self-evident quality of the other [*die gegenseitige Relativierung der beiden Evidenzen*, "the way that these two self-evident truths relativize each other"] leads to ethical skepticism and thereby to the impossibility of "living rightly."[69]

The evident claims of happiness and the evident claims of justice seem to cancel each other out and to leave us with nothing to go on. That would mean the end of philosophical ethics. This is the antinomy that Spaemann will try to resolve in chapter 9.

Chapter 7, "Specifying the Moral," tells the story of how morality came to be differentiated both from the classical reflection on the good life and from religion. Classical eudaimonism in its Aristotelian form did not survive the end of the autonomous *polis* in the Macedonian hegemony. Eudaimonism in its Epicurean and Stoic forms underwent withering criticism from the church fathers, in particular Augustine in *City of God*. Christian morality combined eudaimonism with a morality of unselfish love. Spaemann: "The key to this was to think of the love of God as the fundamental motive of all morality, as *forma virtutum*," that is, the form or inner principle of the virtues. "Unity with the will of God is the Christian formula for morality, being one with God is the Christian formula for *eudaimonia*. That which motivates moral action—namely love—is at the same time that whose fulfillment is thought of as blessedness. Morality is not 'disinterested' any more than blessedness is egotistical."[70]

This Christian synthesis was a response to the problem about eudaimonism and universalism, but a response that is no longer available to us. The synthesis broke down in the seventeenth-century debate over the pure love of God, leaving us with two alternatives: either human beings are totally concerned with themselves, "and then their love of God is a function of the human striving after happiness," or there is a pure, disinterested love of God and "the purity of the motivation would coincide with the disappearance of eudaimonistic thinking." Spaemann's book on Fénelon tells the story of that breakdown. Kant's moral philosophy, arguably the most important statement of modern universalism, reproduces the modern disconnection between happiness and moral action.[71]

Life and Reason

Spaemann's understanding of happiness and benevolence presupposes a certain understanding of the human being, which he outlines in chapter 8 of *Happiness and Benevolence*, "Reason and Life." He starts with the traditional definition of the human being as a rational animal, but gives it a distinctive interpretation. As rational animals we are marked by a constant tension between animal life (*Leben*) and reason (*Vernunft*). Life is what we share with the other animals.[72] As animals, as living beings, we have instincts and drives. We are the centers of our worlds. Other beings are parts of our environment, objects that we cope with. As beings with reason, however, we can decenter ourselves. That is, we can take distance from our animal self-centeredness, our instincts, and our drives. We can recognize others not just as objects for us to cope with but as subjects for whom there is meaning. Humans are thus under a constant tension: as living beings, we construe the world from the standpoint of our own self-preservation; as beings with reason we are open to what Spaemann calls "an infinite horizon."

Spaemann's treatment of life and reason in chapter 2 of *Persons* fills out this picture. Persons, he says, are animals that have their natures. This might seem to be a truism. Doesn't every animal have its own nature? But Spaemann sees a contrast between human beings and other animals. Other animals are simply instances of their natures, nothing more. Human persons, he thinks, are instances of their natures but also something more. Interpreting Boethius's definition of a person—*naturae rationabilis individua substantia*, "an individual substance of a rational nature"—he says that persons are never just instances of their nature or essence, because they are free to take up a stance or attitude with respect to their natures:

With the concept of the person . . . we come to think of the particular individual as being more basic than its nature. This is not to suggest that these individuals *have* no nature, and start out by deciding for themselves what they are to be. What they do is assume a new relation to their nature; they freely endorse the laws of their being, or alternatively they rebel against them and "deviate." Because they are thinking beings, they cannot be categorized exhaustively as members of their species, only as individuals, who "exist *in* their nature." That is to say, they exist as persons.[73]

In chapter 16 of *Persons*, "Freedom," Spaemann returns to his thesis that a person is a being that has its nature: "Freedom, as we saw at the outset, is first and foremost freedom *from* something; but what is the *person* free from? Only from his or her own nature. A person 'has' a nature, but that nature is not what the person *is*, because the person has the power to relate freely to it. But this power is not innate; it comes through encounter with other persons. Only the affirmation of other centres of being, through recognition, justice, and love, allows us the distance on [from?] ourselves and the appropriation of ourselves that is constitutive for persons—in sum, 'freedom from self.'"[74]

Benevolence and Happiness

Chapter 9, "Benevolence," is the turning point of *Happiness and Benevolence*. There Spaemann argues that the key to understanding the compatibility between benevolence and happiness is the correct understanding of benevolence: Leibniz's *delectatio in felicitate alterius*, "a delight in the happiness of another." Benevolence arises when a human being moves beyond the level of animal instinct and awakens to the reality of the other as other. This presupposes that there is an absolute or unconditioned sense of good—good in itself or good as such, as opposed to good for this or that purpose—and that the finite other is an image of the unconditioned good. Awakening to the reality of another person is the necessary condition for awakening to our own reality as persons. Persons, as Spaemann is fond of saying, exist only in the plural: "The ego caught up in instincts has not discovered the self or the other. It remains hidden from itself in the center of everything organic. In the act of awakening to reason, its own reality and that of the other become simultaneously visible . . . . We can only know what it means to be a self through the fact that we live a self [*daß wir ein Selbst leben*], and therefore have instincts but at the same time go out of our centrality and perceive ourselves as the other of the other, and the other as *alter ego*."[75]

This recognition of other persons is inherently benevolent. It is the basis of all moral obligation: "We call the deliberate attitude toward such a being 'respect' or even 'reverence.' This attitude has before all else a negative character. It restricts how much a subject can grasp. It demands the pure 'letting-be' [*Sein-lassen*] of the other in its irreducible otherness."[76]

Spaemann understands the recognition of other persons not as a moral decision but as an enlightenment or awakening: "Just as Buddha's identification with all who suffer was not a moral decision [*moralischer Entschluß*] but an enlightenment [*Erleuchtung*], a sudden awakening [*Innewerden*: becoming aware], so is it with benevolence."[77] So long as we are in the grip of animal instinct, the other is not real to us and we are not real to ourselves. Love of benevolence changes this: "Love as *amor benevolentiae* [love of benevolence] is affirming not negating. *It affirms instinct, because it has totally freed itself from its dominance.* It is no longer instinct which turns itself against itself. The fundamental experience for love is not that of unreality but that of the real. Unambiguous reality is, however, that of the person. In love the other becomes as real to me as I become to myself in this same awakening."[78] As Spaemann uses it, the adjective "real" (*wirklich*) applies first of all to persons rather than to things. "The other becomes real to me" is equivalent to "I become aware that the other is a person."

The adjective "moral" in "was not a moral decision" is important. Spaemann thinks that recognition is free and does involve a decision. That decision, however, is not a specifically *moral* decision, a response to an ought. Oughts only arise within the context of recognition. The decision that makes the enlightenment or awakening of recognition occur is prior to the emergence of oughts. It makes oughts possible.[79]

Recognition

Chapter 9 of *Happiness and Benevolence* takes the notion of recognition (*Anerkennung*) for granted. Chapters 6 and 15 of *Persons* give a fuller account of it. In chapter 6, "Transcendence," Spaemann explains how persons recognize and are recognized by other persons:

> The elementary form of such absolute encounter with reality is the intersection of the other's gaze with mine. I find myself looked at. And if the other's gaze does not objectify me, inspect me, evaluate me, or merely crave for me, but reciprocates my own, there is constituted in the experience of both what we call "personal existence." "Persons" exist only in the plural. It is true that the gaze of the other may in principle be simulated, for the other is never presented to us in the compelling immediacy of pure phenomenon. It is a free decision to treat the other as a real self, not a simulation. What that decision essentially consists in is a refusal to obey the innate tendency of all living things to overpower others. Positively expressed, we may call it "letting-be" [*Seinlassen*]. Letting-be is the act of transcendence, the distinctive hallmark of personality. Persons are beings for whom the self-being of another is real, and whose own self has become real to another.[80]

The reference here to free decision might seem to contradict the claim in *Happiness and Benevolence* that benevolence toward another person arises from an awakening, not from a moral decision. A more literal translation eases the difficulty somewhat: "To take the other for a real self and not a simulation contains an aspect of freedom [*Moment der Freiheit*]." Spaemann's point is that recognizing the reality of persons requires a willingness or readiness to recognize the reality of persons. To put the matter crudely, the reality of persons is not something that we invent or imagine, but neither is it something that hits us over the head.[81]

In chapter 15 of *Persons*, "Recognition," Spaemann says that the recognition of persons is not a simple matter of perception or observation, nor is it a matter of starting with an awareness of our own personhood and then reasoning by analogy to the personhood of others: "On the contrary, we can only conceive of ourself [ourselves?] as a person if there is someone else whom we conceive as one. We do not find out first whether we understand a language, and then whether anyone else understands it, too. To be a person is to occupy a place within a field where other persons have their places."[82] Obviously the other person has to be accessible to us through sense perception, but the other's being a person is not something given in sense perception. It is something noticed in a free act of recognition. Here, as translator Oliver O'Donovan sees, Spaemann plays on the ambiguity of the German verb *wahrnehmen*, which can mean simply "to notice or perceive something," but also "to take something into account": "We say that we 'take note of' another person's interests when we make them our own and defend them before third parties. This is the sense in which persons can be said to be 'noticed.' All obligation begins with taking account of persons."[83] It is not that we have an obligation to recognize persons. On the contrary, it is the recognition of persons that is the source of every obligation.

Spaemann rejects the view that our benevolent recognition of other persons is just speciesism, a preference for our own kind. A passage from chapter 10 of *Happiness and Benevolence* explains why:

> Other humans are unequivocally given to us as "things-in-themselves," as real in the strong sense of the word. That our duties are, first and foremost, duties to other humans finds its reason in this fact and not the biological solidarity of the species, since this has its effect, as we said earlier, instinctively and without reflection, and also because it is unable to ground an obligation for a reflective being. That others belong to the same biological species as I do is not a reason for me to respect or help them; rather the reason lies in the fact that, beyond all biological kinship, these others stand in a relationship with themselves, that is, they are selves.[84]

Chapter 15 of *Persons* complements this point. If recognition were simply a matter of favoring one's own species, it would be compatible with sacrificing some members of the species for the benefit of the species as a whole. But that is precisely what recognition of persons, properly understood, letting them be, forbids: "This prohibition cannot be reached from the claim that humans are more valuable than other animal species. It can only be derived from a claim of incommensurable value—incommensurable even with the dignity of other human beings." This value is the dignity that attaches to each and every person qua person.[85]

Chapter 16 of *Persons*, "Freedom," clarifies to some extent the sense in which Spaemann takes recognition to be free. He distinguishes two basic stances toward reality: self-assertion and self-transcendence. He goes on to say, "A decision [*Entscheidung*] between these alternative motivations is 'arbitrary' [*grundlos*] in the sense that there is no more basic motivation to account for it, no general [*gemeinsam*, "common"] measure by which one or the other of the two contending forces can be shown to be stronger." And again: "The decision [*Entscheidung*] which of the two motives to follow is a fundamental one. It is not a 'choice' [*Wahl*], since a choice needs a reason [*Grund*]."[86] The decision to recognize the reality of other persons is not a choice among other choices or a selection of one alternative among many but a decision at a more basic level.

Benevolence and Happiness, Continued

Toward the end of chapter 9 of *Happiness and Benevolence* we reach the heart of Spaemann's answer to his original question about happiness and benevolence. Benevolent recognition of other persons is at the core of our own happiness:

> Being is that which reveals itself only to the benevolent. And this self-showing precedes all "Shoulds." It is the gift [*Gabe*] which underlies every possible task [*Aufgabe*]. For the benevolent benevolence itself is a gift. It is *eudaimonia*, the turning-out-well of life, which on the level of simply living and instinct appears to us to be subject to irresolvable antinomies. Only the life which is awakened to reason is capable of such a turning-out-well. Life is awake, if reason is no longer merely an instrument in the service of instinct, but becomes a form of life [*zur Form des Lebens wird*, more literally, "becomes the form of life"].[87]

Life can only turn out well when animal life takes on the form of reason. I take it that the level of life and instinct corresponds to what Spaemann in chapter 6 of *Happiness and Benevolence* called an "empirical concept of happiness" and that the level of reason corresponds to what he called the "transcendental concept of happiness." If we confine our thinking to the level of life and instinct, the antinomy of happiness and benevolence is insoluble. It can only be solved on the level of reason, the level on which we recognize ourselves and others as persons.

Later at the end of chapter 10 of *Happiness and Benevolence*, Spaemann returns to Leibniz: "*Delectatio in felicitate alterius* [delight in the happiness of another]—this formula of Leibniz overcomes the opposition between anthropocentrism and love of nature 'for its own sake.' To love something for its own sake is the specific form of human realization [*menschliche Selbstverwirklichung*, "human self-realization"]."[88]

Implementing Benevolence

As a transcendental fundamental option, that is, as a basic attitude, benevolence is universal.[89] In order to become real, however, it has to become concrete and particular. Supposing that we have awakened to the reality of persons, and that our response is one of benevolence, how are we to live out that benevolence in practice? Spaemann answers that question in chapter 10 of *Happiness and Benevolence*, "*Ordo Amoris*" ("Order of Love" or "Ordering of Love"; the phrase comes from Augustine's *City of God* 15.22, where it is his definition of virtue). Benevolence becomes, or should become, concrete and particular through a graduated order of recipients to whom one is responsible: "The finitude of the agent makes it impossible to make everyone the direct goal of action. *Ordo amoris* means there is a hierarchical order of preference within universal benevolence. It is in reference to this order that we speak of justice."[90] In plainer language, our families, friends, fellow workers, neighbors, and fellow citizens have a stronger claim to be the beneficiaries of our actions than those not so related to us.

Spaemann contrasts this *ordo amoris* with the view that our moral responsibility to every other human being is the same. Kant understood benevolence as impartiality, expressed through universalization. Spaemann's rejection of Kant's impartialism might suggest that he holds that our obligations are limited to a narrow circle of family and friends. In fact, he goes beyond that in at least three respects. He recognizes a political obligation, within the limits of our ability, to try to ensure that everyone enjoys the rights of a citizen somewhere. Alluding to the Gospel of Luke's (10:30–37) parable of the Good Samaritan and to German law, he recognizes that the sheer chance of happening on the scene of an accident can make us responsible to help a victim of the accident: "The Samaritan is a foreigner who comes by chance across a man who needs his help. He is the one who happens to be close by. This situation does not somehow exempt one from the *ordo amoris*; rather it is a case for its application." And he recognizes obligations to nonhuman animals: not to kill them without a good reason, not to inflict unnecessary pain on them.[91]

Spaemann says that Kant and the utilitarians agree, mistakenly, that ethics is fundamentally about norms or rules: "It was Kant's opinion that no one could do more than his duty and everyone must do that. Consequentialists of utilitarian and other varieties arrive at a similar result, when they understand moral duty as a duty of universal optimization. . . . It is common to both conceptions to place imperatives, laws, or norms at the beginning of ethics—an 'ought' [*ein Sollen*] then and not a perception of reality [*eine Wahrnehmung der Wirklichkeit*]."[92]

Another passage from chapter 10 of *Happiness and Benevolence* says more about the implications of the benevolence that arises from the recognition of other persons:

A being, which refers to itself [*Seiendes, das sich auf sich selbst bezieht*, "a being that relates to itself"], is not just relative in its relation to others and in the experience of another, but as finite it is also essentially related to others and real only in this relation. But insofar as it knows this, insofar as it realizes its own relativity and, leaving its own centrality, relativizes itself, it overcomes this relativity and becomes a representation of the absolute. This is what is meant by the dignity of humans. A being which has at its disposal such a virtually moral, that is, absolute, perspective prohibits, by its being, being treated in any instrumental fashion which is not justifiable *to* the person himself, that is, which cannot be seen as the sort of action in which the person puts himself or herself at the service of someone else.

I take it this is what Spaemann means by *Seinlassen*, "letting people be": "But what does 'prohibit' mean here? The prohibition which we speak of is not grounded in some further impersonal 'ought' or an abstract imperative, about which we would have to ask why we ought to subordinate ourselves to it. This prohibition is identical with the perception [*Wahrnehmung*] of [the other's] being a self. Plato's thesis that no one knows the good who does not also want it expresses the actual situation."[93] Here there is no passage from is to ought. The ought of respect does not need to be inferred from the is of personhood. It is already given or disclosed in the is of personhood.

In chapter 11 of *Happiness and Benevolence*, Spaemann criticizes the consequentialist approach to implementing benevolence. The core idea of consequentialism or utilitarianism is that agents are responsible for acting in such a way as to optimize the situation of the whole world. The evaluation of any given action depends on its consequences for the world as a whole, not on what the action is in and of itself. But we cannot carry out the consequentialist calculus of benefits, because we do not know the really long-term consequences of our actions. Worse, thinking of morality as optimization does away with any fixed limits or boundaries (*Grenzen*) on human action, because the global end of a better world can supply an argument to relativize any moral rule—a consequence that no one could want. Finally, consequentialism disregards both the self-being or selfhood (*Selbstsein*) of the agent and the self-being or selfhood of the other. Spaemann takes as an example the consequentialist argument for keeping promises: "Someone keeps a promise, not because he made it and because the person to whom it was made has a claim on its being kept, but rather he keeps it in order to further that advantage for human life which comes about from the general trust in promises being kept." But this view misses something that is essential to promising. Consider the case of a promise that someone made to a person who has since died. On a consequentialist view, "Promises given to someone dying would always be somewhat tenuous, since breaking this promise, if it did not hurt anyone, would be justified by any slight advantage. . . . But this teleological view misses precisely that which constitutes the essence of the ethical, the becoming real of a [personal] reality for the agent. Once the dying person to whom one makes a promise has become real, the subsequent calculus of benefits can only appear as a frivolity."[94]

Consequentialism "cannot provide for something like the construction of an *ordo amoris*. In this kind of thinking the incommensurable self-being of the other is lost. This self-being gets reduced to a mere moment in an imagined totality of goodness. For the agent each individual does not grow more, but rather less, real. The only thing which is real in the full sense of the word is a 'whole,' which is, however, in reality, an abstraction."[95] Consequentialism is not the way to make benevolence concrete.

In chapter 12 of *Happiness and Benevolence*, Spaemann criticizes another attempt to make benevolence concrete: the discourse ethics of Jürgen Habermas. This is an attempt "to operationalize the Kantian concept of practical reason while rendering it less individualistic." Instead of individually consulting their own practical reason in the manner of Kant or Rawls, agents are expected to engage in a discourse of justification with those who are affected by their actions, a discourse in which those affected parties speak and are heard. Participants in the discourse have to have an equal chance to influence its conclusion. They have to be competent to state their own interests. And they have to state their interests honestly and be open to those interests being reformulated in the discourse.[96]

Spaemann's response is that a discourse that meets these three conditions cannot be the ground of morality, because the three conditions already presuppose morality: "When one considers these conditions of ideal discourse, it is easily seen that discourse cannot take over the role of rational self-deliberation, but rather that it presupposes it." Such a discourse presupposes mutual recognition: "That which is decisive has to have already occurred, before discourse begins. We saw this already in the context of the three criteria required for making discourse morally relevant. The whole of morality is already contained in these criteria. A mutual recognition of the participants in the discourse underlies every discourse.

The more real they are to each other, the more relevant the discourse but, at the same time, the less necessary, since precisely this recognition was the decisive step, from which the rest followed."[97]

The Sense in Which Nature Is Normative

Spaemann believes that nature gives a norm for human action. What does that mean? It does not mean taking nature, natural drives, or natural processes as grounding moral obligations. In chapter 8 of *Persons*, Spaemann maintains that nature is not and cannot be the source of morality or obligations. Since human persons are not identical with their human nature, but rather *have* their nature and are capable of making decisions about whether to follow its drives, that nature cannot be ultimately normative. There is no question of moral obligation until reason steps in to consider the facts of nature and determine what to do about them: "A person has a nature, nature does not have a person. Human activity is not prescribed by the system of human instincts. Precisely for this reason nature as such has no normative significance for human beings."[98] We could know everything there is to know about human biology and that would not tell us what we ought to do or why we ought to do it. There is thus no question of an inference from what happens in nature to what human beings ought or ought not to do.

Why, then, should human beings submit to their nature? "Religion gives us one answer to this question: nature is not the last horizon, but something we 'have.' Taken as a whole, nature is 'creation,' and its teleological structures allow us to discern the creator's will for humankind. Nothing less than a personal will can be the source of normative 'natural right' for persons."[99]

In what sense *is* nature normative? Chapter 14 of *Happiness and Benevolence*, "Normality and Naturalness" ("Normalität und Natürlichkeit"), gives Spaemann's answer.[100] There he explains what he means by "nature," "normality," "the natural," and that which is "right by nature" and defends these concepts against a variety of misunderstandings and objections. He recalls the debate about nature (*phusis*) and convention (*nomos*) among the Greeks. The Greek sophists criticized the laws and customs of the Greek cities in their day as merely conventional. Plato and

Aristotle—he sees the two as taking essentially the same position on this issue—reject the sophistic antithesis between the natural and the conventional, between a supposedly asocial human nature and artificial social conventions. They make the concept of nature the basis of a new ethics and a new theory of culture. Nature, as known by reason, provides a standard against which human practices can be measured and some conventions judged to be more in line with nature than others.[101]

Spaemann then examines three arguments against taking nature or the natural as a standard for moral judgment. The first is that nature is simply irrelevant to morality. Nature is a necessary condition for subjectivity and freedom, but it cannot and does not tell us what to do with our freedom. And if, instead, nature has already determined action, then it is not morally relevant either. The second argument Spaemann calls "physicalistic" [*physikalistisch*]: everything is nature—Voltaire has nature say, *Je suis le grand tout*, "I am everything there is"—nothing is unnatural, and the unnatural is same as the impossible. Again, nature gives no guidance about what we should or should not do. The third argument is cultural-anthropological: morality is not a matter of natural instincts but of culture or second nature; as such, it transcends human nature and cannot be measured against it.[102]

The three arguments are closely related. The first posits the antithesis of is and ought. The second argument affirms the is and negates the ought: everything is nature, nature is everything, and that is all there is to it. The third argument affirms the ought but negates the is: nature is simply material for human activity, and so cannot be the measure of that activity; there is no such thing as a natural *telos*. All three arguments take for granted a modern mechanistic conception of nature. Spaemann concedes that nature, if understood in that sense, is irrelevant to ethics.[103]

The second and third arguments appear opposed, but together they give rise to the two poles of the modern understanding of the human being: naturalism (a reduction of the human to its material dimension) and what Spaemann calls "spiritualism" and what others might call "angelism" (a denial or neglect of the material dimension of the human). One and the same consciousness looks on nature as an object for it to manipulate and looks on itself as one more natural object to be manipulated:

Only one thing is never to occur within the framework of the modern Weltanschauung: Nature is never to have a spiritual dimension, [n]or is spirit to have a natural one. The ethics which come out of such a civilization are either utilitarian or consequentialistic. For these kinds of ethics there is no intrinsic rightness and certainly no intrinsic falsity [*Falschheit*, "wrongness"] in actions. . . . In principle, the prohibition against torture, against cheating, or the breaking of promises is not different in kind from the prohibition against crossing the street on red. There is no inner nature of action, which limits the universal and preposterous command of optimization.[104]

The classical view of nature distinguishes the natural, or the normal in an evaluative sense, from the statistically normal: "If 90 percent of all people were to have headaches, they would not therefore be the healthy by which the other 10 percent had to measure themselves, but the reverse. For headaches are opposed to that natural tendency to self-preservation and well-being which is characteristic of all natural beings."[105]

The classical view thinks of nature by analogy with human beings' experience of themselves: their nature asserting itself, realizing its own drives, in the context of an environment. Our nature as human beings is to "be out for" (*Aussein auf*) things. This "'being out for' is experienced by us as something which underlies all self-consciousness and all conscious positing of goals, that is, it is experienced by us as something natural."[106]

How, then, is nature in the classical sense supposed to be relevant to morality and ethics? The key terms in Spaemann's answer are "drive" or "appetite" (*Trieb*) and "reason." In the case of humans, appetite is more than a brute fact, a pure is as opposed to an ought:

The position appetite holds vis-à-vis our acting is not at all describable by the "Is-Ought" schema. On the one hand, human action is not simply an event of the appetites. Rather, action begins at that point where we control ourselves as regards our appetites and do not simply hand ourselves over to them. . . . Hunger does not necessitate eating. Still, hunger is not a neutral fact which stands in need of a further premise in order to become a reason for acting. . . . An appetite distinguishes itself from other facts in that it itself already has a vectorial character. It propels, it makes one inclined (*inclinatio*), and that means it is itself a reason for the actions which serve to satisfy it.[107]

Appetite does not simply cause action. It gives a reason to act, but not necessarily a sufficient reason. Hunger gives us a reason to eat, but there may also be a reason not to eat. Action begins at the point where we interpret appetite and make decisions about it. This interpretation and decision is the work of reason. Appetite is only a sufficient reason to act when we accept it as such: "On the one hand, the self-preservation of a free being is, for the most part, guaranteed by powerful drives, while on the other hand, it is constantly tied to free acts, to eating and drinking, which, as opposed to breathing, do not occur 'by nature,' that is, by themselves. *Inclinatio* is not *necessitas* [Inclination is not necessity]." Nature and its appetites are distinct from reason but not opposed to reason. Actions like eating and drinking are taken into culture and remade. They are central to culture, but also inseparable from their basic natural functions. Culture is not nature abrogated but nature humanized.[108]

Some people, Spaemann says, object to the idea of natural moral law that humans are rational by nature, and that the proper standard of action is not nature but reason. But this antithesis between a law of nature and a law of reason is misconceived: "I have tried to show that nature first becomes aware of itself as reason. The law of nature does not consist in obeying non-human nature. . . . One could put it pointedly by saying that only in rational action does the concept of the natural fully come into its own." The norm of action is nature, but nature only as noticed and taken up by reason.[109]

Reason does not, however, take the place of nature. Respect for human beings means respect for *what* they are: "In this, their nature, humans have to be respected, if they are to be respected at all; in this, their nature, they and their dignity are vulnerable [*verletzbar*]. One cannot spit in someone's face and then maintain that one did not intend to affect him as a person."[110]

A common objection to the natural moral law is that it involves an unjustified inference from the facts of nature to moral obligation. That is not the kind of natural moral law that Spaemann is talking about. Nature, he says, only has tendencies, appetites. Nature does not of itself produce an ought. Nature only becomes a source of moral insights when someone takes distance from it and recognizes it in freedom. The recognition of another natural being as a self is not something that happens by nature. So far as nature is concerned, the agent is the center; everything else is just environment. It is only by reason that we step out of the center and recognize the other: "This stepping out of the center position in one's own experience does not cause the natural to disappear, but allows it to make its appearance. One's own nature as well as that of other persons comes forth. To respect others as persons means to affirm them *in their nature*." Reason, not nature, is the ground of respect and benevolence. But the nature of human beings gives respect and benevolence their content.[111]

Action, Responsibility, Conscience

In chapter 13 of *Happiness and Benevolence*, "Action or Functioning within a System?" ("Handlung und Systemfunktion"), Spaemann criticizes what he calls the "system-theoretical interpretation of action," that is, the view that human actions have the function of stabilizing and promoting the survival of social systems. Spaemann's concern about system-functional interpretations goes back to his dissertation on Bonald. He does not object to the claim that human action has effects on social systems. What he opposes is any suggestion that humans should adopt the functional interpretation of action as their own interpretation of what they are doing: "In such a view the unconditioned aspect of morality also becomes obsolete. At most it gets reduced to an *optio fundamentalis* [a fundamental option], a purely mental attitude of benevolence, which never quite finds empirical embodiment, but instead leads to the demand for behavior which is in keeping with the system in some autonomous practical field." Human actions have what Spaemann calls an "absolute or unconditioned character." They, or some of them, are done because they are good in and of themselves, not simply to achieve other goods. The functional or system-theoretical interpretation denies human action this unconditioned character.[112]

For present purposes, however, chapter 13 is important not so much for its criticism of the system-theoretical interpretation of action as for its account of action (*Handlung*) itself. Spaemann's account of action is in key respects Thomistic. He does not say so, but his account of action in this chapter is close to Aquinas's account in *Summa theologiae* I-II, qq. 18–21.[113] Human action involves the behavior itself, the agent's intention, the circumstances, the means employed, and the consequences. Evaluation of an action has to take all these factors into account. Consequentialism errs by focusing on consequences to the neglect of intentions:

> To judge actions only according to their consequences means not to view them as actions at all but as a kind of natural occurrence. To act means to pick out from the infinite number of consequences certain ones as "purposes," in relationship to which the others are reduced to secondary consequences. Further, there are those secondary consequences for which we bear responsibility and others which escape all possible foresight. To judge an action as an action, that is, to judge it morally, does not mean to measure it directly by the totality of its consequences, but to judge it in light of the agent's perception of responsibility for the consequences, that is, how the agent subjectively took account of the objective content of his or her action.[114]

This may sound subjectivist, but it is Spaemann's way of making Aquinas's point that an action takes its *species*, its what-it-is, from what the agent is trying to accomplish. Intention is what makes a piece of behavior the kind of action that it is.[115]

Spaemann is not advocating a morality of intentions apart from consequences. His rejection of consequentialism does not exempt agents from responsibility for the consequences of their actions. He knows perfectly well that the whole point of action is to make a difference in the world. He thinks, however, that a major task of ethics is distinguishing those consequences for which we are responsible from those for which we are not responsible: "In a certain sense the problem of our actions' secondary consequences is the central theme of all normative ethics. . . . Only pure evil, 'diabolical' evil, has evil as evil, the bad as bad for its goal. Normally, evil consists in inattention to, or surreptitiously looking away from, what we bring about and accept. We cannot make all the consequences of our actions the center of our attention, even if we tried. Selection through the focusing of our attention belongs to the essence of finite action."[116]

Spaemann fills out this essentially Thomistic view of action in chapter 11 of *Persons*, "Independence of Context." There he defends two analogies between truth-claims and human actions, both of which echo the Thomistic analysis. The first analogue: as each and every truth-claim in a conjunction is true or false on its own, quite apart from the truth or falsity of the other claims, so each and every human action is good or bad in itself, quite apart from the goodness or badness of the agent's other actions. Human action is not simply a moment in a continuum of action. On the contrary, persons are present as wholes in each of their actions, that is, each and every action is an action of the whole person.[117]

Spaemann's second analogy: "Just as every statement that incorporates a false assertion is false, so an action is wrong if one of its constituent elements is not right: a wrong place, a wrong time, a failure to consider circumstances, an immoral motive, or, indeed, a type of action wrong in itself such that no context could right it. A sentence of Pseudo-Dionysius which Thomas Aquinas quoted more than fifty times sums up the point exactly: 'good arises from a consistent cause, evil from any kind of fault' [*bonum ex integra causa, malum ex quocumque defectu*]."[118] Spaemann's differences with Kantianism and consequentialism are basically differences about the understanding of action: Kantianism focuses on intention, consequentialism on consequences, each to the neglect of other aspects of action.

Chapter 15 of *Happiness and Benevolence*, "Responsibility," extends and in places clarifies the arguments of chapter 9, "Benevolence," and chapter 10, "*Ordo Amoris*." Spaemann reaffirms that benevolence is a response not to an imperative but to an awareness of reality:

> One cannot deduce benevolence from some imperative. It precedes and grounds every moral imperative. But this does not mean that all moral obligation and every moral norm is grounded in an ultimately irrational, absurd, subjective "option." Benevolence is not some absurd option, but the result of a perception, the perception of reality as self-being [*Wahrnehmung der Wirklichkeit als Selbstsein*, "taking account of reality as selfhood"]. Whoever has had this perception finds himself in a peculiar, paradoxical situation. On the one hand, he understands that it is not he himself who grounds this, his own

perception. That would be as if this perception were preceded by something like a moral decision [*sittlicher Entschluß*], when in fact every moral decision is grounded in this perception. He can only understand it as a gift, and indeed as a gift whose absence implies that humans have not yet awakened to being human, that, in spite of all their intelligence, they still dream.[119]

This awareness of personal reality is not, however, something optional for human beings: "Whether we perceive the reality of the real is not only *our* affair; it is a *demand* [*Anspruch*] placed upon us, and we bear responsibility for whether we meet this responsibility or not. Our actions are true or false [*richtig oder falsch*, "right or wrong"] depending upon whether they meet this responsibility or not."[120]

Given the benevolent recognition of other selves, morality in the narrower sense is a matter of dealing responsibly with their reality, that is, acting in a way that takes account of their teleological natures, of what benefits them and what harms them: "For the duty to provide welfare [*Fürsorge*, "care for"], which comes from the perception of reality, grounds duties to act too. One can only speak of responsibility and welfare in reference to a being whose character is teleological by nature, that is, one for whom what occurs has a meaning."[121]

Talk about perception of the other might suggest a neutral awareness of facts to which one might remain indifferent. Spaemann rejects this interpretation, especially in the case of suffering: "Real perception of suffering is not possible in the form of merely neutral observation. It is always connected with an attitude, be it connected with the tendency to alleviate or to do away with the suffering or to be with the sufferer, or be it connected with the opposed tendency not to do just these things. The merely neutral 'taking cognizance' of pain is in reality an act which is opposed to rational benevolence."[122]

Once we are aware of other persons as persons, we realize that we are responsible to them, that we have to be willing to justify to them those of our actions that affect them:

> Responsibility presupposes . . . a "to whom," an addressee, someone who can both demand accountability and be open to reasons. The

only beings we know who demand such accountability are humans. And it is not just other humans who make this demand, but ourselves too. That part of ourselves which demands an interior discourse of justification and is above making deals, we call the conscience. But conscience is not a monological device [*Instanz,* "an authority," especially a court] which releases us from the duty of accountability to others. On the contrary, it is the readiness to give an account in principle [*Bereitschaft . . . prinzipiell Rechenschaft zu Geben,* "readiness in principle to give an account"] to everyone who is affected by our action that renders the claim of one's own conscience credible and distinguishable from arbitrariness or private ideology.[123]

When Spaemann denies that conscience is a monological authority, his point is that conscience is not an oracle. The utterances of an oracle demand to be accepted without question. Not so with conscience: conscience intends truth, and for this reason it can err. What conscience says requires justification and is open to argument.

Being Mindful of Nature

Spaemann talks about being mindful of nature. What does this amount to in practice? In what I have read, he does not answer this question in general terms. The answer has to be gathered from examples that he gives in the latter part of chapter 14 of *Happiness and Benevolence* and elsewhere. The correct interpretation of these examples is not always clear, and my proposed interpretations are correspondingly tentative.

One example of a practice in line with nature is the way in which the human drive to eat and drink has been taken up into the meal: the meal with family, the meal with friends, the marriage feast, even the religious or sacramental meal. The natural function of eating and drinking receives human meaning.[124] Here being mindful of nature would seem to mean bearing in mind how the natural drive to eat has provided the raw material for a variety of meaningful and valuable activities.

Another example of how humanity and naturalness are connected comes from human sexuality and its relationship to the preservation of the species. As Spaemann sees it, human sexuality has been integrated into a personal relationship by a humane and personal remaking. Systematic detachment of sexual pleasure from passing on human life would take away its specifically human dimension: "Whether in the long run the perpetuation of the human race will be assured when it is uncoupled from the satisfaction of the sexual drive, no one can yet say. . . . the systematic detachment of sexual pleasure from the natural context of its function of passing on human life would rob love between the sexes of its specifically human dimension."[125] Here being mindful of nature would seem to mean reading the natural connection between sexual intercourse and procreation as an indication that maintaining the connection safeguards an important human value.

Spaemann then considers the possibility that some future state might seek to ensure the survival of the species by means of artificial reproduction: "One has to make clear to oneself that test-tube reproduction differs from begetting in that it is an action which is a rational means for a goal, a *poiesis* [making, production], and not the natural consequence of relations between humans. . . . A manufactured child, one that comes into being by *poiesis*, is a creature of its parents or of the doctor or of the state in a qualitatively different way from the child which owes its existence 'to nature.'"[126] Spaemann thinks that there may be a sufficient reason not to have a child, but that there is no sufficient reason to have a child. Having a child is not something that someone does for a reason. The existence of a subject for which reasons are reasons cannot be further grounded by other subjects: "The natural growth [*Naturwüchsigkeit*] of the human and the dignity of the human are indissolubly connected."[127] Here being mindful of nature would seem to mean realizing that departing from the natural way of having children may amount to harming or disrespecting persons in their natures.[128]

An important and controversial example of how Spaemann sees the relation between nature and reason concerns the criteria for when a natural being is to be respected as a person. His position is subtle and may appear paradoxical. Spaemann denies that nature of itself gives rise to obligation. Human beings do not deserve respect simply because they belong to the species *Homo sapiens*. They deserve respect because they are persons, that is, rational, potentially moral beings capable of self-determination, beings that can step out of the center and accept the reasonable demands of

others. Some have concluded from this that only human beings who actually exhibit these characteristics are persons and that they alone deserve
respect.[129]

Spaemann strongly resists this inference. Human beings typically
exhibit those characteristics of persons, but those human beings who do
not exhibit them are nonetheless persons: "Who defines where [*wo*, "at
what point"] the human being begins to be a person? In the Aristotelian
tradition the answer was readily available. One concludes from that which
a species 'usually' displays to that which is the essence of a thing of this
kind. From a healthy, adult human one can read off what the essence of
human is, the essence of even those in whom this essential does not show
itself. The essence, which often but not always shows itself, is that which
we call the 'soul.' The soul has to be respected even in those in which it
remains concealed."[130]

Spaemann acknowledges that this line of thought rests on controversial metaphysical presuppositions (that members of a species share a common essence, that normal instances of a species indicate what that essence
is), but he adds that it can also be given what he calls a "transcendental-
pragmatic justification." Genuine human rights are only possible if no one
is entitled to pass judgment on which human beings have those rights. If
human rights make any sense, it is on the presupposition that each human
being enters society on the basis of his or her own claim, as a member of
the species, not because someone else admits him or her. We only have
recognition of the self as such when the person is recognized on the basis
of what he or she is by nature, a human being, not on the basis of fulfill-
ing some other criterion set up by someone else. To set any temporal
boundary for the initial recognition of a human being as a person ("the
developing human being only becomes a person when") would be arbitrary and tyrannical.[131] In this case, then, being mindful of nature would
seem to mean remembering that membership in the human species is the
only defensible criterion we have to determine who is a person and who
deserves respect.

Chapter 14 of *Happiness and Benevolence* gives three other examples
of being mindful of nature. Spaemann argues that torture is naturally
wrong, not simply because it inflicts pain, but because it is an attempt to
make a person abdicate as a free subject. He sees the infliction of torture

as quite different from threatening someone with punishment or death but leaving the choice up to the person: "Above all torture is completely irreconcilable with respect for human persons as persons, not because it hinders them from harmful action, for this hindrance can be necessary, but because it forces them to abdication as free subjects, it reduces them to instinctual beings and wants [*will*: here perhaps "tries"] to beat them down to a subhuman kind of reaction. To affect the body of a human always means to affect a human."[132] Here being mindful of nature would seem to mean remembering that a human person is both reason and nature and that a certain kind of attack on a person's body amounts to an attempt to destroy the person as a subject.

Spaemann argues that feeding a human being against his or her will is wrong: "It cannot be compatible with respect for humans as the subjects of freedom to force nourishment on them against their express will and thereby to make the physical sustenance of humans an affair of external coercion, since this sustenance is by nature a result of free action."[133] To treat human nature in that way is to violate the dignity of a human person. Here being mindful of nature would seem to mean remembering that the things human beings do in response to natural drives are of their nature things that they do freely.

Spaemann also argues that genetic manipulation of human nature is wrong, because human bodies are not simply instruments belonging to subjects. Human beings do not simply *have* their bodies. No, they *are* their bodies. Their bodies are not objects for them to manipulate: "The dignity of the human is inseparably connected with its natural spontaneity. . . . To come to the aid of humans means to come to the aid of natural beings, who are what they are. It does not mean to make something else out of them."[134] In this case it would seem that being mindful of nature means remembering that a human being is both reason and life, not a pure spirit using a body, and mistrusting any proposal for action that disregards this fact about human beings.

The last few pages of "Die Aktualität des Naturrechts" ("The Contemporary Relevance of Natural Right") give three more examples of what Spaemann means by being mindful of nature or, as he calls it there, "natural right thinking."

The first is respect for the environment. In opposition to the utopian view that damage to the environment can always be remedied by further technological interventions, natural right requires that human freedom respect its natural conditions, including the environment. Natural right thinking does not yield a list of prescriptions and prohibitions, but it adopts a certain style or procedure for thinking about environmental issues, namely, to shift the burden of the argument to the side of those who favor expansionist measures.[135] Here being mindful of nature would seem to mean having a presumption in favor of what happens naturally, placing the burden of proof on the party that proposes to tamper with it.

A second application goes against genetic manipulation. Spaemann's argument here is different from the argument in *Happiness and Benevolence*. We cannot legitimately make the biological form of future human beings the object of our own willing, because we lack legitimate criteria to do so.[136] Again, the burden of the argument falls on those who want to manipulate nature, and in this case Spaemann finds that the burden cannot be met. Here being mindful of nature would seem to mean having a presumption in favor of what happens naturally, absent a clear case in favor of change. The burden of proof lies with the party proposing to interfere with what happens naturally.

A third application concerns how to determine who is a subject of rights and duties. One approach would be to base that judgment on someone's contribution to society. On that approach, if the Indians of the Amazon Basin make no contribution to Brazil, they have no claim to recognition, and the Brazilians are free to exterminate them. A second approach would accord recognition on the basis of possessing reason and freedom, thus excluding the unborn, the very young, and the mentally ill. But it would be circular to take freedom as the criterion for recognition as a person. Freedom is not a bare fact independent of recognition. Human beings only develop freedom when they have first been recognized. A third approach would take membership in the human biological species as the criterion for recognition. Spaemann does not try to validate this approach directly, as he does in the last chapter of *Persons*, but he argues that it is at least not open to the objections that lie against the first and the second approaches.[137] Here being mindful of nature would seem to mean having a presumption in favor of biological humanity as the criterion of personhood and a critical attitude with respect to proposed alternative criteria.[138]

Implications for Education

The above summary of Spaemann's ethics has left out much that is important in *Happiness and Benevolence*, and even more of what is important in *Persons*, in order to bring out the main lines of his ethics. It remains to say a few words about his conception of education, because this is closely connected with his conception of ethics.

In what I have read of his work, Spaemann has little to say about the liberal arts and higher education. He does, however, have definite ideas about a more basic level of education. Two citations from *Basic Ethical Concepts* will convey the essentials of his view. The first is from chapter 3, "Education: Self-interest and a Sense of Values":

> Education is the name we give to the process whereby a human being is led out of the animal preoccupation with self to a state where he is able to be objective about his own interests and differentiate between them, in such a way that his capacity to experience joy and pain is increased. It is often said nowadays that the job of education is to teach young people how to stand up for their own interests. Yet there is a much more fundamental task which is to teach people how to *have* interests, that is to say, how to be interested in something. If all a person has learnt is how to stand up for his own interests, but [he] is interested in nothing apart from himself, there is no way that person can be happy. Therefore education, in the sense that it develops interests of an objective nature, and leads to an appreciation of the value content of reality, is an essential element of successful living.[139]

Spaemann follows up on this in chapter 4 of *Basic Moral Concepts*, "Justice: Myself and Others":

> Right living, as we saw in the previous chapters, means dealing fairly with reality. In other words, we should be objective about our own interests and allow them to be formed by the value content of reality.

Education, as we saw, should make us capable of freeing ourselves from the domination of the stimulus of the moment, and enable us to do what we really want to do. We should learn to live our own lives rather than having them lived for us. The object of education should be to disclose the value content of reality and develop a diversity of objective interests. Only then, by being objective about our interests and our wishes, in a way that implies that we should acknowledge universal standards, will we be able to compare those interests with one another, and only then will it be possible for us to come to terms with competing interests, both those within ourselves and those involving other people.[140]

Implications for Politics

Spaemann has much more to say about political theory, most notably in *Zur Kritik der politischen Utopie*, and about contemporary politics, most notably in the second half of *Grenzen*, than I have been able to capture in this summary of his ethics. But the following passage from chapter 15 of *Persons* says much about his political outlook. One of the conditions for political institutions to be legitimate is that

> they should afford real protection to the personal status of each human being within the sphere of their institutional power—which is what it means to be a "state." The relational sphere of personal interaction is universal; from which it follows that the exclusion of even one person from the scheme of recognition brings the personal character of the whole system tumbling down. This occurs . . . the moment any qualitative criteria are imposed, over and above bare membership in the human race, for recognizing a someone as a someone and for co-opting him or her into the community of persons. A political system that imposes such restrictions loses its juridical character and its claim to loyalty. From that point on we can deal with it only through canny calculation [*Klugheitsregeln*, "maxims of prudence"].[141]

Given Spaemann's conviction that all human beings without exception are persons, he would have to judge that many, if not most, contemporary states have already forfeited their legitimacy.

REVISITING ANGLO-AMERICAN MORAL PHILOSOPHY

In chapter 1, we identified a series of overlapping problems that beset Anglo-American ethics in the years 1950 to 1990: (1) the competing claims of deontological and teleological ethics, especially Kantian and utilitarian ethics; (2) the claims of egoism and altruism; (3) the claims of naturalism, intuitionism, and noncognitivism in metaethics; (4) the relations between fact and value; and (5) the challenges of relativism and skepticism. Without suggesting that Spaemann set out to solve these problems precisely as posed, or that he would think success in doing so to be the standard by which his work is to be judged, I find that he addresses them in a number of different ways.

Spaemann's ethics is teleological. He takes the desire for happiness, the desire to make a success of one's life, to be fundamental. Any ethics that did not find a place for this desire would be unmotivated, unable to answer the question, "Why should I do that?" He is strongly critical of what he calls "teleological ethics," but the target of his criticism is utilitarianism or consequentialism, not teleological ethics or eudaimonistic ethics as such. At the same time, Spaemann's ethics is deontological. He regards the benevolent recognition of other persons as a fundamental human experience and the moral obligation to respect other persons, to let them be (*Seinlassen*), as unconditional. The central task of ethics, as he sees it, is to clarify this unconditional experience. This is not to ground it on anything more fundamental, but to show that it is the ground on which we already stand.

Spaemann's ethics thus combines teleological and deontological elements. How precisely to do that has been one of the standard problems of Anglo-American moral philosophy. Spaemann's response in *Happiness and Benevolence* is that our benevolent recognition of other persons is not only compatible with the pursuit of our own happiness but is at the very least a necessary condition for our happiness or (if I am reading chapter 9 correctly) even constitutive of our happiness. Our happiness actually *re-quires* that each of us acknowledge the reality of other selves and of their claims upon us. Spaemann agrees with Kant that persons have dignity and that they owe one another respect, but he holds that according them this respect is not only compatible with, but even required for, our own happiness.

Following Aquinas, Spaemann distinguishes an action itself from the intention behind it, its circumstances, the means employed, and its consequences. For an action to be good, it has to be good in all of these ways, not just good in its consequences: *Bonum ex integra causa, malum ex quocumque defectu,* "good arises from a consistent cause, evil from any kind of fault." Kantian ethics is mistaken insofar as it focuses exclusively on intentions. Utilitarianism is mistaken insofar as it focuses exclusively on consequences. Further, the utilitarian account of moral responsibility is mistaken. The reason why I am responsible for keeping a promise is not that promise-keeping benefits the human race in the long term, but that I made a promise to a fellow human being.

Spaemann regards unrestricted egoism as self-defeating. It would mean renouncing happiness, because it would mean renouncing friendship. This is the lesson he draws from Epicurus: to be happy one must have good friends; to have good friends, one must be a good friend. He recognizes that people can and do have conflicting interests. He regards the notion that all interests can be harmonized and all conflicts avoided as a dangerous error.[142] What he requires is that each person be willing to relativize his or her own interests. To relativize one's interests does not mean to abandon them. It means to subject them to judgment by norms of justice. As he puts it in *Basic Moral Concepts*, justice considers *what* interests are at stake, not *whose* interests they are.[143]

Spaemann's position is not altruistic in any ordinary or obvious sense of the term. He regards ethics as the study of how to make one's life turn out well. At the same time, he thinks that sacrificing one's own interests may be good or even required, depending on circumstances. By this he means not that self-sacrifice is required by some abstract norm—no abstract norm has power to oblige—but that it may be required by respect for another person or persons. For example, someone who is ordered to kill an innocent person may not kill the person and must accept the consequences of refusing to do so. That does not, however, mean accepting responsibility for things that other people do in response to that refusal.[144]

Spaemann does not have much to say about metaethics as such. (In one instance he even applies the term "metaethics" to what appears to be metaethical relativism.) Spaemann uses the German word *Intuition*, but there is no reason to think that he takes goodness to be a nonnatural property or that his metaethics is intuitionist. He shows no sympathy whatsoever for noncognitivist metaethics. His position would seem, then, to be a form of naturalism in which the ground of moral obligation is someone's status as a person, while the content of moral obligation derives from that person's animal nature. This is the sense in which Spaemann takes nature to be normative: not that human nature as such gives rise to moral obligation, but that, once a human being has recognized another human being as a person, that person's human nature spells out what treating them with benevolence requires.

Spaemann is well aware of the passage in Hume's *Treatise* that highlights the passage from is to ought, from fact to obligation. He recognizes that facts, at least some facts, do not entail values or obligations. As he says, a textbook in evolutionary biology may conclude with a plea that we act to preserve endangered species, but the facts in the textbook do not ground any such obligation. At the same time, he takes a teleological view of nature, including human nature with its drives. Drives are not purely neutral facts. Being hungry is a prima facie reason to eat. There may be good reasons not to eat, but hunger, in and of itself, is a reason to eat. And if someone who is hungry comes to me, their hunger is a prima facie reason why I should give them something to eat. No further premise is required. If I see another human being in pain, that pain is a sufficient reason to go to that person's assistance. Someone who recognized that another person was in pain, but received that information with indifference or asked for a reason why they should help the person, would be failing to respect the other person. Respect for persons, Spaemann insists, is always respect for them in their animal natures.

Spaemann criticizes the attempt to argue from the fact of moral disagreement to the truth of ethical relativism. The extent of disagreement, though real and important, is narrower than it is often thought to be. The very fact that the differing parties argue with one another suggests that they assume that there is some truth to be had. And ethical relativism is in fact incompatible with the convictions of the vast majority of ethical agents. More fundamentally, Spaemann sees moral relativism not as a position within philosophical ethics but as an abstention from the enterprise of philosophical ethics.

Spaemann's responses to ethical skepticism are few and far between. He is doing philosophical ethics, not debating whether or not to do philosophical ethics. To my mind, his most telling response to skepticism comes in the foreword to *Happiness and Benevolence*: "The question, Why be moral?, would . . . be incapable of a reasoned answer. . . . One cannot demand to hear reasons why one should listen to reasons."[145]

Spaemann's ethics is informed by a nuanced reading of Western philosophy. This is not a history of decline contrasting the errors of modernity with the wisdom of the ancients and medievals. Modernity improves on the ancients and medievals in many important respects. Modernity's Achilles' heel, however, is the abandonment of natural teleology, with the consequent misunderstanding of the human person and the resulting distortions of Kantian and utilitarian ethics. The abandonment of teleology was not simply modernity's mistake. It had roots in ancient and medieval Christianity.[146] But it is high time to set matters straight by recovering natural teleology and incorporating it into modernity, thus safeguarding modernity against its own liability to degenerate into the radical emancipation that Spaemann sees in the Marquis de Sade, Nazism, Skinner's behaviorism, and other contemporary trends.

SPAEMANN'S APPROPRIATION OF ARISTOTLE

I have called Spaemann's position a personalist Aristotelianism. The term "personalism" has two main senses. In the first and more basic sense, it is the view that the human person ought to be an important subject of philosophical reflection, even the starting point of philosophical reflection, or the central focus of philosophical reflection, or both. It is in this sense that the Scottish personalist John Macmurray spoke of "the form of the personal" as the key philosophical problem of his time.[147] In a second sense, personalism means an insistence on the fundamental and inalienable dignity of persons. It is in the service of this ethical and political commitment that Emmanuel Mounier issued his *Personalist Manifesto* and Jacques Maritain distinguished between the individual who is subject to the political order and the person whose good transcends the political order.[148] Spaemann's ethics is clearly personalist in both of these senses.

One might, however, accept the adjective "personalist" but wonder about the noun "Aristotelianism." Spaemann's position has clearly been influenced by Christian tradition. His analysis of action is largely Thomistic. His emphasis on human dignity echoes Kant. His emphasis on interpersonal recognition echoes Hegel. What exactly is Aristotelian about Spaemann's position?

Spaemann's Aristotelianism is pervasive but unobtrusive. First and most basically, he takes his conception of ethics from Aristotle. He takes for granted a common moral consciousness as the starting point for ethics. Like Aristotle, Spaemann does not try to prove this moral consciousness against skeptical objection. He alludes sympathetically to the point that Aristotle makes at *Topics* 1.11, 105a5–7 ("those who wonder whether we must honor the gods and love our parents need punishment" rather than argument) and in a different way at *Metaphysics* 4.5, 1009a17–18 ("some need persuasion, others need force"). Ethical reflection can and should defend common moral consciousness against relativism, sophistry, and misunderstandings of the human being. Here Spaemann is close to what Aristotle says at *Nicomachean Ethics* 7.1, 1145b6–7, that if the difficulties are solved and the common beliefs are preserved, that is enough by way of proof. He sees the arguments of ethics as largely ad hominem, directed to particular persons holding particular positions. This approach parallels Aristotle's defense of the principles of noncontradiction and excluded middle in *Metaphysics* 4.4–8.

Spaemann's eudaimonism is Aristotelian. Ethical reflection can never neglect the natural human desire for a successful life, for happiness. Any ethics that tried to disregard or prescind from the desire for happiness would be unmotivated. It would offer us an ought without a want. Recognition of other persons, of course, places limits on our pursuit of happiness. We cannot treat anyone purely as a means. But the pursuit of happiness never disappears.

Spaemann's anthropology is also Aristotelian. He affirms the natural teleology of living things, including human beings. Whatever else they may be, human beings are animals with natures, inbuilt tendencies to develop and realize themselves in certain ways. Recognition of a person is recognition of a being with such a nature. Respect for a person is respect for him or her in that nature. Benevolence toward a person is, first of all, letting that person be in his or her human nature and then doing what helps or promotes the development of that nature. Any kind of angelism or spiritualism, any Platonic or Cartesian dualism, obscures the reality of human beings and distorts what it means to respect them.

Spaemann thinks that human beings, because they have reason, *have* their natures. That is, they can make decisions about their natural drives and inclinations. Reason stands over and above human nature in a way that may seem foreign to Aristotle, or to Aristotle as commonly understood. Is this conception of how reason relates to nature Aristotelian?

Spaemann finds this conception in Aristotle himself. I refer to his allusions to Aristotle's remark in *On the Generation of Animals* 2.3, 736b27–28, that intellect (*nous*) alone comes into human beings from outside (*thurathen*).[149] At the beginning of chapter 8 of *Happiness and Benevolence*, Spaemann seems to agree with Aristotle on this point: "Reason and life behave in an antagonistic manner toward each other. . . . even Aristotle could not understand reason simply as a capacity of living beings called humans; rather he saw it as something which comes in 'from the outside.' Why? Because reason is the one human capacity which allows us, so to speak, to see ourselves with the eyes of others, that is, from outside ourselves. Put more exactly, it allows us to know that there exists a view from the eyes of others, whose perspective is not that of the living being which we ourselves are."[150] In "The Natural and the Rational," he also seems to agree with Aristotle: "One can indeed construct a natural history of *amor benevolentiae* [love of benevolence] that can only get at the idea of love by approximation. Yet in the end a leap will always be required, a dramatic *volte face*, even if it is barely noticeable empirically or physically. As Aristotle says, when all is said and done, reason comes 'from outside' (*thyrathen*)."[151]

In chapter 13 of *Persons*, however, reflecting on Aquinas's view of the unity of the human soul and the Council of Chalcedon's (451) affirmation that Jesus Christ has not just a human soul but a human mind or spirit, he writes: "A man, so their argument [the argument of the church fathers at Chalcedon] went, is only a man if he has a *human* spirit [*Geist*], for the spirit is constitutive for the specific humanity of the human soul [*Seele*]. If reason enters man, as Aristotle claimed, 'from outside,' it follows that reason is not a vital function of the soul. If it is part of the soul, however, it makes human existence rational in its totality."[152] Here Spaemann seems to be siding with Chalcedon against Aristotle. But he goes on to say that the position taken at Chalcedon had an unintended and unfortunate consequence—the abolition of soul in the Aristotelian sense of that term:

> The soul found itself caught in a kind of pincer-movement. From one side came all the weight the Christian tradition laid on the spirituality and immortality of the soul; talk about animal souls looked like equivocation, where for Aristotle soul had been the common factor linking man and beast. From the other side, the new natural science and philosophy of the sixteenth century dismissed belief in animal souls as heterodoxy. The functioning of living organisms, it was asserted, could be understood without the Aristotelian form-principle. Organisms must be conceived and explained as machines. Only humans had souls, and even they had them not as the formal power of their organic constitution, but as the substratum of consciousness, as *res cogitans*.[153]

SOME QUESTIONS

Even this short survey of Spaemann's ethics should have made clear that he is rich in insights. Insights, however, do not necessarily come together to form a system, and Spaemann's approach to philosophy is deliberately nonsystematic. As a result, his positions on some important issues may seem ambiguous or even contradictory.

One such ambiguity can be handled fairly easily: the ambiguity of the terms "nature" and "natural." Spaemann is certainly aware that these terms are highly ambiguous.[154] At the risk of making his use of these terms more systematic than it is, I would distinguish five senses in which he uses them: (1) the nature of a species, whether human or other animal, with its natural teleology and drives; (2) the natural world, especially the biosphere or ecosystem; (3) that which is naturally right (*das von Natur Rechte*), as opposed to that which is naturally wrong; (4) merely natural process or development (*Naturwüchsigkeit*), that which happens of itself apart from human reason or decision; and (5) the state of nature, a state without effective moral or legal government. So far as I can see, all or virtually all of Spaemann's uses of "nature" and "natural" fall under one of these headings.

There is at least the appearance of ambiguity in Spaemann's anthropology. On the one hand, the distinction between life and reason is central to his understanding of the person. It is what makes the difference between persons and other animals. It is the reason why human beings are not simply identical with their natures but rather *have* their natures. This distinction of biological life and reason is what leads Spaemann to cite Aristotle's "*nous* from outside" remark with approval. On the other hand, the unity of person and nature is also central to Spaemann's understanding of the person. He strongly criticizes modern, especially Cartesian, dualism. He sees the activities of reason and freedom as aspects of the human essence: "From a healthy, adult human one can read off what the essence of human is, the essence of even those in whom this essential does not show itself. The essence, which often but not always shows itself, is that which we call the 'soul.'"[155] Recognition of persons is recognition of them *in* their nature. Respect for persons is respect for them *in* their nature. One might think that this should lead Spaemann to take distance from Aristotle's "*nous* from outside" remark.

I take it that Spaemann wants to maintain both the contrast between animal life and reason that is essential to persons and the unity of the person with his or her nature. It is not for me to suggest that these two elements of his position are inconsistent. He is too careful and subtle a thinker for that. One could wish, however, that he had worked out the relation between them more explicitly and systematically.[156]

Spaemann's talk about recognition (*Anerkennung*) raises a number of questions, some of which he addresses and some of which he does not address. At the risk of making his thought on this topic more systematic than it is, I will line up some of these questions and try to answer them as best I can.

What is involved in recognition taking place? About this Spaemann has three things to say: recognition is not a moral decision; recognition is a matter of perception, awakening, enlightenment; and recognition involves an aspect of freedom.[157] In chapter 9 of *Happiness and Benevolence*, he says that recognition is not a moral decision but an enlightenment, an awakening to a reality. But in chapter 6 of *Persons*, he speaks of recognition as involving a free decision or at least an aspect of freedom. And in chapter 16 of *Persons*, he speaks of a basic decision between self-assertion and self-transcendence, a decision that is not a choice made for reasons. Are these claims consistent? If recognition involves a decision, or at least an aspect of freedom, then it would seem to be, or involve, a choice.

We can meet this objection by distinguishing specifically *moral* decisions, which already presuppose recognition, from a more basic decision or acceptance that is a necessary condition for recognition to take place. But what, then, is this more basic decision or acceptance? And if recognition is not a moral decision but a perception, awakening, or enlightenment, how does the aspect of freedom come into that perception, awakening, enlightenment?

Here a passage that we have already seen from chapter 6 of *Persons* can help us. Spaemann is explaining how persons recognize and are recognized by other persons:

> The elementary form of such absolute encounter with reality is the intersection of the other's gaze with mine. I find myself looked at. And if the other's gaze does not objectify me, inspect me, evaluate me, or merely crave for me, but reciprocates my own, there is constituted in the experience of both what we call "personal existence." "Persons" exist only in the plural. It is true that the gaze of the other may in principle be simulated, for the other is never presented to us in the compelling immediacy of pure phenomenon. It is a free decision [*enthält ein Moment der Freiheit*, "it contains an aspect of freedom"] to treat the other as a real self, not a simulation. What that decision [*Akt der Freiheit*, "act of freedom"] essentially consists in is a refusal to obey the innate tendency of all living things to overpower others.[158]

The reality of the other person is given to us, but not in a way that hits us over the head. We recognize it freely. But that does not mean that we go through an explicit reflection on whether or not to recognize the being gazing at us as a person.[159]

Is recognition always mutual? Or can A recognize B without B recognizing A? It would seem that recognition is always mutual. Spaemann says that persons only exist in the plural. His analyses of recognition typically feature adult human beings recognizing, and being recognized by, other adult human beings. At the same time, however, his account of human development suggests that recognition need not be mutual and that in one very important case it is, at least initially, not mutual. I refer to what he says in the last chapter of *Persons* about the way parents and other adults treat infants. To recall the context, Spaemann is arguing against the view that the class of persons is limited to those who display specifically personal properties and that human beings who fail to display these properties are not persons: "Recognizing a person is not merely a response to the presence of specific personal properties, because these properties emerge only where a child experiences the attention that is paid to persons. . . . The mother, or her substitute, treats the child from the start as a subject of personal encounter rather than an object to manipulate or a living organism to condition. She teaches the child to speak, not by speaking in its presence but by speaking *to* it."[160]

Does recognizing a person necessarily involve respect for and benevolence toward that person? Or is recognizing a person compatible with disrespect for that person? Spaemann certainly speaks as though recognition necessarily involves respect and benevolence. In *Happiness and Benevolence*, he says, "The prohibition [on treating someone purely as a means to ends] which we speak of is not grounded in some further impersonal 'ought' or an abstract imperative, about which we would have to ask why we ought to subordinate ourselves to it. This prohibition is identical with the perception of [the other's] being a self."[161] In *Persons*, he says, "You cannot first assert that John is a person and then protest that persons matter no more to you than monarchs do. To acknowledge personal status is already to express respect, which is the specific way in which persons are accessible to one another."[162]

Let us dispose of one possible misunderstanding. Is Spaemann saying that from the moment we recognize another person we love that person? The answer has to be no. He distinguishes between a first or basic level of benevolence, which he terms justice, and a higher level that he terms love.[163] Benevolence at the level of respect is primarily negative. It rules out treating the other person purely as a means to my ends. Benevolence at the level of love goes much further. Spaemann's talk about a graduated *ordo amoris* supposes that the expression of benevolence has different levels. But he does claim that recognition of a person necessarily involves at least minimal respect for the person.

There are, however, at least three passages that might seem to suggest that recognition of a person is compatible with disrespect for the person. The first we have just seen: "I find myself looked at. And if the other's gaze does not objectify me, inspect me, evaluate me, or merely crave for me, but reciprocates my own, there is constituted in the experience of both what we call 'personal existence.'"[164] This seems to indicate that someone might recognize a person not with benevolence but with objectification, mere inspection, evaluation, or sheer craving.

The second passage speaks about a kind of detachment or indifference that amounts to disrespect for the other person: "Real perception of suffering is not possible in the form of merely neutral observation. It is always connected with an attitude, be it connected with the tendency to alleviate or to do away with the suffering or to be with the sufferer, or be it connected with the opposed tendency not to do just these things. The merely neutral 'taking cognizance' of pain is in reality an act which is opposed to rational benevolence."[165]

In the third passage Spaemann is discussing sadism: "The temporary suspension of subjective consciousness [under anesthesia], undertaken to restore someone's physical wholeness, has a perverted mirror-image in the sadistic reduction of a person to an object, not by suspending subjectivity but by objectifying the subjectivity itself. The point of this undertaking is to make the suffering person himself or herself experience objectification as a means to the satisfaction of someone else."[166] Here it would seem that the victim's subjectivity is essential to the sadist's satisfaction. Whipping a post is not the same as whipping a person.

How can we square these texts with Spaemann's claim that recognition necessarily involves at least minimal benevolence and respect? The answer, it seems to me, is that the person who objectifies, the callously indifferent person, and the sadist have some awareness of the other person, but an awareness that falls short of full recognition. Spaemann's presentation of animal self-centeredness points the way toward such an explanation. As he sees it, animals without reason are the centers of their own worlds. They are in some sense aware of a world around them. They cope with that world. But they do not recognize any of the objects in that world as other centers. To do so they would need to possess reason. If they did so, they would be persons, and they would recognize other persons. Along this line, we might say that the objectifying person and the callously indifferent person have something more than the kind of awareness that animals have, but not the full awareness made possible by reason. I am not sure how to apply this to the case of the sadist.[167]

There are two further issues about recognition that I can only mention here. What happens to recognition when one person wrongs another? If someone recognizes another person but then later consciously and deliberately injures that person, is that because their recognition of the person has somehow lapsed? In what I have read of his work, Spaemann does not address these questions. I hesitate to answer them on his behalf. But I would suggest that any answer should respect Aristotle's distinction between morally weak action, in which an agent's awareness of some important aspect of a situation is neutralized or clouded over, and vicious action, in which an agent knowingly does what is wrong.

Finally, and most importantly, Spaemann could say more to explain and defend his crucial claim in chapter 9 of *Happiness and Benevolence*, that benevolence *is* (my emphasis) happiness: "For the benevolent benevolence itself is a gift. It is *eudaimonia*, the turning-out-well of life, which on the level of simply living and instinct appears to us to be subject to irresolvable antinomies."[168] This claim lies at the core of Spaemann's solution to the problem of happiness and benevolence, eudaimonism and universalism. But to the best of my knowledge he does not return to it in the later chapters of *Happiness and Benevolence* or in *Persons*. It does not come up for discussion in the section of *Über Gott und die Welt* where he looks back on *Happiness and Benevolence*.[169] Here again one could wish that Spaemann had addressed this issue more thoroughly and systematically.

FURTHER READING

The following suggestions are primarily intended for people who will read Spaemann in English.

Jeanne Heffernan Schindler, introduction to *A Robert Spaemann Reader*, is a brief and accessible introduction to Spaemann's thought. Richard Schenk, O.P., "The Ethics of Robert Spaemann in the Context of Recent Philosophy," in *One Hundred Years of Philosophy*, ed. Brian J. Shanley, O.P. (Washington, DC: Catholic University of America Press, 2001), 156–68, is another brief introduction to Spaemann's ethics by one of his former students. See also Schenk's remarks at the presentation of the Academy of Catholic Theology's John Henry Newman Medal to Spaemann, in Schenk, "Encomium to Robert Spaemann," *Nova et Vetera* 7 (2009): 763–68; and Arthur Madigan, S.J., "Robert Spaemann's *Philosophische Essays*," *Review of Metaphysics* 51 (1997): 105–32; reprinted as an afterword to Spaemann, *Happiness and Benevolence*.

Holger Zaborowski, *Robert Spaemann's Philosophy of the Human Person: Nature, Freedom, and the Critique of Modernity* (Oxford: Oxford University Press, 2010), is essential reading for anyone trying to come to grips with the background and detail of Spaemann's work. Zaborowski's select bibliography of primary and secondary sources is the most useful resource for anyone wishing to access Spaemann's thought. His bibliography of Spaemann's writings goes as far as 2007. His placing English translations of Spaemann's works and important secondary sources about Spaemann's philosophy (not all in English) in separate sections before the book's general bibliography is particularly helpful.

The bibliography in Hanns-Gregor Nissing, ed., *Grundvollzüge der Person: Dimensionen des Menschseins bei Robert Spaemann* (Pößneck: GGP Media on Demand/Munich: Institut für Förderung der Glaubenslehre, 2008), 138–98, is usefully divided into monographs, collections of essays, edited and coedited works, essays and shorter pieces, selected newspaper pieces, selected interviews, two *Festschriften*, and selected secondary literature.

The short bibliography in *A Robert Spaemann Reader*, 232–33, only lists work in English but includes work from as recently as 2014.

A wide-ranging appreciation of Spaemann's oeuvre is Anselm Ramelow, O.P., "Teleology and Transcendence," in *Communio: International Catholic Review* 45 (2018): 567–612.

Matthew A. Schimpf, "The Theory of the Person in Robert Spaemann's Ethical Assessments" (PhD diss., Catholic University of America, 2015), written under the supervision of Robert Sokolowski, addresses a number of aspects of Spaemann's thinking about ethics that I have not tried to address in this chapter.

See reviews: Holger Zaborowski, review of *Happiness and Benevolence*, *Studies in Christian Ethics* 14 (2001): 109–18; Alasdair MacIntyre, review of *Persons*, *Studies in Christian Ethics* 20 (2007): 440–43; Anselm Ramelow, O.P., review of *Persons*, *The Thomist* 72 (2008): 317–21; and Arthur Madigan, S.J., review of *Persons*, *Journal of Religious Ethics* 38 (2010): 373–92.

Sr. Elinor Gardner, O.P., translation of Spaemann's "Was macht Personen zu Personen?," *Philosophisches Jahrbuch* 119 (2012): 3–14, appeared as "What Makes Persons Persons?," *Communio: International Catholic Review* 45 (2018): 613–28.

CHAPTER FIVE

ISSUES FACING ARISTOTELIANS

At the end of Hume's *Dialogues concerning Natural Religion*, the narrator, Pamphilus, passes the following judgment: "So I confess that on carefully looking over the whole conversation I cannot help thinking that Philo's principles are more probable than Demea's, but that those of Cleanthes approach still nearer to the truth."

Alasdair MacIntyre, Martha Nussbaum, and Robert Spaemann are three remarkable contemporary exponents of Aristotelian ethics. I would have liked to conclude this book by comparing their versions of Aristotelian ethics point by point and passing a judgment on their respective merits. But this concluding chapter cannot simply line up a certain number of questions, say how MacIntyre, Nussbaum, and Spaemann answer them, and pass judgment on their answers. They are not asking the same questions, much less asking them in the same ways. Some of their differences run so deep that it would take a much longer book, or even a series of books, to resolve them—if indeed they can ever be resolved.

The preceding three chapters have, I hope, made the case that contemporary Aristotelian moral philosophy possesses important resources with which to interpret our current situation and to understand ourselves as moral agents. They have certainly made the case that the Aristotelian tradition does not speak with one voice, but is divided on important issues. Here I will try to assess the extent to which our three Aristotelians share common ground, try to identify the most important of the differences that divide them, and then close with some suggestions about where contemporary Aristotelians might look for help in addressing the divisions, problems, and difficulties within their tradition.

SEARCHING FOR COMMON GROUND

I have characterized MacIntyre, Nussbaum, and Spaemann as Aristotelians. To what extent does that mean that they share common ground? The honest answer has to be, "Less than one might have expected." Each of them has great debts to Aristotle, but they focus on different Aristotelian insights, and these make for correspondingly different emphases in their own philosophies. What MacIntyre takes from Aristotle is, first, the notion that human being is a functional concept, a concept with standards of evaluation built into it; second, the distinction between human beings as they are and human beings as they would be if they realized their *telos*; and third, the central place of the virtues in their realizing that *telos*. What Nussbaum takes from Aristotle is, first, a conception of philosophical method, the method of appearances; second, a thoroughgoing rejection of the modern antithesis between fact and value; and third, an understanding of human beings as rational but also highly vulnerable animals. What Spaemann takes from Aristotle is, first, a conception of ethics as the elucidation and defense of a common moral experience that student and teacher already share, rather than an attempt to establish moral truths by argument; second, a teleological view of the world and especially of living creatures; and third, an understanding of human beings as rational *animals*, as opposed to Cartesian subjects.

MacIntyre and Nussbaum agree on the basic facts that human beings are vulnerable and interdependent, however differently they describe and interpret those facts. They also agree on the need for human beings to develop and practice a set of virtues, however differently they list and describe the virtues that human beings need. And though Spaemann does not give these two points the same prominence that MacIntyre and Nussbaum do, he would surely join them in affirming that human beings are vulnerable and interdependent and that they stand in need of the virtues.

To this extent, our three Aristotelians share common ground. Beyond that, their differences are many. Let me begin with the roles that they play within the world of philosophy.

MacIntyre and Nussbaum are both North American academics, but they occupy very different places in North American academe. MacIntyre, as he sometimes reminds us, is an immigrant to the New World. He has achieved wide recognition in North America, but he has always remained something of an outsider. He has taught at schools such as Boston University, Vanderbilt, and Duke, but his closest association has been with the University of Notre Dame, a Catholic school. Nussbaum, by contrast, has been an insider in the American academy, with her Harvard doctorate, her appointments at Harvard, Brown, and the University of Chicago, and her long list of lectureships, honorary degrees, and prestigious awards. Yet for all their many differences, MacIntyre and Nussbaum are parties to a conversation that goes on across Anglo-American philosophy. By contrast with both, Robert Spaemann moved in the very different world of the German universities. He drew on English-language moral philosophy, but he took virtually no part in the Anglo-American conversation. Until fairly recently, he was hardly known in Anglo-American circles. That is why, for all their differences, it is often easier to compare MacIntyre and Nussbaum than it is to compare Spaemann with either of them.

Against this background, I will now try to identify the most important of the differences that divide our Aristotelians.

READING OUR CURRENT SITUATION

How should Aristotelians describe, explain, and assess our current situation, both the current state of philosophy and the broader social context in which we do philosophy? From *After Virtue* down to *Ethics in the Conflicts of Modernity*, MacIntyre has consistently criticized the ways in which Western moral and political thinking and practice have evolved from the beginnings of modernity down to the present. He maintains that we are living in an emotivist situation of unsettleable moral disagreement, and that much of our moral vocabulary consists of fragments split off from the contexts in which they once made sense. He is strongly critical of liberal modernity and of what he calls "the dominant order," including its economic, social, and political systems. He accepts the core of Marx's criticism of the capitalist economy—the theory of surplus value. He prefers Aquinas's vision of communities shaped by the virtues and the precepts of the natural law to the dominant economic, social, and political order. He invites his readers to take distance from the dominant order and to live in ways that challenge it.

Nussbaum, by contrast, takes liberal modernity to be basically in good order. The qualification "basically" is important. Both in her Aristotelian period and in her more recent work, Nussbaum has recognized and addressed many of the evils and deficiencies, practical and theoretical, in our current situation. But these evils and deficiencies are failures to redeem the bright promise of modernity: the promise held out by Kant's affirmation of human dignity and Mill's affirmations of liberty and equality. She criticizes narrowly economic criteria of what counts as human development, and she draws on Marx's humanistic writings to point out deficiencies in our current situation and to outline what it would mean to remedy those deficiencies, but I have not found in her Aristotelian work (or, for that matter, in her more recent work) a fundamental critique of capitalism as such, much less anything like the root-and-branch critique of modernity that so pervades MacIntyre's work.

Spaemann's evaluation of our current situation is mixed. Modernity has great positive contributions to its credit—enlightenment, emancipation, human rights, and modern natural science—but it needs to be protected from its own self-understanding and from its own self-assertion. The modern impulse to dominate nature, now strengthened by the latest in technology, poses unprecedented threats to human dignity and even to human survival. In *Philosophische Essays*, *Grenzen*, and elsewhere, Spaemann addresses many of those threats, among them abortion, euthanasia, nuclear warfare, assaults on the environment, and the prospect of genetic engineering. He traces them back to the rejection of natural teleology in the late Middle Ages and early modernity, and he pleads for the revival of a teleological outlook, for an attitude that he calls "being mindful of nature," and for an awareness of our human limits and of the limits of nature itself.

RESPONDING TO ANGLO-AMERICAN MORAL PHILOSOPHY

Anglo-American moral philosophy in the period 1950 to 1990 found itself grappling with five sets of problems: (1) the competing claims of deontological and teleological ethics, especially Kantian and utilitarian ethics; (2) the claims of egoism and altruism; (3) the claims of naturalism, intuitionism, and noncognitivism in metaethics; (4) the relations between fact and value, is and ought; and (5) the challenges of relativism and skepticism. Our three Aristotelians have not made it their project to solve these problems precisely as I have framed them, but they have in fact addressed them in a variety of ways. The most important difference that divides them concerns the extent to which they accept or reject the presuppositions of that moral philosophy.

As MacIntyre sees it, academic moral philosophy "at some point in its past history took a wrong turning, marched off in the wrong direction, set itself the task . . . of climbing the wrong mountain."[1] He challenges that moral philosophy with two main analyses, which I take to be complementary. The first, stated most fully in *After Virtue*, begins with the apparently unsettleable contemporary disputes over moral issues and traces them back to the failure, diagnosed most acutely by Nietzsche, of the Enlightenment's project of justifying morality. This analysis then traces the project of justifying morality back to the rejection of the Aristotelian teleological understanding of the human being in the late medieval and early modern periods. The second analysis, stated most fully in *Ethics in the Conflicts of Modernity*, focuses on what MacIntyre calls "Morality," the generic morality of which deontological, teleological, and contractarian ethical theories are species. It confronts Morality with the challenge of expressivism, the view that in moral matters there is no truth to be had, only choices to be made. MacIntyre finds that Morality has no convincing response to expressivism. Why, then, do people continue to believe in and to let themselves be guided by Morality? MacIntyre explains this by positing that Morality performs the important social function of constraining what people may and may not do in pursuit of their desires, and so helps to sustain what he calls the "dominant order of modernity," including the modern state and the modern capitalist market economy.

In her Aristotelian works, Nussbaum criticizes modern moral philosophy in important respects. She criticizes Kant for treating feeling as essentially nonrational and adopts instead the Stoic view that feelings are cognitive states, along with the Aristotelian view that feelings can make important contributions to moral knowledge. She insists that human dignity is based not only on the possession of reason, as it was for Kant, but on the full range of what is involved in being human, including animality and vulnerability. She criticizes the crude hedonism of Jeremy Bentham and the tendency to aggregate satisfactions that marks utilitarianism generally. She criticizes the fiction of competent adulthood that underlies the social contract tradition, that is, the assumption that in the state of nature everyone is free, equal, and independent. At the same time, she embraces Kant's concern for human dignity, Mill's affirmations of freedom and equality, and a form of political liberalism similar to that articulated by John Rawls. Instead of positing a sharp opposition between Aristotle's ethics and modern ethics, she combines ideas from modern ethics with such important Aristotelian insights as the instrumental character of money and the untenability of hedonism. Most importantly, she reads Aristotle as rejecting, and she herself rejects, the modern antithesis between fact and value. As she sees it, there is no need, in ethics, to pass from premoral fact to moral value.

Spaemann has many debts to modern and contemporary philosophy, including Anglo-American moral philosophy. In the end, however, he stands apart from the Anglo-American tradition in moral philosophy. He understands the task of ethics not as arguing for the truth of ethical or metaethical claims, but as clarifying common moral consciousness, purifying it of inconsistencies, and defending it against sophistic objections. He starts with a teleological understanding of nature in general and of human nature in particular. He takes the concept of person—the being that is not simply identical with its nature but rather *has* its nature—and the recognition of persons to be fundamental to ethics. Spaemann's ethics is, at least in a broad sense, phenomenological: not an attempt to argue from premises to conclusions, but an attempt to lead his audience to a clarified and heightened awareness of a moral consciousness that they already share.

ADAPTING ARISTOTLE'S ETHICS

None of our contemporary Aristotelians has tried to be a "pure" or "originalist" Aristotelian, simply interpreting the letter of Aristotle's text. All three of them are consciously adapting Aristotle, developing, correcting, and supplementing his insights in ways that he could not have envisioned. But there are many different ways to adapt Aristotle's ethics. Which of these adaptations are more illuminating and philosophically fruitful?

Let us begin with an issue that divides both Aristotelian exegetes and contemporary Aristotelians: whether Aristotle's ethics rests on a preethical (metaphysical, natural-scientific) foundation.[2] Nussbaum maintains, most clearly in her exchanges with Bernard Williams, that Aristotle's ethics is not based, and need not be based, on preethical foundations. The concepts of human being and human capabilities are normative from the start.

MacIntyre's position on this issue has developed over time. In *After Virtue*, he declined to rest his broadly Aristotelian ethics of the virtues on what he called Aristotle's "metaphysical biology." Instead, he grounded it on what he later called a "sociological teleology": the necessary conditions for practices to be carried on and for communities and traditions to flourish. In *Dependent Rational Animals*, however, he posited a biological grounding for his ethics. This grounding was not on Aristotle's own biology but rather on the large extent to which human beings resemble certain of the nonhuman animals, and on the fact that the human life cycle always includes, and may at any point include, periods during which we are acutely dependent on other people. This grounding led him to a fuller list of the virtues and a fuller explanation of why human beings need them. In *Ethics in the Conflicts of Modernity*, he went further, along Thomistic lines, positing a metaphysical grounding for ethics: the *telos* that is God, or the vision of God, as established in the part of metaphysics called natural theology.

Spaemann does not appeal to nature as providing a preethical foundation for ethics. Nature as such is not normative for human beings. The ground of benevolence is not nature but the recognition of persons. Once one has recognized persons with benevolence, however, it is human nature that supplies benevolence with its content. To respect persons is to respect them *in* their nature, very much including its physical and animal dimensions.

Our three Aristotelians differ about the project of resting ethics on some sort of preethical foundation, but they seem to be unanimous in endorsing some form of essentialism about human nature. Nussbaum explicitly argues for what she calls an "Aristotelian essentialism." At the same time, consistently with her internal realism, she distinguishes the internal essentialism that she affirms from what she calls "metaphysical essentialism," the view that there is such a thing as human nature prior to our thinking and talking about it. That she denies. In what I have read of their work, MacIntyre and Spaemann do not use the term "essentialism." But insofar as they advance ethical claims about human beings in general, claims not restricted to certain kinds or groups of human beings, they too are for practical purposes essentialists. MacIntyre has, of course, insisted that morality is always the morality of particular groups living at particular times in particular places.

An important question facing Aristotelians is whether or not to supplement Aristotle's ethics with a doctrine of natural law. From *Whose Justice? Which Rationality?* on, MacIntyre has answered this question with a forthright yes. He develops his conception of natural law by reference to the requirements of practices and communities, especially communities that inquire and deliberate together about their goods and about how those goods are to be ordered. Integral to his conception is the idea that the natural law not only forbids such actions as lying, stealing, and killing the innocent, but also requires people to act in line with the virtues. Further, he has had much to say about why natural law, which the Thomistic tradition has held to be accessible to all human beings who possess reason, should be so widely ignored or denied in our times.

Spaemann recognizes what he calls "that which is right by nature" (*das von Natur Rechte*). In "Why There Is No Law without Natural Law," he defends natural law or natural right thinking in opposition to legal positivism. Even so, the concept of natural law plays nothing like the role in Spaemann's thinking that it plays in MacIntyre's, in the older scholastic natural law theorists, or in the New Natural Law theory of Germain

Grisez and John Finnis. Instead, he speaks in a more general way of re-membering nature, being mindful of nature, employing a hermeneutic of nature.

Nussbaum shows some sympathy for classical modern natural law theory: "Typically, thought about 'natural law' in the seventeenth and eighteenth centuries—and thus the core of the classical education given to people bound for politics and government—melded Aristotelian with Stoic elements. Although different combinations of ideas could be made, one attractive and enduring marriage, compatible with mainstream Christian beliefs, was that between Stoic ideas of the equal worth of all human beings and Aristotelian ideas about human vulnerability."[3] But she herself does not supplement Aristotle's ethics with a doctrine of natural law.

Another important issue that faces Aristotelians is whether or not to supplement Aristotle's ethics with a doctrine of rights. Nussbaum characterizes her capabilities approach as "a species of human rights approach. . . . The common ground between the Capabilities Approach and human rights approaches lies in the idea that all people have some core entitlements just by virtue of their humanity, and that it is a basic duty of society to respect and support these entitlements."[4] In what I have read, she does not call these rights "natural" rights. And if a natural right is a right that somehow inheres in human nature prior to human thought and speech, her internal realism would seem to rule that out. But the rights Nussbaum talks about are not simply legal or conventional rights. On her view, they are rooted in the claims that human capabilities have to be realized. People have rights to the development of their capabilities. Those rights deserve to be entrenched in constitutions, and they ought to provide the framework within which political debate takes place. Human rights may not be Baconian hard facts, but Nussbaum sees them as real and objective, whether a given society or legal system recognizes them or not.

From *After Virtue* down to *Ethics in the Conflicts of Modernity*, MacIntyre has steadfastly denied that there even are such things as natural rights, understood as belonging to individuals as such. He affirms that there are certain actions that no human being should ever do to another human being, but he does not ground this on claims that human beings have rights not to be treated in those ways. But he is willing to affirm human rights, provided they are understood as derived from premises about the common good and about the requirements of justice and generosity.

Spaemann certainly speaks of rights. He refers with approval to the list of rights that are guaranteed by Articles 1–19 of the Basic Law of the Federal Republic of Germany. He understands them to be rights that the authors of the Basic Law did not create but rather recognized. In the context of contemporary German debate, he prefers to speak of the rights of human beings (*Menschenrechte*) rather than the rights of persons (*Personenrechte*). At the same time, rights play at most a secondary role in his ethics. And though he agrees with MacIntyre that there are certain kinds of actions that no human being should ever do to another human being, he does not, in what I have seen, argue that this is so because they violate human rights. Instead he argues that certain ways of treating human beings are inconsistent with the recognition of persons as persons and with the benevolence and respect that are implied in that recognition.

Does Nussbaum agree with MacIntyre and Spaemann that certain types of actions may never be done, whatever the circumstances? It would seem that she should not. Her discussion of tragic choices in *Fragility of Goodness* indicates that we may be thrown into situations where none of the choices open to us are good. At the same time, her talk about rights suggests that there may be some absolutes, or something approaching absolutes. The capabilities approach "emphasizes the idea of a fundamental entitlement grounded in the notion of basic justice. It reminds us that people have justified and urgent claims to certain types of treatment, no matter what the world around them has done about that. Even in pursuit of the greatest total or average GDP, or the greatest total or average utility, we may not violate those claims."[5]

ENGAGING WITH OTHER TRADITIONS

All three of our Aristotelians have drawn on other philosophical traditions to develop and supplement Aristotle's insights. In a most careful and subtle way, Nussbaum has drawn on Stoic insights into the intellectual basis of the emotions, on the Stoic and Kantian recognition of human equality and dignity, and on a liberal conception of politics that has roots in the Enlightenment. MacIntyre's position has evolved from Marxism to Aristotelianism and then to a Thomistic Aristotelianism that is enriched by insights from Marx and from contemporary philosophy of science. Spaemann's conception of the recognition of persons has roots in Rousseau, Kant, and Hegel, but he also has debts to Aquinas's account of human action. Those who follow an Aristotelian path today will need to ask which of these borrowings are more fruitful and which, if any, are problematic.

MacIntyre's move to Thomistic Aristotelianism is particularly important and controversial. Thomistic Aristotelianism attempts to synthesize Aristotle with Augustinian Christianity and thus with the worldview of biblical and Christian tradition. Nussbaum would vigorously contest this move. In her 1990 review of Charles Taylor's *Sources of the Self,* she wrote, "Let A be the Aristotelian view that the 'natural' situation of the human being combines capability with limitedness and vulnerability. Let B be the Augustinian view that our fundamental situation is one of sinfulness. To me, it seems most illuminating to narrate the story not going from A to B, but from B to A: people at some time come to realize that their basic situation is not original culpability, but capable finitude, and this is a gain in understanding."[6] One of the great issues dividing Aristotelians such as Nussbaum from Aristotelians such as MacIntyre and Spaemann is how to evaluate the Christian tradition.[7]

FACING THE INSTITUTIONAL DIMENSION

What would it mean for these three different forms of Aristotelian ethics to be embodied in institutions, especially political institutions? What, if any, are the implications of a contemporary Aristotelian ethics for politics?

It is easiest to answer this question for Nussbaum. She calls for a political consensus on the basic requirements of justice, the recognition of a set of basic entitlements for each individual to be brought to a threshold at which they have a real choice about whether and how to exercise their central capabilities, and respect for their freedom to make that choice.

These entitlements are to be entrenched in the constitution of a liberal democracy. Judicial review should be in place to protect and enforce them.

Spaemann has not laid out the political implications of his ethics in a systematic way. In what I have read of his work, the following points stand out. We should not be utopians. We should not expect any political system to do what no political system can do. We should not, for instance, expect that any political system will eliminate conflicts. A political system ought to maintain the rule of law, and it ought to protect the inviolable dignity of each and every human being, from conception to natural death. A political system that fails to do this forfeits its claim to its subjects' allegiance. This is not so much a political program as a statement of the limits (*Grenzen*) that any political system ought to observe.

MacIntyre's approach to institutional embodiment is more definite than Spaemann's but not so determinate as Nussbaum's. He rejects the project of liberal social democracy, the attempt to use the state to cure the ills of capitalism. Convinced that the politics of the nation-state are barren, he has not, so far as I know, committed himself to any side in the quarrels that have divided U.S. politics in recent decades. But, he said in his interview with Giovanna Borradori, "What is not thus barren is the politics involved in constructing and sustaining small-scale local communities, at the level of the family, the neighborhood, the workplace, the parish, the school or clinic, communities within which the needs of the hungry and the homeless can be met."[8] He rejects the label of "communitarian" that some have tried to fasten on him. He espouses no political program. Instead he has advocated a politics of small local communities, communities whose members can pursue common goods and cultivate the virtues. His call, at the end of *After Virtue*, for a new St. Benedict left some readers with the impression that he was counseling a withdrawal from contemporary society. But later writings, especially in the 2007 prologue to *After Virtue* and in *Ethics in the Conflicts of Modernity*, leave no doubt that he is advocating resistance to many aspects of the dominant economic, social, and political order.[9]

Should an Aristotelian ethics ally itself with the dominant contemporary liberalism, or should it, on the contrary, align itself against that liberalism? The question is ambiguous. "Liberalism" is a word with many meanings. In perhaps its most familiar sense, at least in North America, liberalism denotes a set of political attitudes and policies, regularly con-trasted with another set of attitudes and policies labeled "conservatism." In a second sense, liberalism is the liberal individualism that MacIntyre criticizes, the view that human beings are essentially autonomous indi-viduals, the bearers of rights. Liberalism of this sort is, on his view, the genus of which contemporary so-called liberalism and conservatism are species. A third sense is political liberalism of the kind that Nussbaum es-pouses, that is, the view that the legal and constitutional framework of a society should not be based on any particular comprehensive ethical or metaphysical doctrine, that it should be acceptable to people holding dif-ferent comprehensive doctrines. We could list other senses of liberalism and other forms of liberalism. The reason for giving even this short list is simply to point out that someone who wishes to take an Aristotelian di-rection in ethics will need to adopt some stance toward liberalism in its various forms and senses.[10]

Nussbaum's liberalism and MacIntyre's critique of liberalism are op-posed on at least three issues. The first is the issue of rights and rights talk. Rights play a central role in Nussbaum's political thinking. They include both the entitlements that are to be guaranteed in her political conception of justice and the freedom of action about whether and how to actualize one's capabilities. MacIntyre, by contrast, takes the prevalence of rights talk as a sign that people are thinking of themselves as sharply distinct in-dividuals whose interests are opposed to the interests of other individuals. As he sees it, this is one of the fundamental mistakes of liberal modernity. The liberal insistence on the separateness of individuals is the solvent of community. He said in the interview with Borradori, "Liberalism, while imposing through state power regimes that declare everyone free to pursue whatever they take to be their own good, deprives most people of the possibility of understanding their lives as a quest for the discovery and achievement of the good, especially by the way in which it attempts to discredit those traditional forms of human community within which this project has to be embodied."[11] For Nussbaum, by contrast, the first step toward respect for human beings is recognition that they are distinct individuals.

A second issue on which Nussbaum and MacIntyre differ concerns the concept of common goods, especially in the strong sense of goods that are not simply aggregates of the goods of individuals but are actually constituted and enjoyed by people acting together, such as fishing crews and string quartets. Nussbaum occasionally uses the expression "common good," but the concept of common goods in this stronger sense does not do any important work in her Aristotelian writings. Common goods in the stronger sense are central to MacIntyre's thinking. As he sees it, there are important goods that people can only achieve for themselves in and through working together to achieve such common goods.

A third issue is capitalism. In our contemporary situation, liberalism and capitalism are closely connected. Liberalism is the political form that supports and is supported by contemporary capitalism. MacIntyre leaves no doubt that he thinks Aristotelians need to oppose contemporary liberalism and contemporary capitalism. He does not regard social democracy as an effective form of opposition to capitalism. Nussbaum believes that society and the state should see to it that all human beings are brought to the threshold of exercising the main capabilities. Insofar as our current system fails to do that, Nussbaum is critical of it. If I have understood correctly, her capabilities approach requires constraints on how capitalism operates, but not a rejection of capitalism as such. If anything, the project of bringing everyone to the threshold of the ten basic capabilities would seem to require massive public expenditures, and these would seem to require the kind of economic base that capitalism, at least in certain circumstances, provides.

SETTING EDUCATIONAL AGENDA

Education is a particularly important form by which an ethics may be embodied. Given Aristotle's concern, in *Politics* 7 and elsewhere, about the best form of education, it should come as no surprise that MacIntyre and Nussbaum have expressed definite views about education in general and philosophical education in particular.

Nussbaum is well known for her defense of humanistic liberal education against the pressure to reduce education to training in instrumental and marketable skills. She is strongly critical of tendencies to undermine liberal education. She is thus taking a side in a major educational debate going on in the United States, the United Kingdom, and elsewhere. *Cultivating Humanity, Not for Profit*, and other statements witness to her concern to defend and extend liberal education.

Some defenders of liberal education, such as Robert M. Hutchins (1899–1977) and Mortimer J. Adler (1902–2001), have embraced an approach to education that concentrates attention on a canon of writers and works popularly known as the Great Books.[12] Nussbaum has criticized the Great Books (she sometimes writes "great books" in quotation marks) approach on at least two counts: that it inappropriately suggests that these "great books" are authorities to be received with veneration and deference; and that it presents an incomplete and hence distorted picture of the cultures, such as classical Greece, from which the books are taken.[13]

MacIntyre has also criticized the Great Books approach, on rather different grounds: "It is not of course that such texts [a list of Great Books in the preceding paragraph] are not important reading for anyone with pretensions to education. It is rather that there are systematically different and incompatible ways of reading and appropriating such texts and that until the problems of how they are to be read have received an answer, such lists do not rise to the status of a concrete proposal."[14]

Where Nussbaum defends humanistic education against the pressure to reduce it to training in marketable skills, MacIntyre criticizes much of education, especially graduate education, on the ground that it promotes intellectual conformity and thus inhibits challenges to the dominant order.[15] He would favor a subversive or even revolutionary approach to education. Education today should do what Aquinas's teaching on natural law did in its day—provide plain persons with the conceptual tools to challenge governmental authority.[16] As he said in his interview for *Cogito*, "to unfit our students for the contemporary world ought in any case to be one of our educational aims."[17]

In what I have read, Spaemann does not have much to say about university-level education. Instead he focuses on elementary and secondary education, presumably on the ground that these earlier stages of education have more influence than the later stages on how people actually develop morally: "Education is the name we give to the process whereby a human being is led out of the animal preoccupation with self to a state where he is able to be objective about his own interests and differentiate between them, in such a way that his capacity to experience joy and pain is increased. . . . Therefore education, in the sense that it develops interests of an objective nature, and leads to an appreciation of the value content of reality, is an essential element of successful living."[18]

Those who are trying to follow an Aristotelian path in moral philosophy will do well to ask themselves what their Aristotelianism suggests or requires by way of an educational program.

MAKING PROGRESS IN MORAL PHILOSOPHY

MacIntyre's *After Virtue* began with the disquieting suggestion that we live in a situation of unsettleable moral disagreement. Something of the kind is true of our three Aristotelians. Their differences and disagreements are serious. Is there any prospect of their making progress toward settling their disagreements? And if so, how might they do so?

In a fairly obvious sense, it would be progress for our three contemporary Aristotelians to address and resolve the differences that divide them.[19] But how are they to make such progress? A simple and straightforward answer would be that if they keep clarifying their concepts, identifying their assumptions, comparing their perceptions or intuitions, and criticizing and refining their arguments, they should expect to make progress. This progress would come through something like what Nussbaum called Aristotle's "method of appearances," especially through the second of its three phases, in which people work through problems (*aporiae*).

What if this fails to work, or has so far failed to work? Our three Aristotelians may well find that individual arguments take them only so far. They may well find that they do not share sufficient common ground to enable them to make progress on their differences. They may well differ about how to characterize their differences. They may, then, following a lead from MacIntyre, try to understand both their own branches of the Aristotelian tradition, with their respective strengths and weaknesses, and the other branches of the tradition, each with its own strengths and weaknesses, and try to see which branches of their tradition are making progress and which branches are running up against problems that they cannot solve.

This approach is not easy or assured of success. As MacIntyre explains it, it involves the work of understanding another tradition, or in this case another branch of the same Aristotelian tradition, and speaking its language as one would speak a second first language. There is no guarantee that Aristotelians will find it easy to understand one another, to speak one another's languages. They may well find themselves talking past one another. Further, if MacIntyre is right, there is no universal viewpoint from which problems can be addressed and differences resolved, only multiple particular viewpoints whose adherents pass judgments on the successes and failures of their own traditions and other traditions.

Taking this approach a step further, I would suggest that one important way in which our Aristotelians might make progress would be to expand and refine their narratives of the history of Western ethics. MacIntyre, of course, has made this an explicit project from *A Short History of Ethics* through *Ethics in the Conflicts of Modernity*.[20] But the writings of Nussbaum and Spaemann also contain materials from which to construct such narratives. If they, or some of their readers, could construct such narratives, it might be possible to compare and evaluate them and even, perhaps, to judge which of them does the best job of explaining how and why the Western ethical tradition has developed as it has.

I have been speaking of how our Aristotelians or their followers might address one another and try to resolve their differences. It would also make for progress, I think, if they would address the views of philosophers who stand outside the Aristotelian tradition, even broadly conceived. There is room for different judgments about which of these philosophical encounters will be more likely to make for progress, but one philosopher whom Aristotelians might well take more seriously than they do is Ayn Rand. I would not describe Rand as an Aristotelian, certainly not with respect to her ethics, which is highly individualistic. But it remains a fact that in some sense she understood herself as an Aristotelian.[21] It also remains a fact that a number of Aristotelian scholars have identified themselves as followers of Rand.[22] Rand's exaltation of individual freedom and her defense of free market capitalism challenge MacIntyre's Thomistic Aristotelianism with its emphasis on communities and common goods. A trenchant response to her challenge would strengthen MacIntyre's Aristotelianism. Rand would also challenge Nussbaum's attempt to combine commitment to a broad freedom of choice (which Rand would gladly endorse) with commitment to a wide range of entitlements (which Rand would strenuously contest). A successful response to this challenge would strengthen Nussbaum's Aristotelian position.

A second philosopher with whom I suggest that Aristotelians engage is Charles Taylor. Nussbaum and MacIntyre have already engaged with Taylor to some extent.[23] Taylor's work is, of course, many-sided. The part of his work that I think deserves careful attention from Aristotelians is his construction of narratives intended to explain how and why we have arrived at our current situation and to raise critical questions about that situation. Without their necessarily agreeing with the details of the narratives in *Sources of the Self* and *A Secular Age*, I believe Taylor could teach Aristotelians a good deal about how to construct such narratives. Especially important is his identification of what he calls "moral sources"—not simply premises that one might use in ethical arguments, but deep motivating factors, often not consciously articulated, that shape feeling and impel to action—and his concept of a "hypergood," a good that people esteem so highly that they use it as a criterion by which to rank and order other goods. Our three Aristotelians could also teach Taylor a lesson or two about Aristotle and the resources of the Aristotelian tradition, but that is another matter.

In asking how contemporary Aristotelians might make progress, I have presupposed that such progress is both possible and desirable. But Spaemann began *Happiness and Benevolence* by saying, "My hope is that these thoughts on ethics contain nothing fundamentally new. In seeking answers to questions about the right kind of life, only the false could be really new."[24] On Spaemann's view, the practical task of moral philosophy is not to make progress, whatever that would mean, but to defend the moral phenomenon against objections and to make it stand out fully and clearly. If I have understood him correctly, Spaemann understands the role and the responsibility of the moral philosopher quite differently than do MacIntyre and Nussbaum.

How should Aristotelians describe, explain, and evaluate our contemporary situation? How should they respond to the problems of Anglo-American moral philosophy? How can they best adapt Aristotle's ethics to our own times? How should they engage with and draw on other philosophical traditions? What would it mean for a contemporary Aristotelian ethics to be embodied in institutions, especially political and educational institutions? By what path or paths can Aristotelians expect to make progress in moral philosophy? What does it mean to make progress in moral philosophy? These, I suggest, are relevant questions, both for those who are trying to evaluate the achievements of MacIntyre, Nussbaum, and Spaemann and for those who are trying to develop their own forms of contemporary Aristotelian ethics.

NOTES

Chapter One. Anglo-American Moral Philosophy, 1950–1990

Comments from Margaret Holland have greatly improved this chapter. She is not responsible for errors or infelicities that remain.

1. This chapter does not pretend to be an adequate history of moral philosophy in the period. It may well be too soon to write such a history. Presumably, Aristotelians and their rivals would differ about what would count as an adequate history.

2. William K. Frankena, "Moral Philosophy at Mid-Century," *Philosophical Review* 60 (1951): 44–55, gives reason to think that this development had taken place by that time. I extend the category of Anglo-American moral philosophy to include Australians, such as Alan Donagan and J. L. Mackie.

3. The publication of Robert B. Kruschwitz and Robert C. Roberts, eds., *The Virtues: Contemporary Essays on Moral Character* (Belmont, CA: Wadsworth, 1987), of Peter A. French, Howard Wettstein, and Theodore E. Uehling Jr., eds., *Ethical Theory: Character and Virtue*, Midwest Studies in Philosophy 13 (Notre Dame, IN: University of Notre Dame Press, 1988), and of John W. Chapman and William A. Galston, eds., *Virtue*, Nomos XXXIV (New York: New York University Press, 1992), are indications that virtue ethics had come into its own as a field. The diversity of the contributors to these volumes is a reminder that others besides Aristotelians have contributed to the revival of virtue ethics.

4. Readers already familiar with the Anglo-American ethics of this period will recognize the limitations of this survey. Readers who desire to learn more about it will find abundant resources to help them do so. If my summary has been influenced by the responses of the Aristotelians themselves, I accept that influence as the price of making their responses more fully intelligible than they might otherwise be.

5. A. C. Ewing, *Ethics* (New York: Free Press, 1953); Mary Warnock, *Ethics since 1900* (Oxford: Oxford University Press, 1960; 3rd ed., 1978); William K. Frankena, *Ethics*, 2nd ed. (Englewood Cliffs, NJ: Prentice-Hall, 1973); G. J. Warnock, *Contemporary Moral Philosophy* (London: Macmillan; New York: St. Martin's Press, 1967); Gilbert Harman, *The Nature of Morality: An Introduction to Ethics* (New York: Oxford University Press, 1977); James Rachels, *The Elements of Moral Philosophy* (Philadelphia: Temple

University Press, 1986) (the second [1993] and later editions go beyond our period, but for what it may show, the chapter headings of the seventh edition [2012] are for the most part the same as those of the first); David Daiches Raphael, *Moral Philosophy* (Oxford: Oxford University Press, 1981; 2nd ed., 1994).

Frankena, "Ethical Theory," in *Philosophy* (Englewood Cliffs, NJ: Prentice Hall, 1964), 345–463, surveys ethical theory in the United States from about 1930 to the early 1960s. It does not cover work done in the United Kingdom, but it includes pragmatic, existentialist, and religious ethical theories that I am not considering in this chapter. The survey is evidence of Frankena's broad knowledge of twentieth-century moral philosophy.

Kai Nielsen, "Ethics, Problems of," in *The Encyclopedia of Philosophy*, ed. Paul Edwards (New York: Collier Macmillan and Free Press; London: Collier Macmillan, 1967), 3:117–34.

6. Raphael's *Ethics* is somewhat of an outlier in this respect: one index entry for Ayer, two for Hare, none for Moore or Ross or Stevenson. It does, however, have a chapter on logic and language and a chapter on intuitionism.

7. An excellent example of this approach is the interview with R. M. Hare in Bryan Magee, *Men of Ideas* (New York: Viking Press, 1978), 150–67.

8. The term "metaethics" or "meta-ethics" seems to be a twentieth-century invention. The first citation in the latest online *Oxford English Dictionary*, to *Philosophical Review* 47 (1938): 22, is not about metaethics in the Anglo-American sense. The next citation is from Ayer's *Philosophical Essays* (1949), followed by D. M. Mackinnon (1957), G. C. Kerner (1966), and *Nature* (1973). Ayer gives no indication that he is introducing a new word. Apparently "metaethics" was a recognized technical term by 1949. Ayer's thesis that statements in ethics are neither true nor false was a piece of metaethics, and responses to it were bound to be metaethical.

9. The classic formulation of the problem is found in W. D. Ross, *The Right and the Good* (Oxford: Oxford University Press, 1930; repr., Indianapolis: Hackett, 1988).

10. Frankena, *Ethics*, 2nd ed., 14–15.

11. Ibid., 84.

12. See Ross, *The Right and the Good*, 18–36.

13. At the level of Kantian scholarship, the matter is more complicated. For a way into that scholarly discussion, see Christine M. Korsgaard, "The Right to Lie: Kant on Dealing with Evil," *Philosophy & Public Affairs* 15 (1986): 325–49. I owe this reference to Margaret Holland.

14. The scholastic natural law ethics that was taught in Roman Catholic seminaries, colleges, and universities through the 1960s would seem to be an example of this second kind of divine command ethics: God commands people to act in accordance with their human nature, because this is for their good. Scholastic natural law ethics received little attention from mainstream Anglo-American moral philosophers and had little or no influence on them.

15. E.g., Rachels, *Elements of Moral Philosophy*, 53–64. After lining up arguments against psychological egoism, he writes: "In effect the psychological egoist has only announced his determination to *interpret* people's behavior in a certain way, *no matter what they do. Therefore, nothing that anyone could do could possibly count as evidence against the hypothesis.* The thesis is irrefutable, but for that very reason it turns out to have no factual content" (64; emphasis original).

16. Academic philosophy of our period almost completely ignored the work of the most widely read proponent of egoism, the philosopher and novelist Ayn Rand (1905–82), the author of, among many other works, *The Virtue of Selfishness: A New Concept of Egoism* (1961) (New York: Signet Books, 1964). Apart from a response to that book in Rachels, *Elements of Moral Philosophy*, 65, 69–71, I have not noticed any reference to Rand in my survey of introductory ethics texts.

17. Kurt Baier, *The Moral Point of View: A Rational Basis of Ethics* (Ithaca, NY: Cornell University Press, 1958; abridged ed. with a new preface, New York: Random House, 1965). In the first edition, Baier's presentation of the moral point of view occupies chapter 7, "Moral Considerations," and chapter 8, "The Moral Point of View," 169–213. In the second edition it occupies chapter 5, "Moral Reasons," 82–109. Despite this, differences between the two versions are minor. See also Stephen Toulmin, *An Examination of the Place of Reason in Ethics* (Cambridge: Cambridge University Press, 1950; repr. with new preface as *The Place of Reason in Ethics*, Chicago: University of Chicago Press, 1986).

18. Baier, *Moral Point of View* (1958), 314; (1965), 155.

19. Frankena, *Ethics*, 19 and 20 (emphasis original). Harman's position in *The Nature of Morality*, 151, comes close to this: "It is . . . a plausible hypothesis about our use of the word 'moral' that conventions are correctly called moral only if they are conventions of respect for participants. . . . it would follow almost by definition that moral reasons are based on concern for others and not on self-interest."

20. Frankena, *Ethics*, 20, 113, the latter page citing the second edition of Baier, *Moral Point of View*.

21. Rachels, *Elements of Moral Philosophy*, 67–78. Ewing's assertion (*Ethics*, 35–36) that we should be impartial as between ourselves and others comes close to Rachels's position.

22. See Kai Nielsen, "Moral Point of View Theories," *Crítica* 31, no. 3 (1999): 105–16, esp. 109–10; quotation at 109.

23. William K. Frankena, "Moral Philosophy at Mid-Century," *Philosophical Review* 60 (1951): 44–55, gives a fuller account of the three types of metaethics.

24. G. E. Moore, *Principia Ethica*, rev. ed., ed. Thomas W. Baldwin (Cambridge: Cambridge University Press, 1993), 62–72.

25. A. J. Ayer, *Language, Truth and Logic*, 2nd ed. (London: Victor Gollancz, 1946; repr., New York: Dover, 1952); Charles L. Stevenson, *Ethics and Language* (New Haven, CT: Yale University Press, 1944).

26. R. M. Hare, *The Language of Morals* (Oxford: Clarendon, 1952).

27. Alasdair MacIntyre has argued that the common interpretation of Hume is mistaken; see MacIntyre, "Hume on 'is' and 'ought,'" *Philosophical Review* 68 (1959): 451–68. This is reprinted in *Hume: A Collection of Critical Essays*, ed. V. C. Chappell (Garden City, NY: Doubleday and Company, 1966), 240–64, and in MacIntyre, *Against the Self-Images of the Age: Essays on Ideology and Philosophy* (London: Duckworth, 1971; Notre Dame, IN: University of Notre Dame Press, 1978), 109–24.

28. A noteworthy collection is W. D. Hudson, ed., *The Is-Ought Question: A Collection of Papers on the Central Problem of Moral Philosophy* (New York: St. Martin's Press, 1969).

29. See Hilary Putnam, *Reason, Truth and History* (Cambridge, MA: Harvard University Press, 1981), 127–49, 201–16; and Putnam, "Beyond the Fact-Value Dichotomy," *Crítica* 14 (1982): 3–12. For a later statement, see Putnam, *The Collapse of the Fact/Value Dichotomy and Other Essays* (Cambridge, MA: Harvard University Press, 2002).

30. Frankena, *Ethics*, 109–10. Richard B. Brandt, "Ethical Relativism," in Edwards, ed., *Encyclopedia of Philosophy*, 3:75–78, draws essentially the same distinctions.

31. See, for example, Frankena, *Ethics*, 109; Rachels, *Elements of Moral Philosophy*, 16.

32. This may still be the case. The online *Stanford Encyclopedia of Philosophy* deals with these issues in multiple overlapping articles: "Moral Realism," "Moral Anti-Realism," "Moral Relativism," and "Moral Skepticism." Richard Joyce begins the article "Moral Anti-Realism" (revised 2015) as follows: "It might be expected that it would suffice for the entry for 'moral anti-realism' to contain only some links to other entries in this encyclopedia. . . . [Joyce then outlines two ways to do this.] The fact that neither of these approaches would be adequate—and, more strikingly, that following the two procedures would yield substantively non-equivalent results—reveals the contentious and unsettled nature of the topic."

33. Alasdair MacIntyre, *A Short History of Ethics: A History of Moral Philosophy from the Homeric Age to the Twentieth Century*, 2nd ed. (Notre Dame, IN: University of Notre Dame Press, 1998), xxi. The introductions by Frankena (1973), Mary Warnock (1978), and Rachels (1986) cite MacIntyre's *Short History*, as do Raziel Abelson and Kai Nielsen, "Ethics, History of" in Edwards, ed., *Encyclopedia of Philosophy* (1967), 3:81–117.

34. Rachels, *The Elements of Moral Philosophy*, 152. Rachels had in fact made a passing reference to Aristotle on page 51. In later editions he mentions Aristotle more frequently, but less frequently than Kant and the utilitarians.

35. Mary Warnock included a chapter on Sartre in her *Ethics since 1900*. She also wrote about the existentialists in Warnock, *Existentialism* (Oxford: Oxford University Press, 1970; 2nd ed. with postscript, 1996). Still, the 1950s and 1960s saw a great deal of interest in European existentialism, at least in the United States, but this interest had little or no immediate effect on Anglo-American moral philosophy. Abelson and Nielsen, "Ethics, History of" is an honorable exception to the charge of neglecting history.

36. Mary Warnock, *Ethics since 1900* (1960; 3rd ed., 1978), vii.

37. This is not quite fair to Frankena, who recognizes the importance of the virtues of benevolence and justice. See Frankena, *Ethics*, 62–70. Ewing, *Ethics*, also has some references to virtue.

38. Geoffrey Warnock, *Contemporary Moral Philosophy*, 1–2.

39. Bernard Williams, *Morality: An Introduction to Ethics* (New York: Harper and Row, 1972; repr., Cambridge: Cambridge University Press, 1993). The quotation is on page x of the 1972 edition, xvii–xviii of the 1993 reprint. Despite its title, this book is far from being an introductory ethics textbook.

40. See Bernard Williams, *Ethics and the Limits of Philosophy* (Cambridge, MA: Harvard University Press, 1985), esp. chap. 10, "Morality, the Peculiar Institution," 174–96, and the postscript, 197–202.

41. Warnock, *Ethics since 1900*, 143–44.

42. G. E. M. Anscombe, "Modern Moral Philosophy," *Philosophy* 33 (1958): 1–19; reprinted in *The Collected Philosophical Papers of G. E. M. Anscombe*, Vol. 3, *Ethics, Religion and Politics* (Oxford: Basil Blackwell, 1981), 26–42. I cite the reprint, 26–30.

43. Ibid., 30–33.

44. Ibid., 33–42; quotation at 42. By consequentialism Anscombe means the view that agents are responsible for all the consequences of their actions, whether they intended those consequences or not.

45. Wilfrid Sellars and John Hospers, eds., *Readings in Ethical Theory* (New York: Appleton-Century-Crofts, 1952).

46. Wilfrid Sellars and John Hospers, eds., *Readings in Ethical Theory*, 2nd ed. (New York: Appleton-Century-Crofts, 1970). The second edition has only five chapters instead of nine, but these chapters are subdivided into fourteen new sections.

47. I have also consulted Paul W. Taylor, ed., *Problems of Moral Philosophy: An Introduction to Ethics* (Belmont, CA: Dickenson, 1967); and Kenneth Pahel and Marvin Schiller, eds., *Readings in Contemporary Ethical Theory* (Englewood Cliffs, NJ: Prentice-Hall, 1970).

48. W. D. Hudson, *Modern Moral Philosophy* (Garden City, NY: Doubleday, 1970).

49. J. L. Mackie, *Ethics: Inventing Right and Wrong* (Harmondsworth: Penguin, 1977).

50. I have also consulted P. H. Nowell-Smith, *Ethics* (Oxford: Basil Blackwell, 1957); Richard B. Brandt, *Ethical Theory: The Problems of Normative and Critical Ethics* (Englewood Cliffs, NJ: Prentice Hall, 1959); Luther J. Binkley, *Contemporary Ethical Theories* (New York: Philosophical Library, 1961); D. M. Mackinnon, *A Study in Ethical Theory* (New York: Collier, 1962); George C. Kerner, *The Revolution in Ethical Theory* (Oxford: Oxford University Press, 1966); and Alan Donagan, *The Theory of Morality* (Chicago: University of Chicago Press, 1977). G. J. Warnock, *The Object of Morality* (London: Methuen & Co, 1971), is an outlier, perhaps because Warnock stands back somewhat from the standard issues in moral theory to ask what morality itself is about.

Chapter Two.   Alasdair MacIntyre's Revolutionary Aristotelianism

The chapter has been much improved through my personal correspondence with Alasdair MacIntyre, who generously answered my many questions about his writings. This chapter has also been much improved by comments from Christopher Stephen Lutz. Neither man is responsible for errors or infelicities that remain.

1. All three quotations are from "An Interview for *Cogito*," in *The MacIntyre Reader*, ed. Kelvin Knight (Notre Dame: University of Notre Dame Press, 1998), 268. The interview was also published in Andrew Pyle, ed., *Key Philosophers in Conversation: The "Cogito" Interviews* (London: Routledge, 1999), quotations at 77. The collection Alasdair MacIntyre, *Against the Self-Images of the Age: Essays on Ideology and Philosophy* (London: Gerald Duckworth, 1971; repr., Notre Dame, IN: University of Notre Dame Press, 1978), brings together twenty-three essays from MacIntyre's first period.

2. See "An interview with Giovanna Borradori," in *The MacIntyre Reader*, 265–66. The interview appeared earlier, along with an introduction by Borradori, in *The American Philosopher: Conversations with Quine, Davidson, Putnam, Nozick, Danto, Rorty, Cavell, MacIntyre, and Kuhn*, trans. Rosanna Crocitto (Chicago: University of Chicago Press, 1994), in the introduction titled "The Atlantic Wall," 22–25, and in the interview titled "Nietzsche or Aristotle? Alasdair MacIntyre," 137–52.

3. See "A Partial Response to My Critics," in *After MacIntyre: Critical Perspectives on the Work of Alasdair MacIntyre*, ed. John Horton and Susan Mendus (Notre Dame, IN: University of Notre Dame Press, 1994), 283–304.

4. See "What More Needs to Be Said? A Beginning, Although Only a Beginning, at Saying It," in *Revolutionary Aristotelianism: Ethics, Resistance and Utopia*, ed. Kelvin Knight and Paul Blackledge (Stuttgart: Lucius & Lucius, 2008), 261–81.

5. See "How Aristotelianism Can Become Revolutionary: Ethics, Resistance, and Utopia" and "Where We Were, Where We Are, Where We Need to Be," in *Virtue and Politics: Alasdair MacIntyre's Revolutionary Aristotelianism*, ed. Paul Blackledge and Kelvin Knight (Notre Dame: University of Notre Dame Press, 2011), 11–19, 307–34. The introduction to *Virtue and Politics* does a good job of undermining the image of MacIntyre as a conservative or a communitarian.

6. See "On Having Survived the Academic Moral Philosophy of the Twentieth Century" and "Epilogue: What Next?" in the proceedings *What Happened in and to Moral Philosophy in the Twentieth Century?: Philosophical Essays in Honor of Alasdair MacIntyre*, ed. Fran O'Rourke (Notre Dame, IN: University of Notre Dame Press, 2013), 17–34 and 474–86.

7. The interview with Pearson appeared in *Kinesis* 20 (1994): 34–47. It was reprinted in *Kinesis* 23 (1996): 40–50. The interview with Voorhoeve appeared as "Alasdair MacIntyre: The Illusion of Self-Sufficiency," in *Conversations on Ethics*, ed. Alex Voorhoeve (Oxford: Oxford University Press, 2009), 111–31.

8. MacIntyre, *A Short History of Ethics*, 2nd ed. (Notre Dame, IN: University of Notre Dame Press, 1998).

9. Alasdair MacIntyre, *Selected Essays*, Vol. 1, *The Tasks of Philosophy*; Vol. 2, *Ethics and Politics* (Cambridge: Cambridge University Press, 2006).

10. MacIntyre, "Notes from the Moral Wilderness," in *The MacIntyre Reader*, 31–49. This was originally published in two parts in the British New Left journal *The New Reasoner* in 1958 and 1959. It is also found in Paul Blackledge and Neil Davidson, eds., *Alasdair MacIntyre's Engagement with Marxism: Selected Writings 1953–1974* (Leiden: Brill, 2008), 45–68.

11. In his interview with Thomas D. Pearson, MacIntyre said, "My critique of liberalism is one of the few things that has gone unchanged in my overall view throughout my life. Ever since I understood liberalism, I have wanted nothing to do with it— and that was when I was about seventeen years old"; see *Kinesis* 20 (1994): 43; *Kinesis* 23 (1996): 47.

12. C. B. Macpherson, *Democratic Theory: Essays in Retrieval* (Oxford: Clarendon, 1973). MacIntyre's review was first delivered at the Pacific Division of the American Philosophical Association in March 1975; see MacIntyre, review of *Democratic Theory*, by C. B. Macpherson, *Canadian Journal of Philosophy* 6 (1976): 177–81.

13. C. B. Macpherson, *The Political Theory of Possessive Individualism: Hobbes to Locke* (Oxford: Oxford University Press, 1962).

14. Ibid., 263.

15. MacIntyre, review of *Democratic Theory*, 179.

16. Ibid., 180.

17. Ibid., 181. I take it that MacIntyre is referring to the practice of enclosing formerly common land in modern England. Of this E. P. Thompson, *The Making of the English Working Class* (London: Victor Gollancz, 1980 [1963]), writes, "Enclosure (when all the sophistications are allowed for) was a plain enough case of class robbery, played according to fair rules of property and law laid down by a parliament of property-owners and lawyers" (237–38).

18. MacIntyre, *After Virtue: A Study in Moral Theory*, 3rd ed. (Notre Dame, IN: University of Notre Dame Press, 2007), 2. Readers unfamiliar with *After Virtue* may wish to begin with "The Claims of *After Virtue*," in *The MacIntyre Reader*, 69–72.

19. G. E. Moore (1873–1958) brought out his *Principia Ethica* in 1903. In it he argued that goodness was a simple nonnatural property, not definable in terms of any other property, that claims about what is good cannot be proven or disproven, and that we know what is good by a direct intuition, somewhat in the way that we recognize colors by sense perception. Moore taught philosophy in the University of Cambridge and was friends with a number of members of the so-called Bloomsbury Group.

20. MacIntyre, *After Virtue*, 17.

21. Ibid.

22. Ibid., 6–22. Christopher Lutz has drawn my attention to the parallel between the way Moore was using moral language and the way in which eighteenth-century

Polynesian used the term *taboo* as a word for something forbidden, but they could not explain why it was forbidden, and the parallel between Stevenson's emotivism and King Kamehameha II's abolition of the *taboos*. See *After Virtue*, 111–13, where MacIntyre suggests that our current use of moral language resembles the Polynesians' use of the language of *taboo*.

23. MacIntyre, *After Virtue*, 6–8.

24. Ibid., 23–25.

25. MacIntyre's dismissal of natural rights at ibid., 68–70, is brief. He explains his position more fully in his Charles F. Adams Lecture, "Are There Any Natural Rights?" (Brunswick, ME: Bowdoin College, 1983), and in "Community, Law, and the Idiom and Rhetoric of Rights," *Listening* 26 (1991): 96–110. In the Adams Lecture, he argues at length against the claim that natural rights can be defended on the ground that they are self-evident. In the 1991 article, he argues that appeals to rights in contemporary debates systematically obscure what is actually going on in those debates.

26. *After Virtue*, 68–72.

27. Ibid., 52–55.

28. Ibid., 39–50.

29. Ibid., 51–53, 57–59. MacIntyre analyzes another aspect of the Enlightenment in "Some Enlightenment Projects Reconsidered," in *Selected Essays*, 2:172–85. In the preface, he summarizes the essay as follows: "Effective as the theses and argument of Enlightenment thinkers were in exposing what was unjust and oppressive in various eighteenth-century regimes, the form that their institutionalization has since taken has had outcomes very different from those hoped for by Kant, by the utilitarians, and by other Enlightenment thinkers. The Enlightenment has failed by its own standards" (x).

30. MacIntyre, *After Virtue*, 113–20. Even if someone were to question this or that detail of MacIntyre's readings of Aristotle and Nietzsche, the basic alternative between discovering the content of morality through practical reasoning and imposing moral value through an act of will would remain. I owe this point to Christopher Lutz.

31. By "eudaimonism" I mean an attempt to spell out the meaning, necessary conditions, and sufficient conditions for *eudaimonia*, human fulfillment. Aristotle's *Nicomachean Ethics* is the paradigm case of a eudaimonistic ethics. "Happiness" is a common but arguably misleading translation for *eudaimonia*, because in contemporary English it commonly denotes a state of subjective contentment. Aristotelian *eudaimonia*, by contrast, consists in a pattern of worthwhile activity.

32. MacIntyre, *After Virtue*, 187.

33. Ibid., 188–91.

34. Ibid., 191.

35. Ibid., 190–93.

36. Ibid., 197

37. Ibid., 197–99.

38. Ibid., 199.

39. Ibid., 196–97. The phrase "metaphysical biology" occurs at 196. MacIntyre was to revise his view in *Dependent Rational Animals*.

40. Ibid., 191, 201–3.

41. Ibid., 204–15.

42. Ibid., 215–19.

43. Ibid., 215–16.

44. Ibid., 219.

45. I owe this formulation to Christopher Lutz.

46. MacIntyre, *After Virtue*, 222.

47. Ibid., 223.

48. Ibid., 194.

49. Ibid., 259.

50. Ibid., 263.

51. Ibid., xvi.

52. Ibid., 259–60. Here and in other quotations from MacIntyre the emphasis is in the original.

53. MacIntyre, *Whose Justice? Which Rationality?* (Notre Dame, IN: University of Notre Dame Press, 1988).

54. MacIntyre, "Moral Relativism, Truth and Justification," in *The MacIntyre Reader*, 202–20; quotation at 202. The essay also appears in *Selected Essays*, 1:52–73; quotation at 52.

55. MacIntyre, "Moral Relativism, Truth and Justification," in *The MacIntyre Reader*, 202–4; in *Selected Essays*, 1:52–54. The first essay in *Selected Essays* is "Epistemological Crises, Dramatic Narrative, and the Philosophy of Science," 1:3–23, in which MacIntyre indicates how an encounter with the philosophers of science Thomas Kuhn and Imre Lakatos led to a turning point in his thinking about how to make progress in philosophy. This turning point can be understood as a step toward the positions of *After Virtue*, *Whose Justice? Which Rationality?*, and "Moral Relativism, Truth and Justification."

56. MacIntyre discusses these conceptions of truth in "Moral Relativism, Truth and Justification," 205–16; in *Selected Essays*, 1:56–68. A more extended discussion of his (and Aquinas's) conception of truth is MacIntyre, "Truth as a Good: A Reflection on *Fides et Ratio*," in *Thomas Aquinas: Approaches to Truth: The Aquinas Lectures at Maynooth, 1996–2001*, ed. James McEvoy and Michael Dunne (Dublin: Four Courts Press, 2002), 141–57.

57. MacIntyre, "Moral Relativism, Truth and Justification," 216–20; in *Selected Essays*, 1:68–73. See also MacIntyre's summary of his position on this issue in the 2007 prologue to the third edition of *After Virtue*, xii–xiv.

58. MacIntyre, "Moral Relativism, Truth and Justification," 220; in *Selected Essays*, 1:73.

59. *After Virtue*, 267, quoting David Lewis, *Philosophical Papers* (Oxford: Oxford University Press, 1983), 1:x–xi. The ellipses in the quotation from Lewis are MacIntyre's.

60. MacIntyre, *Marxism: An Interpretation* (London: SCM Press, 1953). Chapters 8–10 of this book appear in Blackledge and Davidson, eds., *Alasdair MacIntyre's Engagement with Marxism*, 1–23. Blackledge and Davidson have done the great service of documenting MacIntyre's critical engagement with Marx and Marxism in the period from 1953 to 1974.

61. MacIntyre, *Marxism and Christianity* (New York: Schocken, 1968; repr., Notre Dame, IN: University of Notre Dame Press, 1984).

62. MacIntyre, *Marxism and Christianity*, rev. ed. with new introduction (London: Duckworth, 1995).

63. The introduction is available as MacIntyre, "Three Perspectives on Marxism: 1953, 1968, 1995," in *Selected Essays*, 2:145–58; "Whereas in 1953 I had, doubtless naively, supposed it possible to be in some significant way both a Christian and a Marxist, I was by 1968 able to be neither, while acknowledging in both standpoints a set of truths with which I did not know how to come to terms" (152). The introduction also appears as the epilogue to Paul Blackledge and Neil Davidson, eds., *Alasdair MacIntyre's Engagement with Marxism*, 411–25. There the quotation appears, with slightly different punctuation, at 419. Despite its title, "Three Perspectives on Marxism," chapter 8 of the 1968/1984 *Marxism and Christianity*, is quite different from the 1995 introduction.

64. Preface to MacIntyre, *Selected Essays*, 2:x.

65. MacIntyre, "Three Perspectives on Marxism," 148.

66. Ibid., 149.

67. Ibid.

68. Ibid., 150.

69. Ibid., 153.

70. Ibid.

71. Ibid., 153–54.

72. Ibid., 155.

73. He refers the reader to his 1994 paper, MacIntyre, "The *Theses on Feuerbach*: A Road Not Taken," now in *The MacIntyre Reader*, 223–34. See Karl Marx, *Theses on Feuerbach*, in *Marx and Engels: Basic Writings on Politics and Philosophy*, ed. Lewis S. Feuer (Garden City, NY: Doubleday, 1959), 243–45; in *Writings of the Young Marx on Philosophy and Society*, ed. Loyd D. Easton and Kurt H. Guddat (Garden City, NY: Doubleday, 1967), 400–402; and in *The Marx-Engels Reader*, 2nd ed., ed. Robert C. Tucker (New York: W. W. Norton, 1978), 143–45. The third thesis is concerned with the relationship of theory and practice.

74. This was published in Italian in 1997 and first appeared in English in *The MacIntyre Reader*, 235–52.

75. MacIntyre, "Politics, Philosophy and the Common Good," 236–39.

76. Ibid., 237.

77. Ibid., 244. See also *Whose Justice? Which Rationality?*, 392, and *After Virtue*, xv.

78. I owe much of this formulation to Christopher Lutz.

79. MacIntyre, "Politics, Philosophy and the Common Good," 240.

80. Cf. ibid., 247–50. For more on compartmentalization, see MacIntyre, "Social Structures and Their Threats to Moral Agency," in *Selected Essays*, 2:186–204.

81. MacIntyre, "Three Perspectives on Marxism," 149.

82. Cf. MacIntyre, "Politics, Philosophy and the Common Good," 243–46. See also "An Interview with Giovanna Borradori," in *The MacIntyre Reader*, 265, and in Borradori, *The American Philosopher*, 151: "I am not a communitarian. I do not believe in ideals or forms of community as a nostrum for contemporary social ills. I give my political loyalty to no program."

83. Cf. MacIntyre, "Politics, Philosophy and the Common Good," 252. See also "An Interview with Giovanna Borradori," in *The MacIntyre Reader*, 258, and in Borradori, *The American Philosopher*, 143: "Liberalism, while imposing through state power regimes that declare everyone free to pursue whatever they take to be their own good, deprives most people of the possibility of understanding their lives as a quest for the discovery and achievement of the good, especially by the way in which it attempts to discredit those traditional forms of human community within which this project has to be embodied."

84. MacIntyre, *Whose Justice? Which Rationality?*, 183–208.

85. MacIntyre, "Natural Law as Subversive: The Case of Aquinas," in *Selected Essays*, 2:42–43. Note 1 on page 43 indicates that "elsewhere" is MacIntyre, "Aquinas on Practical Rationality and Justice," in *Whose Justice? Which Rationality?*, chap. 11.

86. MacIntyre, *Whose Justice? Which Rationality?*, 199.

87. Ibid.

88. Ibid.

89. Ibid., 200.

90. Ibid.

91. Ibid., 200–201.

92. MacIntyre, "The Only Vote Worth Casting in November," http://perennis .blogspot.com/2004/10/alasdair-macintyre-only-vote-worth.html.

93. MacIntyre, *After Virtue*, x. MacIntyre credits the Notre Dame philosopher Ralph McInerny with showing him why he needed to be not only an Aristotelian but a Thomist, so that (MacIntyre is speaking) "I came to understand not only that Aquinas is the finest interpreter of Aristotle, but that Thomism is what Aristotelianism had to become, if it was to transcend its limitations, the limitations of Aristotle's time, place, and prejudices, and if it was to extend its questioning into further areas of enquiry"; see MacIntyre, "After McInerny," in *O Rare Ralph McInerny: Stories and Legends about a Legendary Notre Dame Professor*, ed. Christopher Kaczor (South Bend, IN: St. Augustine's Press, 2011), 104.

94. MacIntyre, *After Virtue*, xi.

95. This sentence begins "One such failure," but "failure" cannot be correct.

96. MacIntyre, *Dependent Rational Animals: Why Human Beings Need the Virtues* (Chicago: Open Court, 1999), x.

97. Ibid., 21–51.

98. Ibid., 155–56.

99. Ibid., 87.

100. Ibid., 99.

101. Ibid., 126–27.

102. Ibid., 119. MacIntyre quotes Smith's remark at 117.

103. Cf. ibid., 120–26.

104. Ibid., 133.

105. Ibid., 134.

106. Ibid., 111.

107. Ibid.

108. MacIntyre, "Theories of Natural Law in the Culture of Advanced Modernity," in *Common Truths: New Perspectives on Natural Law*, ed. Edward B. McLean (Wilmington, DE: ISI Books, 2000), 91–115. MacIntyre, "Intractable Moral Disagreements," in *Intractable Disputes about the Natural Law: Alasdair MacIntyre and Critics*, ed. Lawrence S. Cunningham (Notre Dame, IN: University of Notre Dame Press, 2009), 1–52. Sections 8 and 9 of this piece incorporate parts of chapter 18 of *Whose Justice? Which Rationality?*

109. MacIntyre, "Intractable Moral Disagreements," 4–5 (emphasis original).

110. Ibid., 5.

111. Ibid., 40.

112. MacIntyre, "Theories of Natural Law in the Culture of Advanced Modernity," 109–10 (emphasis original). MacIntyre has more to say about the exceptionless negative precepts of the natural law in MacIntyre, "How Can We Learn What *Veritatis Splendor* Has to Teach?," *The Thomist* 58 (1994): 171–95, esp., 176–77.

113. MacIntyre, "Intractable Moral Disagreements," 6.

114. MacIntyre, "Theories of Natural Law in the Culture of Advanced Modernity," 110–11. This is close to what the Canadian philosopher Charles Taylor has called "social atomism"; see Taylor, *Philosophical Papers 2: Philosophy and the Human Sciences* (Cambridge: Cambridge University Press, 1985), 187–210.

115. Christopher Lutz points out to me that this is essentially the same point that MacIntyre made in "Notes from the Moral Wilderness." Cf. *The MacIntyre Reader*: "Why do the moral standards by which Stalinism is found wanting have authority over us? Simply because we choose that they should. The individual confronting the facts with his values condemns. But he can only condemn in the name of his own choice" (34).

116. The New Natural Law theorist Robert P. George has charged that MacIntyre's admission that large numbers of people do not acknowledge the natural law puts him at a distance from the position of Aquinas; see George, "Moral Particularism, Thomism, and Traditions," *Review of Metaphysics* 42 (1989): 593–605. Christopher Lutz has defended MacIntyre against this charge in Lutz, *Tradition in the Ethics of Alasdair MacIntyre: Relativism, Thomism, and Philosophy* (Lanham, MD: Lexington Books, 2004), 141–55.

117. MacIntyre, "Theories of Natural Law in the Culture of Advanced Modernity," 113. See also MacIntyre, "Natural Law as Subversive: The Case of Aquinas," in *Selected Essays*, 2:41–63.

118. MacIntyre, *Ethics in the Conflicts of Modernity: An Essay on Desire, Practical Reasoning, and Narrative* (Cambridge: Cambridge University Press, 2016), 89.

119. MacIntyre, "On Having Survived the Academic Moral Philosophy of the Twentieth Century," in *What Happened in and to Moral Philosophy in the Twentieth Century? Philosophical Essays in Honor of Alasdair MacIntyre*, ed. Fran O'Rourke (Notre Dame, IN: University of Notre Dame Press, 2013).

120. Ibid., 24–25 (emphasis mine).

121. Ibid., 27.

122. Ibid., 28–29.

123. Ibid., 29.

124. Ibid., 29–30.

125. Ibid., 33.

126. As the prefix suggests, NeoAristotelianism has roots in Aristotle but is not simply identical with the position of the historical Aristotle.

127. MacIntyre, *Ethics in the Conflicts of Modernity*, chap. 1, esp. 64–65.

128. Ibid., 17–24.

129. Ibid., 24–31.

130. Ibid., 59–64.

131. Ibid., 114–16.

132. Ibid., 116–17.

133. Ibid., 117–19.

134. Ibid., 119, 139–41. Lutz points out that morality and expressivism are complementary errors, and MacIntyre's NeoAristotelianism is intended to diagnose and correct both at the same time.

135. Ibid., 77.

136. Ibid., 77–78.

137. MacIntyre, *After Virtue*, 69.

138. Ibid., 78 (emphasis mine).

139. MacIntyre, "What More Needs to Be Said? A Beginning, Although Only a Beginning, at Saying It," in Knight and Blackledge, eds., *Revolutionary Aristotelianism*, 272.

140. MacIntyre, *Ethics in the Conflicts of Modernity*, 144–45.

141. Ibid., 148–49.

142. Ibid., 151. MacIntyre is drawing on chapter 10 of Bernard Williams, *Ethics and the Limits of Philosophy* (Cambridge, MA: Harvard University Press, 1985), "Morality, the Peculiar Institution," 174–96 and 221–24.

143. MacIntyre, *Ethics in the Conflicts of Modernity*, 96–97.

144. Ibid., 97.

145. Ibid., 95–96.

146. MacIntyre explains the difference in ibid., 54: "In contemporary English, to be happy is to be and feel satisfied with one's present state or with some aspect of it, whether one has good reason to be and feel satisfied or not. But the state to which Aristotle gave the name *eudaimonia* and Aquinas the name *beatitudo* is that state in which one is and feels satisfied with one's condition only because one has good reason to be and to feel satisfied."

147. Ibid., 98.

148. Ibid., 108. Elsewhere MacIntyre credits McNabb with seeing clearly how radical Distributivism was; see MacIntyre, "The Irrelevance of Ethics," in *Virtue and Economy: Essays on Morality and Markets*, ed. Andrius Bielskis and Kelvin Knight (Farnham: Ashgate, 2015), 16: "What McNabb recognised was that the concepts of just wages and just exchanges, of the proper relationships of workers to their work and to the products of their work, of the proper relationship of the household to the work place and of both to arenas of politics, as understood by the distributivists, were so much at odds with the norms governing the British political, economic and monetary system of the 1930s that what was implied by distributivist doctrine was a total withdrawal from that system." For more on Distributism or Distributivism, see Jay P. Corrin, *G. K. Chesterton and Hilaire Belloc: The Battle against Modernity* (Athens: Ohio University Press, 1981), 78–171.

149. MacIntyre, *Ethics in the Conflicts of Modernity*, 124–29.

150. Ibid., 129.

151. Ibid., 101–2.

152. Ibid., 103.

153. Ibid.

154. Ibid., 103–4; quote at 104. MacIntyre expands on these points in "The Irrelevance of Ethics."

155. Ibid., 170.

156. Ibid., 172.

157. Ibid., 237–38 (emphasis original). Toward the end of "An Interview for *Cogito*," in *The MacIntyre Reader*, 274–75, MacIntyre says what subjects students ought to study in school and as undergraduates. He concludes, "Of course an education of this kind would require a major shift in our resources and priorities, and, if successful, it would produce in our students habits of mind which would unfit them for the contemporary world. But to unfit our students for the contemporary world ought in any case to be one of our educational aims" (275).

158. MacIntyre, *Ethics in the Conflicts of Modernity*, xi.

159. Ibid., 243. I have added the numbers in brackets.

160. Ibid., 8.

161. Ibid.; see also 73.

162. Ibid., 37.

163. Ibid., 37–38; 38n12 references *After Virtue*, 187–96, on practices, internal goods, and virtues, indicating that MacIntyre still endorses the account given there.

164. Ibid., 73–74.

165. Ibid., 74.

166. Ibid., 75.

167. Ibid., 76–77.

168. Ibid., xi, 165.

169. Ibid., 74.

170. Ibid., 57.

171. Ibid., 193. In chapter 5, MacIntyre illustrates the kind of narrative he is talking about by studying the relationship of theory to practice and of desire to practical reasoning in the lives of the Russian Jewish novelist Vasily Grossman, U.S. Supreme Court justice Sandra Day O'Connor, the Trinidadian writer and political activist C. L. R. James, and the Irish monsignor and activist Denis Faul.

172. Ibid., 241.

173. Cf. ibid., 230: "What *we* have to ask is whether or not Aquinas's philosophical theses on God's existence are able to withstand not only the objections that he entertained, but the strongest contemporary objections." In the last lines of the book, MacIntyre says, "The perfection and completion of a life consists in an agent's having persisted in moving toward and beyond the best goods of which she or he knows. So there is presupposed some further good, an object of desire beyond all particular and finite goods, a good toward which desire tends insofar as it remains unsatisfied by even the most desirable of finite goods, as in good lives it does. But here the enquiries of politics and ethics end. Here natural theology begins" (315). MacIntyre gives a fuller account of his theism in "On Being a Theistic Philosopher in a Secularized Culture," in *Proceedings of the American Catholic Philosophical Association* 84 (2010): 23–32.

174. MacIntyre, *Ethics in the Conflicts of Modernity*, 241 (emphasis original).

175. Ibid., 206–7.

176. Ibid., 208–10.

177. Ibid., 210–11; quote at 211.

178. Ibid., 211.

179. Ibid., 213.

180. Ibid., 210. The internal quotations are from David Lewis, "Introduction," in *Philosophical Papers*, 1:x–xi.

181. MacIntyre, *Ethics in the Conflicts of Modernity*, 140.

182. Ibid., 153. MacIntyre is drawing on Bernard Williams, "Morality and the Emotions," in *Problems of the Self: Philosophical Papers 1956–1972* (Cambridge: Cambridge University Press, 1973), 207–29.

183. MacIntyre, *Ethics in the Conflicts of Modernity*, 153–54. The quotation from Williams and MacIntyre's comment are at 154. The quotation comes from 227 of Williams, "Morality and the Emotions."

184. MacIntyre, *Ethics in the Conflicts of Modernity*, 41 and n24.

185. Ibid., 62.

186. This and the preceding sentence owe much to suggestions by Christopher Lutz.

187. As we saw in chapter 1, MacIntyre dissents from the common interpretation of Hume as arguing that nonmoral premises cannot entail moral conclusions is mistaken. See MacIntyre, "Hume on 'is' and 'ought,'" *Philosophical Review* 68 (1959): 451–68; reprinted in *Hume: A Collection of Critical Essays*, ed. V. C. Chappell (Garden City, NY: Doubleday , 1966), 240–64, and in MacIntyre, *Against the Self-Images of the Age: Essays on Ideology and Philosophy* (London: Duckworth, 1971; Notre Dame, IN: University of Notre Dame Press, 1978), 109–24.

188. MacIntyre, "On Having Survived the Academic Moral Philosophy of the Twentieth Century," in O'Rourke, ed., *What Happened in and to Moral Philosophy in the Twentieth Century?*, 17–34.

189. MacIntyre, *Ethics in the Conflicts of Modernity*, 34–35. For MacIntyre's criticisms of the way moral philosophy is practiced in contemporary Anglo-American academe, see ibid., 70–72. For his alternative approach, see MacIntyre, "Philosophical Education against Contemporary Culture," in *Proceedings of the American Catholic Philosophical Association* 87 (2014): 43–56. MacIntyre, *God, Philosophy, Universities: A Selective History of the Catholic Philosophical Tradition* (Lanham, MD: Rowman and Littlefield, 2009), places this approach in a broader context.

190. The phrase comes from "An Interview for *Cogito*," in *The MacIntyre Reader*, 269; in Pyle, ed., *Key Philosophers in Conversation*, 77. MacIntyre discusses various ways in which the history of moral philosophy has been written and different conceptions of how it should be written in MacIntyre, "Histories of Moral Philosophy," in *The Oxford Companion to Philosophy*, ed. Ted Honderich (Oxford: Oxford University Press, 1995), 357–60.

191. See MacIntyre, "On Having Survived the Academic Moral Philosophy of the Twentieth Century," 29–30: "It is . . . of some importance that in arriving at a certain kind of Aristotelian standpoint I was not taking up one more theoretical position within the ongoing debates of contemporary moral philosophy. It is because I have been thought to have done just this that I have been unjustly accused of being one of the protagonists of so-called virtue ethics, something that the genuine protagonists of virtue ethics are happy to join me in denying."

192. Aristotle, *Nicomachean Ethics* 1.2, 1094b20; 1.11, 1101a27; 2.2, 1104a1; 2.7, 1107b14; 5.1, 1129a11.

193. Lutz points out that "following the natural law" is ambiguous. For secular humanists or nontheists who recognize the natural law, following it would be a matter of practical wisdom. For people who see the natural law as coming from God, following it would (also) be a matter of obeying divine law.

194. MacIntyre does not regard the fall of various communist regimes as refuting or discrediting Marxism. At the end of MacIntyre, "The *Theses on Feuerbach*: A Road

Not Taken" (1994), in *The MacIntyre Reader*, 234, he writes: "I have noted how Marx was unable to develop his own insights in the theses. But the important thing now about the errors that resulted is not so much that they were Marx's errors, as that for so many of us they were *our* errors and the defeat of Marxism has been *our* defeat. But Marxism was not defeated, and we were not defeated, by the protagonists of the standpoint of civil society, who now mistakenly congratulate themselves on the collapse of communist rule in so many states. Marxism was self-defeated and we too, Marxists and ex-Marxists and post-Marxists of various kinds, were the agents of our own defeats, in key part through our inability to learn in time some of the lessons of the theses on Feuerbach. The point is, however, first to understand this and then to start out all over again."

195. MacIntyre rejects the view that Marx was a philosophical materialist. See MacIntyre, "The *Theses on Feuerbach*: A Road Not Taken," in *The MacIntyre Reader*, 224–25.

196. Kelvin Knight, "Revolutionary Aristotelianism," in *Contemporary Political Studies*, ed. Iain Hampsher-Monk and Jeffrey Stanyer, *Proceedings of the Political Studies Association* 3 (1996): 885–96. This is reprinted in Blackledge and Knight, eds., *Virtue and Politics*, 20–34. Kelvin Knight, *Aristotelian Philosophy: Ethics and Politics from Aristotle to MacIntyre* (Cambridge: Polity Press, 2007), 102–221, expands on this description in chapter 4.

197. See MacIntyre, "How Aristotelianism Can Become Revolutionary: Ethics, Resistance, Utopia," in Blackledge and Knight, eds., *Virtue and Politics*, 11–19. See also MacIntyre, "Politics, Philosophy and the Common Good," in *The MacIntyre Reader*, 235: "For an accurate and perceptive discussion of my political views, see Kelvin Knight, 'Revolutionary Aristotelianism.'"

198. MacIntyre, *Ethics in the Conflicts of Modernity*, 219–20.

199. See, for instance, the essays in Aristide Tessitore, ed., *Aristotle and Modern Politics: The Persistence of Political Philosophy* (Notre Dame, IN: University of Notre Dame Press, 2002).

200. See https://iep.utm.edu/mac-over/.

201. See https://iep.utm.edu/p-macint/.

202. MacIntyre, *Three Rival Versions of Moral Enquiry*, includes a brief but penetrating criticism of the Great Books approach to education: "It is not of course that such texts [a list of Great Books in the preceding paragraph] are not important reading for anyone with pretensions to education. It is rather that there are systematically different and incompatible ways of reading and appropriating such texts and that until the problems of how they are to be read have received an answer, such lists do not rise to the status of a concrete proposal. Or to make the same point in another way: proponents of this type of Great Books curriculum often defend it as a way of restoring to us and to our students what they speak of as *our* cultural tradition; but we are in fact the inheritors, if that is the right word, of a number of rival and incompatible traditions and there is no way of either selecting a list of books to be read or advancing a determinate account of how they are to be read, interpreted, and elucidated which does not involve taking a partisan stand in the conflict of traditions" (228).

203. For the quotation and other information about the ISME, see https://www
.macintyreanenquiry.org/mission.

Chapter Three.   The Liberal Aristotelianism of Martha Nussbaum

I am grateful to Martha Nussbaum for help on various points, especially for clarifying the differences between her earlier Aristotelian position and her current position. Margaret Holland and Paulette Kidder have improved this chapter with their comments. They are not responsible for errors or infelicities that remain.

1. Martha Craven Nussbaum, *Aristotle's "De Motu Animalium": Text with Translation, Commentary, and Interpretive Essays* (Princeton, NJ: Princeton University Press, 1978).

2. A recent statement of hers is Nussbaum, *Anger and Forgiveness: Resentment, Generosity, Justice* (Oxford: Oxford University Press, 2016), 174: "My view, then, is neither Benthamite nor similar to most familiar forms of economic Utilitarianism. But it is quite Millian in spirit and it seems not inappropriate to categorize it as, overall, a philosophically informed type of welfarism. It certainly has deontological elements, in the sense that a capability violation is an injustice, whatever wealth or other good it produces; and the protection of each capability is an intrinsic political good. Moreover, the capabilities are a partial political doctrine of (minimal) welfare, not a comprehensive doctrine. The view as a whole, however, seems to me correctly classified as a form of political welfarism that has a richer, more variegated picture of welfare than many of its competitors."

3. Nussbaum, *The Fragility of Goodness: Luck and Ethics in Greek Tragedy and Philosophy* (Cambridge: Cambridge University Press, 1986; updated ed. 2001), 240.

4. Ibid., 245–47.

5. Ibid., 242–43.

6. Ibid., 252. Here and elsewhere, unless noted otherwise, the emphasis is in Nussbaum's original.

7. Ibid., 254–55.

8. Ibid., 256, both quotations. The translation in the first quotation is Nussbaum's. Elsewhere on 256, Nussbaum explains *teretismata* as "meaningless sounds you make when you are singing to yourself."

9. Ibid., 260. Nussbaum will develop this point at length in *Hiding from Humanity*.

10. Ibid., 257.

11. As Nussbaum notes, the view that she finds in Aristotle resembles the "internal realism" of the late Harvard philosopher Hilary Putnam; cf. ibid., 257 and 482n37, where she makes reference to Putnam, *Reason, Truth, and History*.

12. Nussbaum, *Fragility of Goodness*, 291.

13. Ibid., 290–91.

14. Ibid., 290. Nussbaum uses "Platonic" to refer to the dialogues of Plato's "middle period" (quotation marks hers), not the *Phaedrus*, the *Laws*, or the *Statesman*. Cf. ibid., 291, asterisked note.

15. Ibid., 291.

16. Ibid., 293. She returns to the function argument in Nussbaum, "Aristotle on Human Nature and the Foundations of Ethics," in *World, Mind, and Ethics: Essays on the Ethical Philosophy of Bernard Williams*, ed. J. E. J. Altham and Ross Harrison (Cambridge: Cambridge University Press, 1995), 86–131. This will be discussed below.

17. Nussbaum, *Fragility of Goodness*, 294.

18. Ibid., 299. There Nussbaum introduces this as one view of the place of rules in ethical deliberation. At 300–305 she argues that it is in fact Aristotle's view.

19. Ibid., 306.

20. Ibid.

21. Ibid., 308, both quotations. "Itself by itself" translates the Platonic catchphrase *auto kath' hauto*.

22. Ibid., 264.

23. Ibid., 288.

24. Ibid., 309.

25. Ibid., 341.

26. Ibid., 353–69.

27. Ibid., 328.

28. Ibid., 334.

29. Ibid., 334–35.

30. Ibid., 413–21.

31. Charles Taylor, review of *Fragility of Goodness*, by Martha Nussbaum, *Canadian Journal of Philosophy* 18 (1988): 805–14.

32. "Transcending Humanity" is chapter 15 of Nussbaum, *Love's Knowledge: Essays on Philosophy and Literature* (Oxford: Oxford University Press, 1990), 365–91; quotes at 379.

33. *Fragility of Goodness*, xv.

34. Ibid., xvii.

35. Ibid., xix.

36. Ibid.

37. Ibid., xxiv.

38. Ibid., xxv.

39. Ibid., xxvi.

40. Annette Baier (1929–2012) was born in New Zealand and taught philosophy for many years at the University of Pittsburgh. She was both a scholar of Hume and a follower of Hume. Hume famously, or notoriously, claimed that moral distinctions are derived not from reason but from a moral sense.

41. Nussbaum, *Fragility of Goodness*, xxvii–xxviii. For a fuller discussion, see Nussbaum, "Virtue Ethics: A Misleading Category?" *Journal of Ethics* 3 (1999): 163–201;

Nussbaum discusses Baier at 194–96 and MacIntyre at 196–98. For an extended defense of the project of ethical theory, see Nussbaum, "Why Practice Needs Ethical Theory: Particularism, Principle, and Bad Behavior," in *"The Path of the Law" and Its Influence: The Legacy of Oliver Wendell Holmes, Jr.*, ed. Steven J. Burton (Cambridge: Cambridge University Press, 2000), 50–86. It would seem unfair to describe MacIntyre's project as theory-bashing.

42. Nussbaum, "The Discernment of Perception: An Aristotelian Conception of Private and Public Rationality," first appeared in *Proceedings of the Boston Area Colloquium in Ancient Philosophy* 1 (1985): 151–201. The revised and expanded version used here appears in Nussbaum, *Love's Knowledge*, 54–105.

43. Nussbaum, "Discernment of Perception," 55.

44. Ibid., 63–64.

45. Ibid., 66. The phrase appears at *Nicomachean Ethics* 2.9, 1109b23, and 4.5, 1126b3–4.

46. Ibid., 76. Nussbaum is frequently critical of utilitarianism, but she has expressed appreciation for certain aspects of the thought of Jeremy Bentham and John Stuart Mill; see Nussbaum, "Mill between Aristotle & Bentham," *Daedalus* (Spring 2004): 60–68. A somewhat different version of this essay appeared as "Mill between Aristotle and Bentham," in *Economics and Happiness: Framing the Approach*, ed. Luigino Bruni and Pier Luigi Porta (Oxford: Oxford University Press, 2005), 170–83.

47. Nussbaum, "Discernment of Perception," 84.

48. Ibid., 96.

49. Nussbaum, "Aristotle on Human Nature," 87. Williams responds to Nussbaum's paper at 194–202.

50. Ibid., 88–90, 102.

51. Ibid., 102.

52. Ibid., 113–17; quotation at 113; see also 120–21: "Nature comes into the ethical enterprise . . . not as an external fixed point, but as a humanly experienced context for human lives, evolving in history, yet relatively constant, presenting certain possibilities and foreclosing others, our sphere of hope and finitude."

53. Ibid., 118.

54. Ibid., 118–19.

55. Ibid., 119.

56. Nussbaum, "Non-Relative Virtues: An Aristotelian Approach," *Midwest Studies in Philosophy* 13 (1988): 32–53. The expanded version used here appears in *The Quality of Life*, ed. Martha C. Nussbaum and Amartya Sen (Oxford: Clarendon, 1993), 242–69.

57. Ibid., 244.

58. Ibid., 243.

59. Ibid. This article, first published in 1988 and then again in 1993, could not take account of MacIntyre, *Dependent Rational Animals* (1999).

60. Nussbaum, "Non-Relative Virtues, 243–44.

61. This contrast between "thin" and "thick" draws on the anthropologist Clifford Geertz, "Thick Description: Toward an Interpretive Theory of Culture," in *The Interpretation of Cultures: Selected Essays* (New York: Basic Books, 1973), 3–30. Geertz was drawing on two papers by Gilbert Ryle, "Thinking and Reflecting," and "The Thinking of Thoughts: What Is 'Le Penseur' Doing?," in Ryle, *Collected Papers* (London: Hutchinson, 1971), 2:479–93 and 494–509. To the question, "What is so-and-so doing?" the answer, "Moving his right eyelid in a certain way," would be a relatively thin description, but the answer, "Winking to a friend," would be a thicker description. Social scientists have refined the concept of thick description in various ways. Philosophers contrast "thick" and "thin" in a rough-and-ready way: "thick" meaning more informative or having more content, "thin" meaning less informative or having less content.

62. Nussbaum, "Non-Relative Virtues," 245.

63. Ibid., 246. The wording is Nussbaum's, but I condense her lists of spheres and virtues and make no attempt to reproduce her two-column presentation.

64. Ibid., 247.

65. Ibid.

66. Ibid., 251–52.

67. Ibid., 260. Cf. 261: "The grounding experiences will not, the Aristotelian should concede, provide precisely a single, language-neutral bedrock on which an account of virtue can be straightforwardly and unproblematically based."

68. Ibid., 261.

69. Ibid., 262.

70. Ibid., 263.

71. Ibid., 263–65. I give Nussbaum's list, including her numbering, but omit her explanations.

72. Ibid., 265.

73. Particularly noteworthy is Nussbaum, introduction to *Rawls's "Political Liberalism,"* ed. Thom Brooks and Martha C. Nussbaum (New York: Columbia University Press, 2015), 1–56. For more general appreciations of Rawls, see Nussbaum, "The Enduring Significance of John Rawls," *The Chronicle Review*, July 20, 2001, and Nussbaum, "Making Philosophy Matter to Politics," *New York Times*, December 2, 2002. See also Paul Weithman, "John Rawls: A Remembrance," *Review of Politics* 65 (2003): 5–10.

74. Nussbaum, *Frontiers of Justice: Disability, Nationality, Species Membership* (Cambridge, MA: The Belknap Press of Harvard University Press, 2006). The book was based on Nussbaum's Tanner Lectures in Human Values in 2002 and 2003. It is dedicated to Rawls's memory.

75. Ibid., ix.

76. Ibid., 5.

77. Ibid., 6.

78. Nussbaum, "Nature, Function, and Capability: Aristotle on Political Distribution," was first delivered to the Eleventh Symposium Aristotelicum in 1987. It appeared in *Oxford Studies in Ancient Philosophy*, Supplementary Vol. 1 (1988): 145–84. There it is followed by David Charles, "Perfectionism in Aristotle's Political Theory," 185–206, and then by Nussbaum, "Reply to David Charles," 207–14. A fuller version of Nussbaum's paper later appeared in *Aristoteles' "Politik,"* Akten des XI. Symposium Aristotelicum, ed. Günther Patzig (Göttingen: Vandenhoeck & Ruprecht, 1990), 152–86. There it is followed by David Charles, "Comments on M. Nussbaum," 187–201. I will use the shorter version in *Oxford Studies*, taking the view that readers are more likely to have access to it.

79. Nussbaum, "Nature, Function, and Capability," 149.

80. See John Rawls, *A Theory of Justice: Revised Edition* (Cambridge, MA: The Belknap Press of Harvard University Press, 1999), 347–49. Rawls drew a contrast between a thin (basic, minimal) theory of the good and what he called "a full theory of the good."

81. Nussbaum, "Nature, Function, and Capability," 152.

82. Ibid., 154.

83. Ibid., 155. Nussbaum credits the Nobel Prize–winning economist Amartya Sen with developing this criticism of utilitarianism.

84. Ibid., 174–75.

85. Ibid., 177.

86. Ibid., 181.

87. Ibid., 183, quoting Karl Marx, *Economic and Philosophical Manuscripts of 1844*, trans. Martin Milligan, in *The Marx–Engels Reader*, 2nd ed., ed. Robert C. Tucker (New York: W.W. Norton, 1978), 88–89; ellipsis is Nussbaum's. It allows Marx's main point to stand out from a mass of detail.

88. Ibid., 184.

89. Nussbaum, "Aristotelian Social Democracy," in *Liberalism and the Good*, ed. R. Bruce Douglas, Gerald M. Mara, and Henry S. Richardson (New York: Routledge, 1990), 203–52; reprinted in *Aristotle and Modern Politics: The Persistence of Political Philosophy*, ed. Aristide Tessitore (Notre Dame, IN: University of Notre Dame Press, 2002), 47–104; the reprinted version adds a postscript from 2001, 90–92; pagination here follows the 1990 version except for that postscript. Manuel Knoll has argued that Nussbaum departs from Aristotle at many points; see Knoll, "How Aristotelian Is Martha Nussbaum's 'Aristotelian Social Democracy'?," *Revista di Filosofia* 105 (2014): 207–22. Here I am treating the essay as evidence for Nussbaum's own position.

90. Nussbaum, "Aristotelian Social Democracy," 203. Aristotle does not count women or slaves as citizens. Nussbaum's use of ideas from his *Politics* does not commit her to his restrictive view of citizenship.

91. Ibid., 205–6, 217.

92. Ibid., 206.

93. Ibid., 209.

94. Ibid., 219–24, highly compressed. Compare the list in Nussbaum, "Non-Relative Virtues," 263–65.

95. Nussbaum, "Aristotelian Social Democracy," 224.

96. Ibid., 225. Nussbaum's list of the basic capabilities has developed over time: "The list is an attempt to summarize the empirical findings of a broad and ongoing cross-cultural inquiry. As such, it is open-ended and humble; it can always be contested and remade. It does not claim to read facts of 'human nature' off of biological observation, although it does of course take account of biology as a relatively constant element in human experience. Not does it deny that the items on the list are to some extent differently constructed by different societies. Indeed, part of the idea of the list is that its members can be more concretely specified in accordance with local beliefs and circumstances"; Nussbaum, "Capabilities and Human Rights," *Fordham Law Review* 66 (1997): 273–300; quotation at 286. I will not attempt to follow all the changes and refinements in the list of capabilities. Here I have given the version found in Nussbaum, "Aristotelian Social Democracy" (1990). Later in this chapter I will present the version found in Nussbaum, *Creating Capabilities* (2011).

97. Nussbaum, "Aristotelian Social Democracy," 228.

98. Ibid.

99. Ibid., 234.

100. Ibid., 235.

101. Ibid., 236.

102. Ibid., 237.

103. Ibid., 238.

104. Ibid.

105. Ibid.

106. The postscript follows Nussbaum, "Aristotelian Social Democracy," in *Aristotle and Modern Politics*, 90–92.

107. Nussbaum, "Human Functioning and Social Justice: In Defense of Aristotelian Essentialism," *Political Theory* 20 (1992): 202–46. A shortened version appears in *Moral Issues in Global Perspective*, ed. Christine M. Koggel (Toronto: Broadview Press, 2006), 4–25. The pagination here is that of the original article.

108. Nussbaum, "Human Functioning," 204.

109. Ibid.

110. Ibid., 205.

111. Ibid., 206.

112. Ibid., 207. This comes close to her criticism of Plato in *Fragility of Goodness*.

113. Ibid.

114. Ibid., 212–13.

115. Ibid., 213. Nussbaum distinguishes relativism and subjectivism as follows: "By relativism I mean the view that the only available standard to value is some local

group or individual; by subjectivism I mean the view that the standard is given by each individual's subjective preferences; thus relativism, as I understand it here, is a genus of which subjectivism is one extreme species" (243n14).

116. Ibid., 208 (the objection) and 224–25 (the reply).

117. Ibid., 208–9 (the objection) and 225–26 (the reply).

118. Ibid., 209 (the objection) and 226–27 (the reply); quote at 226.

119. Ibid., 227. On human being as an evaluative concept, see also Nussbaum, "Nature, Function, and Capability": "The question as to whether a certain function is or is not a part of our human nature is a certain special sort of evaluative question, namely, a question about whether that function is so important that a creature who lacked it would not be judged to be properly human at all" (177).

120. Nussbaum, "Human Functioning," 227. The emphasis in this and the next three quotations is mine.

121. Ibid., 228.

122. Ibid.

123. Ibid., 229. These four quotations are important for understanding Nussbaum's internal realism. She clearly takes it to be a fact that human powers and capabilities exert claims on other human beings and on society. People who do not recognize this fact nonetheless ought to recognize it.

124. Ibid., 230.

125. Ibid.

126. Ibid., 231.

127. Ibid.

128. Ibid., 232.

129. Ibid.

130. Ibid., 233, all four quotations.

131. Nussbaum, "Transcending Humanity," in *Love's Knowledge*, 391. Nussbaum refers to page 218, where she lists the four papers.

132. Nussbaum, "The Future of Feminist Liberalism," *Proceedings and Addresses of the American Philosophical Association* 74 (2000): 47–79; reprinted in *Setting the Moral Compass: Essays by Women Philosophers*, ed. Cheshire Calhoun (Oxford: Oxford University Press, 2004), 72–88. The reprinted version omits six paragraphs on the capabilities approach, an appendix listing the central capabilities, and more than half the footnotes. Pagination here follows the original. An earlier defense of liberalism is Nussbaum, "The Feminist Critique of Liberalism," in *Sex and Social Justice* (Oxford: Oxford University Press, 1999), 55–80. More of her thinking about the situation of women can be gathered from Nussbaum, "Aristotle, Feminism, and Needs for Functioning," *Texas Law Review* 70 (1991–92): 1019–28; it also appears in *Feminist Interpretations of Aristotle*, ed. Cynthia A. Freeland (University Park: University of Pennsylvania Press, 1998), 248–59; and Nussbaum, "Justice for Women!," her 1992 review of Susan Moller Okin, *Justice, Gender, and the Family*, in *Philosophical Interventions: Reviews 1986–2011* (New York: Oxford University Press, 2012), 115–29. Nussbaum, "Women in the Sixties," in *Reassessing the*

Sixties: Debating the Political and Cultural Legacy, ed. Stephen Macedo (New York: W. W. Norton, 1997), 82–101, gives additional background on Nussbaum's feminist liberalism.

133. Nussbaum, "Future of Feminist Liberalism," 48.

134. Ibid., 49.

135. Ibid., 49–50.

136. Ibid., 54–55; quote at 55.

137. Ibid., 56.

138. Ibid., 58.

139. Ibid., 59.

140. Ibid., 59–63.

141. Ibid., 63.

142. Ibid., 63–67.

143. Ibid., 67.

144. Nussbaum, *Women and Human Development: The Capabilities Approach* (Cambridge: Cambridge University Press, 2000).

145. Nussbaum, *Sex and Social Justice* (New York: Oxford University Press, 1999). The introduction, 3–25, gives an excellent overview of her position.

146. Nussbaum, "Discernment," in *Love's Knowledge*, 101–4.

147. Ibid., 103.

148. Ibid., 104.

149. Nussbaum, *Cultivating Humanity: A Classical Defense of Reform in Liberal Education* (Cambridge, MA: Harvard University Press, 1997).

150. Ibid., 84.

151. Nussbaum, *Not for Profit: Why Democracy Needs the Humanities* (Princeton, NJ: Princeton University Press, 2010; with a new afterword, 2012).

152. Nussbaum, *The Therapy of Desire: Theory and Practice in Hellenistic Ethics* (Princeton, NJ: Princeton University Press, 1994; reprinted with new introduction 2009).

153. Ibid., 507.

154. Ibid., 101.

155. Ibid., 102–3. See also 490: "Finally, the Hellenistic schools are the first in philosophy's history in the West to *recognize the existence of unconscious motives and beliefs.* This innovation—again both substantive and methodological—leads, as I have argued, to a radical change in the methods of Aristotelian dialectic" (emphasis is Nussbaum's).

156. These agenda were also foreshadowed in other works. In the concluding section of Nussbaum, "Human Functioning" (1992), she explored the relationship between the moral sentiments of compassion and respect, arguing that both of them require an essentialist notion of common human functioning (237–41). (The reprinted version in *Setting the Moral Compass* omits this section.) She explored the political implications of the emotion of pity; see Nussbaum, "Compassion: The Basic Social Emotion," *Social*

Philosophy and Policy 13 (1996): 27–58. "The friend of pity should argue, I think, that pity is our species' way of connecting the good of others to the fundamentally eudaimonistic (though not egoistic) structure of our imaginations and our most intense cares. The good of others means nothing to us in the abstract or antecedently. Only when it is brought into relation with that which we already understand—with our intense love of a parent, our passionate need for comfort and security—does such a thing start to matter deeply" (48).

157. Nussbaum, *Creating Capabilities: The Human Development Approach* (Cambridge, MA: The Belknap Press of Harvard University Press, 2011), 59.

158. Ibid., 126–27; first two quotations at 126, the third at 127.

159. Ibid., 127.

160. Ibid., 128–31; quote at 128.

161. Ibid., 124.

162. Ibid., 132.

163. Ibid., 140. For Nussbaum's account of Smith and Paine, see 133–40.

164. Ibid., 33–34 (emphasis original).

165. Ibid., 40.

166. Ibid., 31–32, 71, 73, 75, 166–70, 178.

167. Ibid., 24–26, 97–100, 110–11. Nussbaum is not saying or implying that individuals should be free to do anything they please. Her point is that it is not for government to decide for people how they will exercise their capabilities.

168. John Rawls, *Political Liberalism* (New York: Columbia University Press, 1993), 2.

169. Nussbaum, *Creating Capabilities*, 75–76. Nussbaum had earlier articulated her position in the 2009 introduction to *Therapy of Desire*, xv: "This is a good place to clarify an issue that has caused considerable misunderstanding. From about 1995 on, I have held the view that in a pluralistic society political principles ought to be built out of materials that all reasonable citizens can endorse—and thus ought to avoid any sort of metaphysical or epistemological grounding that would slant them toward one religious or secular comprehensive doctrine more than another. In other words, I agree with John Rawls: we should seek a form of *political liberalism*, meaning a political doctrine that is fair to all the different ways in which citizens pursue the good, refusing to endorse one of them over the others."

170. Nussbaum, *Creating Capabilities*, 89.

171. Ibid., 90. Cf. 93: "The point that is relevant here is that the Capabilities Approach is a political doctrine only, and one that aspires to be the object of an Overlapping Consensus. As such, it should not recommend any comprehensive ethical doctrine or be built upon one."

172. Ibid., 92–93. Nor is Nussbaum herself committed to cosmopolitanism. Cf. 93: "Whether my own comprehensive ethical doctrine is cosmopolitan or not is a separate question (it isn't, but it is close)." Nussbaum, "Patriotism and Cosmopolitanism" (1994) may have suggested to some that her position was a form of cosmopolitanism.

That essay was the lead chapter in *For Love of Country: Debating the Limits of Patriotism*, ed. Joshua Cohen (Boston: Beacon Press, 1996), 2–17, with Nussbaum's reply to the other contributors at 131–44. When the essay was reprinted in *The Cosmopolitanism Reader*, ed. Garrett Wallace Brown and David Held (Cambridge: Polity, 2010), 155–62, the editors added the following note: "The author would like us to alert you to the fact that her views on this topic have changed in significant ways. For her latest argument, please see M. Nussbaum, 'Toward a Globally Sensitive Patriotism,' *Daedalus*, vol. 137, n. 3 (2008): pp. 78–93." There Nussbaum argues that a patriotic commitment to one's own nation is legitimate, even necessary, provided it is purified in certain ways and globally conscious. As of this writing, her latest book is Nussbaum, *The Cosmopolitan Tradition: A Noble but Flawed Ideal* (Cambridge, MA: The Belknap Press of Harvard University Press, 2019).

173. Nussbaum, *Creating Capabilities*, 35.

174. Ibid., 66–67. Cf. 147: "As John Stuart Mill pointed out, this move [conceiving of the family as a private sphere] was an inconsistency within classical liberalism, not its natural outgrowth, since liberalism at its core is committed to equal liberty and opportunity for all. Leaving the family uncriticized was leaving a little piece of feudal hierarchy uncriticized, and liberalism is rightly subversive of all hierarchies based on birth or status."

175. Ibid., 96.

176. Nussbaum, *Fragility of Goodness*, 252–54. For Nussbaum's criticism of ancient Pyrrhonian skepticism and the contemporary skepticism of Stanley Fish and Richard Rorty, see Nussbaum, "Equilibrium: Scepticism and Immersion in Political Deliberation," in *Ancient Scepticism and the Sceptical Tradition*, ed. Juha Sihvola (Helsinki: The Philosophical Society of Finland, 2000), 171–97.

177. Nussbaum, *Fragility of Goodness*, appendix to part III, 373–77.

178. Nussbaum's reading of Aristotle's "method of appearances" has been critically examined by John M. Cooper, review of *The Fragility of Goodness*, by Martha Craven Nussbaum, *Philosophical Review* 97 (1988): 543–64. This also appears as Cooper, "Aristotle on the Authority of 'Appearances,'" in *Reason and Emotion: Essays on Ancient Moral Psychology and Ethical Theory* (Princeton, NJ: Princeton University Press, 1999), 281–91. Another critical examination is William Wians, "Saving Aristotle from Nussbaum's *Phainomena*," in *Essays in Ancient Greek Philosophy V: Aristotle's Ontology*, ed. Anthony Preus and John P. Anton (Albany: State University of New York Press, 1992), 133–49.

179. We have met some of these disagreements in the 2001 preface to *Fragility of Goodness*, in "Nature, Function, and Capability," and in "Non-Relative Virtues." See also Nussbaum, "Recoiling from Reason: Alasdair MacIntyre, *Whose Justice? Which Rationality?*," in Nussbaum, *Philosophical Interventions*, 53–68. This review first appeared in the *New York Review of Books*, December 7, 1989.

180. In MacIntyre, *Whose Justice? Which Rationality?*, 169, he writes as follows: "A key word in the formulation of this kind of internalism [MacIntyre is writing about

Hilary Putnam's position in *Reason, Truth and History*] in respect to truth and reality is 'we.' The assumption underlying its use is that there is one and only one overall community of enquiry, sharing substantially one and the same set of concepts and beliefs. But what if there appears a second community whose tradition and procedures of enquiry are structured in terms of different, largely incompatible and largely incommensurable concepts and beliefs, defining warranted assertibility and truth in terms internal to its scheme of concepts and beliefs?" This would seem to be a fair question to raise about Nussbaum's internal realism and about the method of appearances.

181. The adversarial character of some of the reviews collected in Nussbaum, *Philosophical Interventions*, points in the same direction. Besides Nussbaum's review of MacIntyre, *Whose Justice? Which Rationality?*, I am thinking of her reviews of Roger Scruton, *Sexual Desire* (1986), Allen Bloom, *The Closing of the American Mind* (1987), and Harvey C. Mansfield Jr., *Manliness* (2006). In addition, many of her books from *Upheavals of Thought* through *The Monarchy of Fear* suggest that significant numbers of people are influenced by irrational feelings of disgust, envy, shame, and anger that stand in need of criticism.

182. Nussbaum's proposal that the fundamental entitlements should be entrenched in the U.S. Constitution suggests an awareness that they may not always command sufficient political support and that they may need to be enforced through the judicial process.

183. The distinctions between reasonable and unreasonable comprehensive doctrines and between reasonable and unreasonable disagreements come from Rawls. Nussbaum explores them in her 2015 introduction to Rawls's *"Political Liberalism,"* 22–31. At 27 she criticizes Rawls's attempt to offer theoretical, as distinct from practical, criteria for reasonableness: "What dooms the whole project of offering theoretical criteria for reasonableness, however, so far as I can see, is that the major religions, his central cases, fail to meet them, and they fail for reasons that, in the case of Christianity, go deep: a repudiation of theoretical reason that lies at the heart of that religion's account of faith, at least in some central instances."

184. I borrow this term from Charles Taylor, "Atomism," in *Philosophical Papers 2: Philosophy and the Human Sciences* (Cambridge: Cambridge University Press, 1985), 187–210.

185. Nussbaum, "Future of Feminist Liberalism," 63.

186. The theological ethicist Lisa Sowle Cahill has argued that Nussbaum could strengthen the capabilities approach by taking more account of the sociality and social interdependence of persons that are stressed in Roman Catholic social teaching. "What Catholic social teaching could bring to Martha Nussbaum is greater recognition of the sociality of persons, and of the social dimensions of every aspect of human embodiment. What Martha Nussbaum could bring to Catholic social teaching is the commitment to see women's basic human needs and rights as primary, in no way to be subordinated to their reproductive roles"; see Cahill, "Justice for Women: Martha Nussbaum and Catholic Social Teaching," in *Transforming Unjust Structures: The Capability Approach*, ed. Séver-

ine Deneulin, Mathias Nebel, and Nicholas Sagovsky (Dordrecht: Springer, 2006), 83–104; quotation at 86.

187. Charles Taylor made a similar point in his response to Nussbaum, "Patriotism and Cosmopolitanism": "A citizen democracy can only work if most of its members are convinced that their political society is a common venture of considerable moment and believe it to be of such vital importance that they participate in the ways they must to keep it functioning as a democracy"; see Taylor, "Why Democracy Needs Patriotism," in Cohen, ed., *For Love of Country*, 120.

Chapter Four.   The Personalist Aristotelianism of Robert Spaemann

This chapter has been much improved by comments from Jeremiah Alberg, Oliver O'Donovan, and Robert Sokolowski. They are not responsible for errors or infelicities that remain.

1. The following summary of Spaemann's education and publications draws heavily on the introduction to Spaemann, *Philosophische Essays* (Stuttgart: Reclam, 1983; exp. ed. 1994), 3–18. This appears in English as "A Philosophical Autobiography," in *A Robert Spaemann Reader: Philosophical Essays on Nature, God, and the Human Person*, ed. D. C. Schindler and Jeanne Heffernan Schindler (Oxford: Oxford University Press, 2015), 11–21.

2. Spaemann, *Der Ursprung der Soziologie aus dem Geist der Restauration: Studien über L. G. A. de Bonald* (Munich: Kösel, 1959).

3. Spaemann, *Reflexion und Spontaneität: Studien über Fénelon* (Stuttgart: Kohlhammer, 1963; exp. ed., Stuttgart: Klett-Cotta, 1990). Chapter 2 of this work is available in English as "Bourgeois Ethics and Non-Teleological Ontology," in Schindler and Schindler, eds., *A Robert Spaemann Reader*, 45–59.

4. Spaemann, *Zur Kritik der politischen Utopie: Zehn Kapitel politischer Philosophie* (*A Critique of Political Utopia: Ten Chapters in Political Philosophy*) (Stuttgart: Klett, 1977). The volume includes an exchange between Spaemann and Jürgen Habermas.

5. Spaemann, *Rousseau—Bürger ohne Vaterland: Von der Polis zur Natur* (Munich: Piper, 1980). This later appeared as *Rousseau—Bürger ohne Vaterland: Das Dilemma der Moderne* (Stuttgart: Kletta-Cotta, 2008). Chapter 1 of this work is available in English as "Natural Existence and Political Existence in Rousseau," in *A Robert Spaemann Reader*, 125–38. Chapter 2 is available in English as "From the Polis to Nature: The Controversy Surrounding Rousseau's *First Discourse*," in *A Robert Spaemann Reader*, 60–76.

6. Spaemann, *Die Frage Wozu? Geschichte und Wiederentdeckung des teleologischen Denkens* (*The Question "To What End?" The History and Rediscovery of Teleological Thinking*) (Munich and Zurich: Piper, 1981; exp. ed., 1985), was based on lectures that Spaemann had delivered in 1976 and 1977. The expanded edition added a new concluding chapter, "Teleologie und Teleonomie," to which we shall return. Spaemann was Löw's scientific assistant. Löw died in 1994. He later brought out a new edition with a

revised foreword, now Spaemann, *Natürliche Ziele* (*Natural Ends*) (Stuttgart: Klett-Cotta, 2005).

7. Spaemann, *Moralische Grundbegriffe* (Munich: Beck, 1982); available in English as *Basic Moral Concepts*, trans. T. J. Armstrong (London: Routledge, 1989). The idea that ethics should start with a prephilosophical awareness of right and wrong that all or most human beings share goes back at least as far as Kant's *Groundwork for the Metaphysics of Morals*, the first section of which is entitled "Transition from Common Rational Moral Cognition to Philosophical Moral Cognition." I am using Wood's translation in Immanuel Kant, *Groundwork for the Metaphysics of Morals*, trans. Allen W. Wood (New Haven, CT: Yale University Press, 2002), vii, 9.

8. Spaemann, *Philosophische Essays* (1994).

9. Spaemann, *Das Natürliche und das Vernünftige* (*The Natural and the Rational*) (Munich and Zurich: Piper, 1987); now in English as *Essays in Anthropology: Variations on a Theme*, trans. Guido de Graaff and James Mumford (Eugene, OR: Cascade Books, 2010).

10. Spaemann, *Glück und Wohlwollen: Versuch über Ethik* (Stuttgart: Klett-Cotta, 1989); Spaemann, *Happiness and Benevolence*, trans. Jeremiah Alberg (Notre Dame, IN: University of Notre Dame Press, 1998).

11. Spaemann, *Personen: Versuche über den Unterschied zwischen "etwas" und "jemand"* (Stuttgart: Klett-Cotta, 1996); *Persons: The Difference between "Someone" and "Something,"* trans. Oliver O'Donovan (Oxford: Oxford University Press, 2006); hereafter cited as *Persons*.

12. Spaemann, *Grenzen: Zur ethischen Dimension des Handelns* (Stuttgart: Klett-Cotta, 2001). *Grenzen* means "borders," "boundaries," or "limits."

13. Spaemann, *Das unsterbliche Gerücht: Die Frage nach Gott und die Täuschung der Moderne* (Stuttgart: Klett-Cotta, 2007); Spaemann, *Der letzte Gottesbeweis* (with Rolf Schönberger) (München: Pattloch, 2007). Chapter 1 of *Das unsterbliche Gerücht* appears as "The Undying Rumor: The God Question and the Modern Delusion," in *A Robert Spaemann Reader*, 179–91.

14. Spaemann, *Schritte über Uns Hinaus: Gesammelte Reden und Aufsätze*, Vol. 1 (Stuttgart: Klett-Cotta, 2010); Spaemann, *Schritte über Uns Hinaus: Gesammelte Reden und Aufsätze*, Vol. 2 (Stuttgart: Klett-Cotta, 2011); the title "Steps beyond Ourselves" is a critical allusion to Hume's remark that we never really advance a step beyond ourselves.

15. Spaemann, *Love and the Dignity of Human Life: On Nature and Natural Law* (Grand Rapids, MI: William B. Eerdmans, 2012).

16. Spaemann, *Über Gott und die Welt: Eine Autobiographie in Gesprächen* (Stuttgart: Klett-Cotta, 2012). Stephan Sattler was the interviewer and edited the book.

17. See https://thetrueeurope.eu/a-europe-we-can-believe-in/. Other signatories included Rémi Brague, Pierre Manent, and Roger Scruton.

18. Max Horkheimer and Theodor Adorno, *Dialektik der Aufklärung*; in English as *Dialectic of Enlightenment*, trans. John Cumming (New York: Seabury/Continuum, 1972), and as *Dialectic of Enlightenment: Philosophical Fragments*, trans. Edmund Jeph-

cott (Stanford, CA: Stanford University Press, 2002); C. S. Lewis, *The Abolition of Man* (London: Geoffrey Bles, 1967).

19. As Robert Sokolowski points out, this is comparable to Aristotle's approach in *Nicomachean Ethics* 7.1, 1145b2–8: if we can lay out the phenomena, work through any difficulties arising from the phenomena, and leave most of the common opinions and the most important of them standing, we have done enough.

20. Spaemann, *Happiness and Benevolence*, vii.

21. Sokolowski points out that this is Aristotle's procedure in defending the principle of noncontradiction in *Metaphysics* 4.

22. For more on this point, see Spaemann, "Die kontroverse Natur der Philosophie," in *Philosophische Essays*, 104–29. Richard Schenk, O.P., who studied with Spaemann in Munich, writes, "The same Socratic preference for arguments over global claims brought to Spaemann's seminars both a relative freedom from the conflicts of ideological camps and something of the excitement of a gambling casino. . . . This preference for the disputed question over the indisputable system means of course that philosophy itself can never be considered finished." See Schenk, "The Ethics of Robert Spaemann in the Context of Recent Philosophy," in *One Hundred Years of Philosophy*, ed. Brian J. Shanley, O.P. (Washington, DC: Catholic University of America Press, 2001), 156–68; quotation at 161–62. Spaemann sometimes speaks of anarchy as a necessary condition for philosophy. See also Spaemann, "Philosophie als institutionalisierte Naivität" ("Philosophy as Institutionalized Naiveté"), *Philosophisches Jahrbuch* 81 (1974): 139–42.

23. Spaemann, "A Philosophical Autobiography," in *A Robert Spaemann Reader*, 16–17.

24. Spaemann characterizes the Marquis de Sade's worldview as a form of materialism in which the whole world, human and nonhuman, is without any objective meaning: "Now he of course is an extreme and abnormal case, yet those who share his materialistic worldview have no way of understanding their revulsion to his behavior other than as subjective dislike. Their displeasure is as indifferent as the Marquis's pleasure that causes it. In fact, their disgust can be seen to top off his own satisfaction!"; see Spaemann, "Evolution," in *Essays in Anthropology*, 30.

25. Spaemann, "Human Dignity," in *Essays in Anthropology*, 49–72, esp. 68–72; also appears in *A Robert Spaemann Reader*, 97–110.

26. His fullest and most systematic characterization of modernity appears in Spaemann, "Ende der Modernität?" (1986), in *Philosophische Essays* (1994), 232–60; and Spaemann, "The End of Modernity?," in *A Robert Spaemann Reader*, 211–29. See also Spaemann, "Christianity and Modern Philosophy," in *One Hundred Years of Philosophy*, ed. Brian J. Shanley, O.P. (Washington, DC: Catholic University of America Press, 2001), 169–80.

27. Spaemann, "A Philosophical Autobiography," in *A Robert Spaemann Reader*, 18.

28. One such essay that is translated is Spaemann, "Nature," in *A Robert Spaemann Reader*, 22–36. The German original, "Natur," is the first essay in Spaemann,

Philosophische Essays, 19–40; first published in *Handbuch philosophischer Grundbegriffe*, ed. Hermann Krings, Hans M. Baumgartner, and Christoph Wild (Munich: Kösel, 1973).

29. Spaemann, *Persons*, 42. To speak of pursuit or drive as the basic structure of subjective experience is not to deny that pursuits and drives are grounded on the more basic needs arising from our teleological nature.

30. Spaemann, "Naturteleologie und Handlung," in *Philosophische Essays*, 42–46; in *Grenzen*, 38–41.

31. Spaemann, "Zur Ontologie der Begriffe 'Rechts' und "Links,'" in *Grenzen*, 263–64; Spaemann, "Remarks on the Ontology of 'Right' and 'Left,'" *Graduate Faculty Philosophy Journal* 10 (1984): 95.

32. Spaemann, "Natur," in *Philosophische Essays*, 25; "Nature," in *A Robert Spaemann Reader*, 26.

33. Spaemann, *Persons*, 137.

34. Ibid., 140.

35. Ibid., 144.

36. The chapter "Teleologie und Teleonomie" appears in the expanded edition of Spaemann, *Die Frage Wozu?*, and in Spaemann, *Natürliche Ziele*. In his foreword, Spaemann described the chapter as a short statement of the position for which the book as a whole is arguing. The book he describes as a plea "to reconsider the prejudice that has become dear to science, that sense is a variant of un-sense, reason is a variant of un-reason, and that the human being itself is an anthropomorphism" (quotation in *Die Frage Wozu?*, 11, and *Natürliche Ziele*, 9).

37. This comparison seems to go back to the British geneticist J. B. S. Haldane. See the letter of Colin Pittendrigh reproduced in Ernst Mayr, "The Multiple Meanings of Teleological," in *Toward a New Philosophy of Biology: Observations of an Evolutionist* (Cambridge, MA: The Belknap Press of Harvard University Press, 1988), 63.

38. Spaemann, "Teleologie und Teleonomie," in *Die Frage Wozu?*, 300; in *Natürliche Ziele*, 249. Here Spaemann appears to be thinking of Pittendrigh. So too in Spaemann, "Naturteleologie und Handlung," in *Grenzen*, 42. The earlier version of this essay in Spaemann, *Philosophische Essays*, 48, had cited Jacques Monod rather than Pittendrigh. Mayr says in *Toward a New Philosophy of Biology: Observations of an Evolutionist* that Pittendrigh's "placing the term *teleonomic* in opposition to Aristotle's *teleology* is unfortunate" (47). Mayr's project is not to reject teleological language but to distinguish different classes of teleological phenomena, to one of which he applies the term "teleonomic"; see his conclusions, 59–60. Spaemann cites an earlier version of Ernst Mayr, "Teleological and Teleonomic: A New Analysis," in *Methodological and Historical Essays in the Natural and Social Sciences*, Boston Studies in the Philosophy of Science XIV, ed. Robert S. Cohen and Marx Wartofsky (Dordrecht: D. Reidel, 1974), 91–117. The conclusions of this earlier paper, 113–14, are essentially the same. It includes Pittendrigh's reference to Haldane's remark (115), and Mayr's criticism of Pittendrigh (101).

39. Spaemann, "Teleologie und Teleonomie," in *Die Frage Wozu?*, 301; in *Natürliche Ziele*, 249–50.

40. Spaemann, "Teleologie und Teleonomie," in *Die Frage Wozu?*, 305–6; in *Natürliche Ziele*, 253–54.

41. Spaemann, "Teleologie und Teleonomie," in *Die Frage Wozu?*, 301–2; in *Natürliche Ziele*, 250. This is a reference to a statement in section 75 of Kant's *Critique of Judgment* (1790): "For it is quite certain that in terms of merely mechanical principles of nature we cannot even adequately become familiar with, much less explain, organized beings and how they are internally possible. So certain is this that we may boldly state that it is absurd for human beings even to attempt it, or to hope that perhaps some day another Newton might arise who would explain to us, in terms of natural laws unordered by any intention, how even a mere blade of grass is produced"; Kant, *Critique of Judgment*, trans. Werner Pluhar (Indianapolis: Hackett, 1987), 282.

42. Spaemann, "Teleologie und Teleonomie," in *Die Frage Wozu?*, 306; in *Natürliche Ziele*, 254–55. For example, an acorn has the potentiality to become an oak tree, but acorns themselves come from actual oak trees; an egg has the potentiality to develop into a chicken, but eggs come from actual chickens. Aristotle argues for the priority of actuality to potentiality in *Metaphysics* 9.8.

43. Spaemann, "Teleologie und Teleonomie," in *Die Frage Wozu?*, 307; in *Natürliche Ziele*, 255. The expression "first philosophy" goes back to Aristotle, who presented his metaphysics as the primary or most basic form of philosophy.

44. Spaemann, "Teleologie und Teleonomie," in *Die Frage Wozu?*, 304–5; in *Natürliche Ziele*, 253. In Spaemann's original German, this sentence is italicized for emphasis.

45. Spaemann, "Teleologie und Teleonomie," in *Die Frage Wozu?*, 304; in *Natürliche Ziele*, 252–53. In simplest terms, "being out for" (*Aus-sein-auf*) is that which manifests itself in drives such as hunger and thirst. Spaemann sometimes writes *Ausseinauf* without hyphens. I drop the hyphens in translation.

46. Spaemann, "Teleologie und Teleonomie," in *Die Frage Wozu?*, 307–8; in *Natürliche Ziele*, 256.

47. Spaemann, "Naturteleologie und Handlung," in *Philosophische Essays*, 48–57, and *Grenzen*, 42–48; quotation from *Philosophische Essays*, 57, and *Grenzen*, 48 (my translation). He expands on this idea in Spaemann, "Wirklichkeit als Anthropomorphismus" ("Reality as Anthropomorphism") (2008), in *Schritte über Uns Hinaus: Gesammelte Reden und Aufsätze II*, 188–215, which appears in English as "In Defense of Anthropomorphism," in *A Robert Spaemann Reader*, 77–96.

48. The phrase "hermeneutic of nature" (*Hermeneutik der Natur*) comes from Spaemann, "Naturteleologie und Handlung," in *Philosophische Essays*, 49, and *Grenzen*, 43.

49. Spaemann, *Persons*, 156.

50. Spaemann, "Die Aktualität des Naturrechts," in *Philosophische Essays*, 60–79. I translate *Naturrecht* as "natural right" rather than "natural law" in order to preserve the connection between *Naturrecht* and *das von Natur Rechte*, "that which is naturally right" or "that which is right by nature." We will return to this essay later in this chapter.

51. Ibid., 66–69; slogan at 68. I have not been able to trace its origin, but Spae-mann criticizes Karl Marx and Jürgen Habermas for thinking that freedom from domination requires the overcoming of scarcity, presumably through more effective domination of nature; see Spaemann, "Die Utopie der Herrschaftsfreiheit" ("The Uto-pia of Freedom from Being Ruled"), in *Zur Kritik der politischen Utopie*, 121. The point that domination over nature can turn into domination over human beings echoes the first chapter of Horkheimer and Adorno, *Dialectic of Enlightenment*, and, even more closely, chapter 3 of Lewis, *Abolition of Man*.

52. Spaemann, *Grenzen*, 15–26; first appeared in *Ethik-Lesebuch: Von Platon bis Heute*, ed. Robert Spaemann (Munich and Zurich: Piper, 1987), 9–24. A slightly dif-ferent version appeared in a revised edition of this collection, *Ethik Lehr- und Lesebuch: Texte—Fragen—Antworten*, ed. Robert Spaemann and Walter Schweidler (Stuttgart: Klett-Cotta: 2006), 11–24. This version adds a concluding paragraph not found in the original or in the version in *Grenzen*.

53. Spaemann, "Was ist philosophische Ethik?," in *Grenzen*, 16–17.

54. Ibid., 17–18.

55. Ibid., 15, 18; the German at 18 is [*eine*] *"Metaethik" historischer, soziologischer, psychologischer oder ethnologischer Art*, "a historical, sociological, psychological, or ethno-logical kind of 'metaethics'" (translations from this essay are mine).

56. Ibid., 18–19.

57. Ibid., 19–20.

58. Ibid., 20–22; quotation at 22.

59. Kant, *Critique of Practical Reason*, postulated the reality of God, human free-dom, and immortality not on theoretical grounds—in his *Critique of Pure Reason* he had argued that there were no sufficient theoretical grounds for these affirmations—but on practical grounds, as required to make sense of our moral experience.

60. Spaemann, "Was ist philosophische Ethik?," 22–23. Spaemann uses "real" (*wirklich*) and "reality" (*Wirklichkeit*) to refer to the recognition of specially personal re-alities. "A becomes real to B" is Spaemann's way of saying that B recognizes that A is a person.

61. Spaemann, *Happiness and Benevolence*, foreword, vii–ix; quotation at vii–viii. The wording recalls Kant's formulation of the categorical imperative: "Act only in accor-dance with that maxim through which you can at the same time will that it become a universal law" (see Kant, *Groundwork for the Metaphysics of Morals*, 37). See also Spae-mann, "A Philosophical Autobiography," in *A Robert Spaemann Reader*, 20: "But all the differentiation [of the ethical phenomenon] does not change the fact that no obligation possesses the power to move if it is not grasped as a necessary condition for the *vita beata* [the happy life], or more precisely, if it is not grasped as this good life itself."

62. Spaemann, *Happiness and Benevolence*, viii–ix.

63. Ibid., 40–41. Spaemann cites R. M. Hare. This is most likely a reference to Hare, *Moral Thinking: Its Levels, Method, and Point* (Oxford: Clarendon, 1981), 143.

There Hare credits Smart in J. J. C. Smart and Bernard Williams, *Utilitarianism For and Against* (Cambridge: Cambridge University Press, 1973), 18 and n1.

64. Spaemann, *Happiness and Benevolence*, 39, 43, 47–50.

65. Ibid., 53–55, 57–59; quotation at 54–55.

66. Ibid., 56–57. Aristotle discusses this point in *Nicomachean Ethics* 1.10.

67. Ibid., 64.

68. Ibid., 61–69.

69. Ibid., 69.

70. Ibid., 73–79; quotations at 77 and 78–79.

71. Ibid., 77–78; quotations at 78.

72. Spaemann is not denying that plants are alive, but affirming that human life is a form of animal life.

73. Spaemann, *Persons*, 33 (emphasis is O'Donovan's). In the German original, Spaemann places *in einer solchen Natur existieren* ("exist in such and such a nature") in quotation marks.

74. Ibid., 216. The German original emphasizes the words for "from" and "is" but not the word for "person." Here Spaemann draws on Harry Frankfurt's distinction between primary and secondary volitions. By secondary volitions, Frankfurt means volitions *about* our primary volitions, our everyday desires and reactions. He gives the example of an addict who wants what he or she is addicted to, but who also wants *not* to be addicted to it; see Harry G. Frankfurt, "Freedom of the Will and the Concept of a Person," *Journal of Philosophy* 68 (1971): 5–20. Spaemann believes that these secondary volitions are really our primary volitions because they bear on who we are and what we most fundamentally want.

75. Spaemann, *Happiness and Benevolence*, 92–98; quotation at 98.

76. Ibid., 96. A passage from chapter 15 of *Persons*, 182, makes the same point: "To acknowledge personal status is already to express respect, which is the specific way in which persons are available to one another."

77. Ibid., 103.

78. Ibid. (emphasis original). Cf. 91: "Being oneself becomes possible only in free affirmation, in an act of acceptance. This act, however, in which life transcends itself and in this self-transcendence comes to a whole which examines its various states, is only possible through the highest powers of life. This self-transcendence of life is the rational: In its most elementary form we speak of justice; in its highest, of love."

79. I owe the formulations in these last two sentences to Robert Sokolowski.

80. Spaemann, *Persons*, 77.

81. A passage from one of Spaemann's essays on evolution makes the same point: "To recognize a thing as similar to us is not an act of theoretical science but remains in every case an act of free recognition [*ein Akt freier Anerkennung*] that can also be denied"; see Spaemann, "Being and Coming to Be: What Does the Theory of Evolution Explain?," in *A Robert Spaemann Reader*, 157. The passage is also found, in a different

translation, in Spaemann, *Essays in Anthropology*, 31: "Recognizing something as some-how similar to us . . . is not an act of theoretical science; it will always remain an act of free recognition, which could also be refused"; original German from "Sein und Ge-wordensein: Was erklärt die Evolutionstheorie?," in *Philosophische Essays*, 190, and in *Das Natürliche und das Vernünftige*, 50. Also: "Indeed, we saw earlier that being in the sense of reality is not an empirical datum. It does not force itself upon us. Realizing it requires a free act of reason. This does not have to be an explicit and reflexive act, but freedom nevertheless lies implicit in the experience, in the possibility of relinquishing my position at the center and acknowledging that there exists a self outside of me, which is not defined by its being my object. It is only in an act of recognition that the person is given as a person"; Spaemann, "In Defense of Anthropomorphism" (2008), in *A Robert Spaemann Reader*, 84–85.

82. Spaemann, *Persons*, 182.

83. Ibid., 183.

84. Spaemann, *Happiness and Benevolence*, 114. The statement that other human beings are unequivocally given to us might seem to contradict the statements at *Persons*, 77 and 183, that persons are not simply given but rather noticed in a free act of recog-nition. Lower down on page 114, however, Spaemann writes, "Plato's thesis that no one knows the good who does not also want it expresses the actual situation. *Amor oculus est* [love is an eye]." The recognition of what is given includes an aspect of freedom.

85. Spaemann, *Persons*, 185.

86. Ibid., 201–4; quotations at 203 and 204. Much earlier, Spaemann says "that when we apply the term 'person' to individuals we accord a special status to them, that of inviolability [*Unantastbarkeit*]" (ibid., 16). Compare the first sentence of the Basic Law (*Grundgesetz*) of the Federal Republic of Germany: "Die Würde des Menschen ist unantastbar" ("The dignity of the human being is inviolable").

87. Spaemann, *Happiness and Benevolence*, 103. Here Spaemann alludes to a quo-tation from Heraclitus DK B 89 that appears on page 1 of *Happiness and Benevolence*: "While awake, we have one common world. But dreamers turn each to their own." When we awake to the reality of other persons, benevolence toward them becomes part of our happiness. By "dreamers" Spaemann means people who have not awoken to the reality of other persons.

88. Ibid., 118.

89. Some Roman Catholic moral theologians speak of a "fundamental option" in the sense of a basic choice for or against God. The notion is controversial. Here and at *Happiness and Benevolence*, 150, Spaemann is taking "fundamental option" in a more general sense, not entering into that controversy. But see also note 117, below.

90. Spaemann, *Happiness and Benevolence*, 110.

91. Ibid., 111–12; quotation at 112.

92. Ibid., 112. In chapter 1, we saw that Elizabeth Anscombe understood conse-quentialism as the view that we are responsible for all the consequences of our actions,

not just those that we intend. As Spaemann uses the word, it means the view that agents are under an obligation to bring about the best possible state of affairs.

93. Ibid., 114. The claim is that recognition of a person is inseparable from (at least minimal) respect for the person. Spaemann, *Persons*, 182: "You cannot first assert that John is a person and then protest that persons matter no more to you than monarchs do. To acknowledge personal status is already to express respect, which is the specific way in which persons are accessible to one another." The German original of the first sentence is highly compressed and O'Donovan's English reflects the compression. I would expand, "You can say 'So and so is a monarch, but I don't respect monarchs.' You cannot say 'So and so is a person, but I don't respect persons.'" See Spaemann, *Persons*, 16–17: "We can declare that someone is a king, a city-freeman [*Ehrenbürger*, "an honored or honorary citizen"], or an officer, and yet be opposed to kings and officers and think the title 'freeman' an anachronistic survival. But if we do not intend to *respect* human beings as persons, we either deny that they *are* persons, or we consider the designation vacuous and unserviceable. To employ the term 'person' is to acknowledge definite obligations to those we so designate."

94. Spaemann, *Happiness and Benevolence*, 123–30; first quotation at 127, second at 128.

95. Ibid., 131. For a more detailed criticism of consequentialism, see Spaemann, "Über die Unmöglichkeit einer universalteleologischen Ethik" ("The Impossibility of a Comprehensive Teleological Ethics"), in *Grenzen*, 193–212. Here Spaemann is using "teleological" not in an Aristotelian sense but as equivalent to "consequentialist."

96. Spaemann, *Happiness and Benevolence*, 131–34; quotation at 132.

97. Ibid., 134–42; first quotation at 134, second at 138. Sokolowski says that discourse does not cause recognition, it presupposes it.

98. Spaemann, *Persons*, 96–97; quotation at 96. On the same page, Spaemann writes, "Textbooks in evolutionary biology are wont to conclude with urgent appeals that we should take responsibility for the survival of species; but those appeals have no logical connection with the contents of the textbooks."

99. Ibid., 96.

100. The chapter's title is somewhat misleading. The distinction between the statistically normal and the natural is just one of several points that Spaemann makes about the concept of nature and how it bears on implementing benevolence.

101. Spaemann, *Happiness and Benevolence*, 158–60.

102. Ibid., 160–61; quotation at 161. *Je suis le grand tout* appears in Voltaire's *Dialogue entre le philosophe et la nature* (*Dialogue between a Philosopher and Nature*), in his *Questions sur l'Encyclopédie par des amateurs*, Vol. 7, ed. Nicholas Cronk and Christiane Mervaud, Vol. 42B of *Les Oeuvres Complètes de Voltaire* (Oxford: Voltaire Foundation, 2012); the dialogue occupies 286–90; quotation at 287.

103. Spaemann, *Happiness and Benevolence*, 161.

104. Ibid., 161–62; quotation at 162.

105. Ibid., 163.

106. Ibid., 165.

107. Ibid.

108. Ibid., 165–67; quotation at 166. I have altered the translation slightly. Sokolowski points out, that there is no virtue or vice with respect to breathing, but there are virtue and vice with respect to eating and drinking.

109. Ibid., 168.

110. Ibid., 168–69; quotation at 168. I have altered the translation slightly.

111. Ibid., 169–70; quotation at 169 (my emphasis).

112. Ibid., 147–53; quotation at 150.

113. In his introduction to Rolf Schönberger's translation of and commentary on Aquinas's account, Spaemann summarizes that account and apparently endorses it; see Schönberger, *Thomas von Aquin: Über sittliches Handeln* (*Summa theologiae* I-II q. 18–21) (Stuttgart: Philipp Reclam, 2001), 7–18.

114. Spaemann, *Happiness and Benevolence*, 144–45.

115. Aquinas, *Summa Theologiae* I-II, q. 18, a. 6, says that an interior act of the will receives its *species* from the agent's end.

116. Spaemann, *Happiness and Benevolence*, 146. Spaemann, "Wer hat wofür Verantwortung?" ("Who Is Responsible for What?"), cites the case of a policeman whose superior officer ordered him to shoot a twelve-year old Jewish girl; if he refused, the superior would shoot twelve innocent people. The policeman shot the girl and went insane. In Spaemann's view the policeman was responsible for what he did, shooting the girl. He would not have been responsible for what his superior would have done, shooting the twelve innocent people; see *Grenzen*, 237.

117. Spaemann, *Persons*, 128–31. This is in opposition to a school of thought in Roman Catholic moral theology that would hold back from evaluating individual human acts in favor of evaluating a person's deeper options or commitments. For more on this point, see Spaemann, "Einzelhandlungen," in *Grenzen*, 49–64; in English as "Individual Actions," in *A Robert Spaemann Reader*, 139–53.

118. Spaemann, *Persons*, 131. In Spaemann's text and O'Donovan's translation the Latin is in a footnote.

119. Spaemann, *Happiness and Benevolence*, 173. This is another allusion to Heraclitus DK B 89.

120. Ibid., 173 (emphasis also in German original).

121. Ibid.

122. Ibid., 178.

123. Ibid., 181.

124. Ibid., 166.

125. Ibid., 167. Spaemann is aware of the debate in Catholic circles about the morality of artificial contraception. Here, however, he is speaking at a high level of generality, about a systematic detachment of sexual intercourse from procreation, not about individual contraceptive acts.

126. Ibid., 167–68.

127. Ibid., 168. Spaemann applies the adjective *naturwüchsig*, "merely natural," to events and processes that "just happen" rather than being the results of reasoned decision.

128. For more on this point, see Spaemann, "Begotten, Not Made," *Communio: International Catholic Review* 33 (2006): 290–97.

129. Spaemann, *Happiness and Benevolence*, 170. In a German context, this is the debate about whether it is better to speak in terms of human rights (*Menschenrechte*) or the rights of persons (*Personenrechte*). For some proponents of *Personenrechte* it is an open question which human beings are persons and which are not. Spaemann's view is that it is better to speak of the rights of human beings and that all human beings are persons. For more on this, see Spaemann, *Persons*, chap. 18, "Are All Human Beings Persons?"; Spaemann, "Is Every Human Being a Person?" *The Thomist* 60 (1996): 463–74; and Spaemann, "Sind alle Menschen Personen? Über neue philosophische Rechtfertigungen der Lebensvernichtung," in *Grenzen*, 417–28. Despite their similar titles, these three statements differ in a number of respects.

130. Spaemann, *Happiness and Benevolence*, 170.

131. Ibid., 170–71. In *Persons* and other writings Spaemann extends this to the mentally handicapped, the mentally ill, and the senile.

132. Ibid., 168–69. He makes this point: "There is . . . one proceeding that is simply ruled out: the use of physical torture to destroy another person's capacity to be the subject of his or her own acts, to induce performances that could not be described as acting freely. To threaten death does not destroy anyone's freedom. Life may be the price one has to pay for refusal to perform certain acts. But torture does not aim to prove freedom [*stellt die Freiheit nicht auf die Probe*, "does not put freedom to the test"] but to eradicate it, and it is incompatible with the a priori relation that obtains between persons" (ibid., 178). Coercion and torture are different. Coercion involves setting up alternatives and forcing a person to choose between them. Torture tries to destroy the possibility of the person's choosing. I owe this point to Robert Sokolowski.

133. Ibid., 169.

134. Ibid., 171.

135. Spaemann, "Die Aktualität des Naturrechts," in *Philosophische Essays*, 75–76. "The debate [about whether the human race is overstepping itself and hastening to its end] is as yet undecided. But since the debate is undecided, and since the human environment at a planetary level has for the first time become a dependent variable, natural right can only mean the demand, in any case revolutionary, perhaps even more revolutionary today, to fix the terms of the debate in a new way, to place the burden of proof on expansionist interventions. This may perhaps be incompatible with the relations of production under capitalism. But that would be an argument against those relations of production—and a total reversal of the Marxist argument, which takes the progressive expansion of technology as the standard of criticism" (ibid., 76; my translation).

136. Ibid., 76.

137. Ibid., 76–78.

138. In Spaemann, "Why There Is No Law without Natural Law," *Proceedings of the American Catholic Philosophical Association* 86 (2012): 17–21, he defends natural law or natural right thinking in opposition to legal positivism: "The constitution of my country contains a catalog of basic rights that is not subject to change by parliamentary majorities. If nothing is right by nature, then such basic rights constitute an unjustified submission on the part of those living today to the will of the dead, namely of the fathers and mothers of the Constitution. But they did not think their catalog of basic rights was an imposition on later generations. They did not understand themselves as creators of these basic rights; they did not think of themselves as authorized to bind the hands of their descendants. Rather, they wanted to codify for all time the recognition of a standard that they themselves had not posited" (20). Spaemann is referring to the rights recognized in Articles 1–19 of the Basic Law (*Grundgesetz*) of the Federal Republic of Germany.

139. Spaemann, *Basic Moral Concepts*, 26.

140. Ibid., 35. Further indications of his approach to education can be found in Spaemann, "The Courage to Educate," *Communio: International Catholic Review* 40 (2013): 48–63. This is a translation of a speech that Spaemann delivered at the conference Mut zur Erziehung (Courage to Educate) in 1978. The conference and the manifesto that it issued sparked a considerable debate. Spaemann's speech appeared under the title "Die Herausforderung" ("The Challenge") in the proceedings of the conference, *Mut zur Erziehung: Beiträge zu einem Forum am 9./10. Januar 1978 im Wissenschaftszentrum Bonn-Bad Godesberg* (Stuttgart: Klett-Cotta, 1979), 16–34; under the title "Über den Mut zur Erziehung," in *Grenzen*, 490–503. See also Spaemann, "Education as an Introduction to Reality: A Speech Commemorating the Anniversary of a Children's Home (1988)," in *A Robert Spaemann Reader*, 111–120; "What Does It Mean to Be Cultured?," in *A Robert Spaemann Reader*, 121–24; "Emanzipation: Ein Bildungsziel?" ("Emancipation: A Goal of Education?"), in *Grenzen*, 476–89; and "Zum Sinn des Ethikunterrichts in der Schule" ("The Point of Teaching Ethics in Schools"), in *Grenzen*, 516–25.

141. Spaemann, *Persons*, 196.

142. See ibid., 187: "It has been a consistently cherished ideal that humans, being related to each other, should organize their endeavours cooperatively, understand their interests as common interests, never instrumentalize each other or compete, but cooperate as effectively as they can through a discursive communication about the common good. Equally consistently, every attempt to implement this ideal has led to disillusion."

143. Spaemann, *Basic Moral Concepts*, 36.

144. See the example in note 116, above.

145. Spaemann, *Happiness and Benevolence*, viii.

146. See the earlier discussion in this chapter of "natural teleology" and the modern tendency to restrict teleology to "conscious purpose." See also Francis Slade, "Ends

and Purposes," in *Final Causality in Nature and Human Affairs*, ed. Richard F. Hassing (Washington, DC: Catholic University of America Press, 1997), 83–35; cf. Robert Sokolowski, "What Is Natural Law? Human Purposes and Natural Ends," *The Thomist* 68 (2004): 507–29; and Sokolowski, "Recovering Classical Philosophy in the Modern Content: The Works of Francis Slade," *Perspectives on Political Science* 45 (2016): 4–8.

147. John Macmurray, *The Self as Agent* (London: Humanities Press International, 1978 [1957]), 17–38, esp. 17 and 21.

148. Emmanuel Mounier, *A Personalist Manifesto* (London: Longmans, Green and Co., 1938). Jacques Maritain, *The Person and the Common Good* (Notre Dame, IN: University of Notre Dame Press, 1985 [1947]), esp. 31–46.

149. *Leipetai de ton noun monon thurathen epeisienai kai theion einai monon*, "it remains that *nous* ["mind," "intellect"; Spaemann translates it with the German *Vernunft*, "reason"] alone comes in from outside and alone is divine."

150. Spaemann, *Happiness and Benevolence*, 82 (translation slightly altered).

151. Spaemann, "The Natural and the Rational," in *Essays in Anthropology*, 91.

152. Spaemann, *Persons*, 153 (I have italicized "human" in line with the German original). Discussion of whether Christ had a human mind or spirit (*nous*) took place in response to Apollinaris of Laodicea, who claimed that Christ's mind or spirit was divine rather than human. The Council of Chalcedon (451) declared that Christ has both a complete divine nature and a complete human nature.

153. Ibid., 154.

154. This comes out clearly in "Natur," the first essay in Spaemann, *Philosophische Essays*, 19–40. It now appears as "Nature," in *A Robert Spaemann Reader*, 22–36.

155. Spaemann, *Happiness and Benevolence*, 170. Cf. *Persons*, 47: "Rationality is a form of life," (*Vernunft ist eine Form des Lebens*).

156. In what I have read, when Spaemann speaks of "life," he means animal life. It is not clear what he thinks about the life of plants. Sokolowski drew my attention to this point.

157. Here I am assuming that perception, awakening, and enlightenment are three descriptions of the same event, not three different events.

158. Spaemann, *Persons*, 77.

159. Sokolowski has helped me to see this point. He has also reminded me of Aristotle's distinction between voluntary action (discussed in *Nicomachean Ethics* 3.1) and deliberate choice (discussed in 3.2). Given this distinction, Spaemann's saying that recognition is free but not a choice poses no problem.

160. Spaemann, *Persons*, 240–41. At the end of chapter 4 of *Basic Moral Concepts*, 23, Spaemann writes, "In general the mother is the first self-sufficient reality a child comes across. The result of this is that the child initially experiences reality as something kind and helpful. The legacy of this experience, what psychologists call 'primitive trust,' is the most significant gift a good upbringing can bestow."

161. Spaemann, *Happiness and Benevolence*, 114.

162. Spaemann, *Persons*, 182. I would expand, "You can say 'So and so is a monarch, but I don't respect monarchs.' You cannot say 'So and so is a person, but I don't respect persons.'"

163. See Spaemann, *Happiness and Benevolence*, 91.

164. Spaemann, *Persons*, 77.

165. Spaemann, *Happiness and Benevolence*, 178.

166. Spaemann, *Persons*, 79–80.

167. Oliver O'Donovan has suggested that the sadist does not recognize the personal status of the victim, but must recognize the victim's subjective capacity to feel the objectification. If I am understanding this correctly, the sadist is aware of one aspect of the person, but without recognizing the person as such. I am grateful for this suggestion and grateful to O'Donovan, Jeremiah Alberg, and Robert Sokolowski for other helpful observations about recognition.

168. Spaemann, *Happiness and Benevolence*, 103.

169. Spaemann, *Über Gott und die Welt*, 251–61.

Chapter Five.   Issues Facing Aristotelians

1. MacIntyre, *Ethics in the Conflicts of Modernity*, 34–35.

2. Terence Irwin is perhaps the best-known contemporary proponent of the view that it does; see Irwin, *Aristotle's First Principles* (Oxford: Clarendon, 1988).

3. Nussbaum, *Creating Capabilities*, 132.

4. Ibid., 62, and, more generally, 62–68.

5. Ibid., 68.

6. Nussbaum, "Our Pasts, Ourselves," in *Philosophical Interventions*, 91.

7. For more on this topic, see Harry V. Jaffa, *Thomism and Aristotelianism: A Study of the Commentary by St. Thomas Aquinas on the Nicomachean Ethics* (Chicago: University of Chicago Press, 1952; repr., Westport, CT: Greenwood Press, 1979). See also the remarks of Frederick D. Wilhelmsen, "Jaffa, the School of Strauss, and the Christian Tradition," in *Christianity and Political Philosophy* (Athens: University of Georgia Press, 1978), 209–25 and 238–39.

8. "An Interview with Giovanna Borradori," in *The MacIntyre Reader*, 265.

9. A number of philosophers who sympathize with MacIntyre have investigated how his approach might be implemented on a variety of local and professional levels. See, in particular, the collections Kelvin Knight and Paul Blackledge, eds., *Revolutionary Aristotelianism: Ethics, Resistance and Utopia* (Stuttgart: Lucius & Lucius, 2008), and Andrius Bielskis and Kelvin Knight, *Virtue and Economy: Essays on Morality and Markets* (Farnham: Ashgate, 2015). These collections explore ways in which MacIntyre's project can be extended and realized in practice.

10. The reader does not need to be told that the literature on liberalism is vast. Out of many possible resources, I would suggest John Gray, *Liberalism* (Minneapolis:

University of Minnesota Press, 1986); Pierre Manent, *An Intellectual History of Liberalism*, trans. Rebecca Balinski (Princeton, NJ: Princeton University Press, 1995); and Alan Ryan, *The Making of Modern Liberalism* (Princeton, NJ: Princeton University Press, 2012).

11. "An Interview with Giovanna Borradori," in *The MacIntyre Reader*, 258.

12. The Great Books approach has sometimes been criticized as elitist, privileging a certain canon of classical and modern texts, but fairness to Adler requires the admission that his intention was the very reverse of elitist: to make these texts accessible to people in every walk of life. Adler, who strongly criticized the academic establishment of his day, did not want the Great Books to be the preserve of professors.

13. See Nussbaum, *Cultivating Humanity*, 33–35, 170–71, 186, 198–99.

14. MacIntyre, *Three Rival Versions of Moral Enquiry*, 228.

15. MacIntyre says that university faculty go through "two successive apprenticeships, one aimed at the PhD, and a second aimed at achieving tenure. During both what is rewarded is the successful completion of those short-term tasks approved by their seniors. So respect for the prejudices of those seniors is inculcated, while long-term adventurous risk-taking and unfashionable projects tend to go unrewarded, and are therefore increasingly rarely undertaken"; see MacIntyre, "The End of Education: The Fragmentation of the American University," *Commonweal*, October 20, 2006, 10–11.

16. See, for instance, MacIntyre, "Natural Law as Subversive: The Case of Aquinas," in *Selected Essays*, 2:42–43; MacIntyre, "Aquinas's Critique of Education: Against His Own Age, against Ours," in *Philosophers on Education: Historical Perspectives*, ed. Amélie Oksenberg Rorty (London: Routledge, 1998), 95–108; MacIntyre, "Philosophical Education against Contemporary Culture," *Proceedings of the American Catholic Philosophical Association* 87 (2013): 43–56.

17. "An Interview for *Cogito*," in *The MacIntyre Reader*, 275.

18. Spaemann, *Basic Moral Concepts*, 26.

19. Here I am speaking loosely. Spaemann died in November 2018. MacIntyre turned ninety-four in January 2023. Nussbaum has moved on from the Aristotelian phase of her work. My hope is that younger minds who are attracted by their different forms of Aristotelian ethics will address one another and try to resolve their differences.

20. As he said in his interview for *Cogito*, one of his colleagues described his project as writing an interminably long history of ethics; see "An Interview for *Cogito*," in *The MacIntyre Reader*, 269.

21. In her review of John H. Randall, *Aristotle*, she wrote, "Aristotle may be regarded as the cultural barometer of Western history. Whenever his influence dominated the scene, it paved the way for one of history's brilliant eras; whenever it fell, so did mankind. . . . There is only one fundamental issue in philosophy: the cognitive efficacy of man's mind. The conflict of Aristotle versus Plato is the conflict of reason versus mysticism. It was Plato who formulated most of philosophy's basic questions—and doubts. It was Aristotle who laid the foundation for most of the answers"; Rand, "Review of

Randall's *Aristotle*," in Ayn Rand, *The Voice of Reason: Essays in Objectivist Thought* (New York: New American Library, 1988), 6.

22. I am thinking, for example, of James G. Lennox, Fred D. Miller Jr., Robert Mayhew, Gregory Salmieri, and the late Allan Gotthelf, who authored a brief introduction to Rand's thought, Gotthelf, *On Ayn Rand* (Belmont, CA: Wadsworth/Thomson Learning, 2000). See also Gotthelf and Salmieri, eds., *A Companion to Ayn Rand* (Malden, MA: John Wiley & Sons, 2016). Lennox and Miller contributed to this volume. Mayhew has edited collections of essays on several of Rand's works, collections to which Gotthelf and Salmieri contributed.

23. See the extensive Charles Taylor, "Critical Notice" on *The Fragility of Goodness*, by Martha Nussbaum, *Canadian Journal of Philosophy* 18 (1988): 805–14. Nussbaum, "Transcending Humanity," in *Love's Knowledge*, chap. 15, 365–91, responded favorably to Taylor's review. Earlier in this chapter and in chapter 3 we have referred to Nussbaum, "Our Pasts, Ourselves: Review of Charles Taylor, *Sources of the Self: The Making of the Modern Identity*," in *Philosophical Interventions*, 79–92. MacIntyre, "Critical Remarks on *The Sources of the Self* by Charles Taylor," in *Philosophy and Phenomenological Research* 54 (1994): 187–90, and MacIntyre, "Charles Taylor and Dramatic Narrative: Argument and Genre," *Philosophy and Social Criticism* 44 (2018): 761–63.

24. Spaemann, *Happiness and Benevolence*, vii.

INDEX

International Society for MacIntyrean Enquiry (ISME), 77
intuitionism, 11, 15, 68
inverted teleology, 143
Inwood, Brad, 134
"is-ought problem," 12, 164, 167, 168

J

James, William, 16
Joyce, Richard: "Moral Anti-Realism," 218n32
justice: capabilities approach to, 123–24, 125; family and, 125–26; happiness and duty of, 154–55; minimum requirements of, 123, 124, 131, 132; vs. natural law, 49; political conception of, 123–25; Thomistic conception of, 39; virtue of, 31
just wages, concept of, 228n148

K

Kant, Immanuel: on benevolence, 162–63; categorical imperative of, 6, 248n61; conception of practical rationality, 51; criticism of, 51; *Critique of Judgment*, 247n41; on discernment of perception, 92; on emotions, 89; on ethics, 6, 16, 182; on happiness, 152; on human dignity, 106, 200; influence of, 120; on mechanical principles of nature, 247n41; morality of, 27; on passions, 92; on virtues, 90
Kantianism, 7, 8, 50, 51, 172
Kenny, Anthony, 18
Kierkegaard, Søren, 16, 27
Knight, Kelvin, 72, 74, 75, 77; *Revolutionary Aristotelianism* (Knight and Blackledge), 24

L

Leibniz, Gottfried Wilhelm, 157, 162
Levmore, Saul, 135

Lewis, C. S.: *The Abolition of Man*, 139
Lewis, David, 34, 65
liberal education, critique of, 208–9
liberalism: capitalism and, 36, 208; criticism of, 24–25, 37, 114–15, 198, 207; family and, 126, 241n174; feminism and, 113–15; forms of, 112; individualism and, 36; meanings of, 206–7; as politics of elites, 37
liberal social democracy, 36–37
local specification, 105, 109
local tradition relativism, 111
Locke, John, 140, 144
Love's Knowledge (Nussbaum), 91, 112–13
Löw, Reinhard, 138
Luhmann, Niklas, 140
Lutz, Christopher Stephen, 73, 75, 76, 221n22, 226nn115–16, 227n134, 230n193

M

MacIntyre, Alasdair: academic career of, 23, 24, 74, 197; on Aquinas, 39, 40, 41; Aristotelian reflections, 23, 28–30, 32, 70, 72, 195–96; on common goods, 37–39, 44, 206, 207–8; on communities, 37–39, 44, 206, 241n180; on conservatism, 37; criticism of, 34; on desire, 29, 43, 53, 60–61, 65; on dominant order, 56, 57, 58; on education, 75, 209, 228n157, 231n202; on emotivist situation, 26, 28; on Enlightenment project, 27–28, 222n29; on ethics, 69, 201; on evolution of moral philosophy, 49–50; on expressivism, 66–67; on God, 63; on good human life, 49–50, 229n173; on happiness, 56–57; on human activity, 62; on human beings, 196; on institutional embodiment, 206; interview for *Cogito*, 23, 74; "Intractable Moral Disagreements," 45; on

justification, 33, 64–65, 68; on
Kantianism and utilitarianism, 50,
51; on liberalism, 24–25, 36, 207,
208, 221n11; on liberal social democracy, 36–37; on Marxism,
35–37, 72, 224n63, 230n194;
metaethics of, 68; on modern individualism, 47; on modernity, 73,
198; on moral disagreements,
129–30; on morality and Morality,
53–56, 57–58, 65, 202; on moral
philosophy, 52, 67–68, 69, 199;
"Moral Relativism, Truth and Justification," 33, 64, 68; on narrative,
28, 30, 41, 62–64, 68–69; on
natural law, 45–49; on natural
rights, 55, 203–4, 222n25; "Notes
from the Moral Wilderness," 24;
Nussbaum and, 91, 197; "On
Having Survived the Academic
Moral Philosophy of the Twentieth
Century," 69; philosophical views
of, 41, 42; political implications of
view of, 72–73; "Politics, Philosophy and the Common Good,"
37, 38; on politics, 36, 37, 38,
40–41, 44, 206; on practical reasonableness, 61–62; on progress, 62,
63–64; on rationality, 32–33, 34;
rejection of rights talks, 25, 26; on
relativism, 34, 68; scholarly works
about, 73–77; *Selected Essays*, 74; *A
Short History of Ethics*, 16, 24, 69;
on sociological self-knowledge, 65;
teleology of, 71–72; theism of,
229n173; "Theories of Natural Law
in the Culture of Advanced Modernity," 45; as theorist of virtue ethics,
52, 230n191; on Thomism, 225n93;
Thomistic Aristotelianism of,
52–53, 60, 64–65, 205, 210–11;
*Three Rival Versions of Moral
Enquiry*, 23; on tradition and ratio-

nality, 76; on truth, 33; on virtues,
29, 42–45, 62, 69, 70, 95; on
Western moral and political think-
ing, 197. *See also individual works by
MacIntyre*
Mackie, J. L.: *Ethics*, 22
Macmurray, John, 184
Macpherson, C. B., 24, 25
Madigan, Arthur, S.J., 74, 76
Maritain, Jacques, 139, 185
Marx, Karl: Aristotle and, 102, 128; on
capitalism, 35, 56, 198; criticism of,
248n51; influence of, 16, 28, 120;
Theses on Feuerbach, 37
Marxism, 35–37, 72, 230n194
Mayr, Ernst, 145
McInerny, Ralph, 225n93
McMylor, Peter, 75
McNabb, Vincent, O.P., 57, 228n148
Mendus, Susan, 74; *After MacIntyre*, 24
metaethical relativism, 13–14
metaethics, 3, 4, 11, 15, 149, 183, 216n8
metaphysical realism, 108
metaphysical teleology, 71
Metaphysics (Aristotle), 82, 185
method of appearances, 81–84, 128–30,
131, 133, 196, 210
Mill, John Stuart, 2, 6, 16, 25, 80, 120,
200, 241n174
modal fallacy, 12
modern individualism, 47–48
modernity, 47, 141, 142, 184, 198
Moore, G. E., 14, 16, 19, 21, 26, 221n22;
Principia Ethica, 2, 20, 221n19
Moore, Geoff, 76
moral anti-realism, 218n32
moral convictions, 149
moral disagreements, 129–30, 210
morality: choice and, 27; criticism of, 18;
desire and, 27; nature and, 166, 167,
168, 169–70; practical reason and,
27; religion and, 155–56; scholarly
debates on, 10, 217n19; secular doc-

Stalin, Joseph, 24
Stevenson, C. L., 11, 14, 16, 21, 26; *Ethics and Language*, 2
Stoics, 89, 120, 128, 145, 153, 203
Strauss, Leo: *Natural Right and History*, 139
Strawson, Galen, 63–64
subjectivism, 13, 14
suffering, 191
Sullivan, Robert E., 75

T
taboos, 221–22n22
Taylor, Charles, 18, 73, 77, 88, 226n114, 243n187; *A Secular Age*, 212; *Sources of the Self*, 205, 212
teleological ethics, 3, 4–5, 15, 181
teleology: Aristotelian concept of, 145; biology and, 145, 146; classical vs. modern, 141; modernity and, 148, 184; vs. teleonomy, 146, 147; universal, 145–46
teleonomy, 145, 146, 147
telos, 27, 30, 41, 63, 196, 201
theological voluntarism. *See* divine command theory
Theory of Justice, A (Rawls), 18, 99
thick description, 235n61
thick vague conception of the good, 102–3, 104, 105, 106
thin theory of the good, 99, 103, 128, 235n61
Thomas Aquinas: Aristotle and, 41; on communal life, 39, 198; on happiness, 56–57, 228n146; on human action, 171; influence of, 16; on justice, 39–40; on lending money, 40; on natural law, 45–46, 47, 48; on ownership, 39; on prudence, 51; *Summa theologiae*, 139; teleology of, 143; on virtues, 44
Thomism, 225n93

Thomistic Aristotelianism, 50, 52–53, 64–65, 67–68, 205, 211
torture, 176–77, 253n132
traditions, 30, 31, 33, 34
tragedy, 87–88
Treatise of Human Nature (Hume), 12, 195
truth, 31, 33
two-world theories, 148
tyranny, 40

U
unconscious motives, 239n155
universalism, 151, 152
usury, 40
utilitarianism: attractiveness of, 7; as best-known version of teleological ethics, 8; criticism of, 181, 182; introductory texts on, 6; vs. Kantianism, 50, 51; on passions, 92; practical rationality and, 91; principles of, 6, 7, 111; on virtues, 90
utility, 25, 55, 111

V
values, 12, 15, 106
vices, 29
Virtue and Politics (Blackledge and Knight), 24
virtue ethics, 52, 90–91, 230n191
virtues: of acknowledged dependence, 44; Aristotelian account of, 29–30, 95–96; biological grounding of, 70; definitions of, 29, 97, 98; desires and, 43, 70; of giving and receiving, 43; human experience and, 95–97; institutions and, 31, 32; modern nation-state and, 44–45; teleological basis of, 30; theories of, 17, 90; traditions and, 31
volition, primary vs. secondary, 249n74
Voltaire, 167

ARTHUR MADIGAN, S.J., is professor emeritus of philosophy at Boston College. He is the author and translator of many books and essays about Greek philosophy, including Aristotle's *Metaphysics: Books B and K 1–2*.

Printed in the USA
CPSIA information can be obtained
at www.ICGtesting.com
CBHW062317050324
5012CB00003B/63

9 780268 207595